Dark Continent

"River Navigation in Equatorial Africa." An example of the illustrative material included in American reports from Africa. This one is from Paul B. Du Chaillu, *Explorations and Adventures in Equatorial Africa* (1861).

Dark Continent

AFRICA AS SEEN BY AMERICANS

Michael McCarthy

HENRY WHITTEMORE
LIBRARY

STATE COLLEGE
FRAMINGHAM, MASS

CONTRIBUTIONS IN AFRO-AMERICAN AND
AFRICAN STUDIES, NUMBER 75

GREENWOOD PRESS
Westport, Connecticut • London, England

Acknowledgment

Grateful acknowledgment is made to Cambridge University Press for permission to reprint Michael McCarthy, "Africa and the American West," in *Journal of American Studies* Vol. 11, no. 2 (August 1977), pp. 187-202.

Library of Congress Cataloging in Publication Data

McCarthy, Michael, 1942-
 Dark continent.

 (Contributions in Afro-American and African studies,
ISSN 0069-9624 ; no. 75)
 Bibliography: p.
 Includes index.
 1. Africa—Relations—United States. 2. United States
—Relations—Africa. 3. Africa—Public opinion.
4. Public opinion—United States. 5. Africa—Study and
teaching—United States. I. Title. II. Series.
DT38.1.M38 1983   303.4'826'073   83-8878
ISBN 0-313-23828-6 (lib. bdg.)

Copyright © 1983 by Michael McCarthy

All rights reserved. No portion of this book may be
reproduced, by any process or technique, without the
express written consent of the publisher.

Library of Congress Catalog Card Number: 83-8878
ISBN: 0-313-23828-6
ISSN: 0069-9624

First published in 1983

Greenwood Press
A division of Congressional Information Service, Inc.
88 Post Road West
Westport, Connecticut 06881

Printed in the United States of America

10 9 8 7 6 5 4 3 2 1

DT
38.1
M38
1983

For Mary and Michael

To Bishop Desmond Tutu

Contents

Illustrations

Series Foreword

The paucity of creative and scholarly works available for library and classroom use remains a crucial barrier to the adequate study of African and Afro-American arts and letters. Despite a flood of hastily conceived and rashly executed monograph and bibliographical series that ostensibly meant to address this quandary, students, scholars, and librarians agree that African and Afro-American materials continue to be either inadequate as research tools or, more often, simply unavailable at all.

Despite the intention of well-meaning publishers and eager Afro-Americanists, the 1880 lament of the black critic, Richard T. Greener, retains its poignancy as an account of knowledge of black arts and letters: "It would be interesting, were it not painful, to observe how little even educated Americans, judging from articles in current literature, know of the capacity, disposition, achievements, services, or sacrifices of the Negro in general and the Negro-American in particular." The American academy has only a limited notion of the manner in which black writers and scholars have structured their responses to the complex fate of institutionalized racial and economic discrimination. Nor does the academy have a sufficient idea of the peculiar manner in which black texts respond to considerations raised in other, related texts, which responses themselves constitute an aspect of intellectual history. What's more, there exists no systematic publishing venture that has addressed this problem intelligently, by commissioning major Africanists and Afro-Americanists to prepare sophisticated studies on the vast and challenging subject of black arts and letters.

To sharpen the definition of African and Afro-American Studies and to present a more coherent view of the continuum of black thought and action, a new departure is necessary. This series is designed to fill this need. Often inter-disciplinary and cross-cultural, it seeks to address not only the complexities of the cultural and aesthetic confrontation of black cultures with nonblack ones, but also the nature and function of African and Afro-American arts and letters themselves.

While Michael McCarthy's study of Africa as a trope in American discourse is one of the general order of a number of works by excellent scholars on the broad subject of the "image of the black," McCarthy's emphasis upon representations, or images, of Africa as a *physical space* is remarkably unique and impressively original. While others in this crucial subfield of so very many disciplines (literature, history, sociology) have studied the depiction of black figures within this medium or that, McCarthy has explored the complex relation between the physical and, as it were, the metaphysical "Africa." We cannot stress too much the importance of this gesture, or its novelty. Everyone who addresses the subject subsequently shall be forced to do so through McCarthy's analysis, which is the hallmark of the truly seminal work. There can be no question that this study is a major work, and that it alone certifies his place in the field, a central place indeed.

Dark Continent is one of a number of emerging systematic studies concerned with the image of the black in Western consciousness. In the last five years, scholars have published *The Image of the Black in Western Art* (2 volumes, of 3); *On Blackness Without Blacks: Essays on the Image of the Black in Germany*; *The Image of the Black in German Literature*; *The Popular Image of the Black Man in English Drama 1550-1688*; *Sambo Sahib*; *The African Link*; *Presence and Prestige: Africans in Europe*; and *The French Encounter with Africans*, among a dozen more titles. *Dark Continent*, therefore, must be reviewed in the context of those texts that it complements or supplements.

The scholarship analyzed here has not, we are pleased to say, been duplicated elsewhere. At long last, someone has turned to geographical accounts specifically to chart the idea of "Africa" in American writings. In literary studies, we would call this an evocation of the sense of place. But sense of place, it is crucial to recall, is evoked essentially to convey, to reflect, a sense of self. This is as true of geographical and anthropological studies as it is of literary studies. Exotic landscapes contain exotic peoples: from Homer and Herodotus to Richard Nixon, this has remained consistently the case among Western commentators upon "the Other," especially others of color. And it is this relationship between descriptions of Africa the place, and Africans, the people upon which the success of this book is founded.

John W. Blassingame
Henry Louis Gates, Jr.

Preface

As a young man, Malcolm Little listened to his father tell of a remote and exotic land known as Africa. The young man's father spoke often about the many desirable aspects of life in Africa and passionately about the attractiveness of making it a future home for black Americans. He believed that Africa offered black Americans what life in America had denied them for so long—the freedom to live without prejudice and discrimination. After listening to his father's talks about Africa, Malcolm Little, later to be remembered by the name that authored *The Autobiography of Malcolm X*, remarked how his view of the continent and that of his father did not quite coincide. In contrast to his father's portrayal of the many positive aspects of things African, Malcolm X recalled that his image was somehow different. "My image of Africa," he writes in his autobiography, "was of naked savages, cannibals, monkeys and tigers and steaming jungles."[1]

Malcolm X's observation is both intriguing and troubling since it—and not the positive view of his father—has captured the essence of American thinking about Africa. From seventeenth-century America to the more recent past, it has been well documented that a majority of Americans have rendered Africa in a number of ill-conceived, imprecise, and inaccurate portraits because they have lacked a basic understanding of the continent.[2] Africa, on the one hand, a land that is four times the size of the continental United States and equally as varied, has been condensed by them into a powerful geographic stereotype. When Americans have formed pictures of Africa, they have imagined that a major portion of the topography of the continent is either desert, jungle, or an ill-defined combination of both. African people, on the other hand, comprise literally hundreds of distinct cultural societies and are as different from one another as the many ethnic groups in America. Yet they have been seen, all too frequently, as a single homogeneous race with their strange customs and "savage" behavior being their only distinguishing marks.

Until recently such speculative thinking characterized American commentary about Africa. Samuel P. Verner, an American missionary-explorer and commercial entrepreneur, and an individual who had spent considerable time in various parts of Africa, wrote in the early part of the twentieth century of a "popular impression" of Africa as a continent "cursed with pestilential fevers, malarial marshes and deserts, burning sands and deadly atmospheric conditions." This highly impressionistic picture was further supplemented, Verner relates, by American "visions" of Africa that were composed exclusively of "black people" and "burning sunshine."[3] Even today, by concentrating almost exclusively upon the sensational and unusual, much of the writing in American newspapers and magazines and much of the focus in American films and documentaries have done little to counter the idea that Africa must be a strangely unreal land. As it might be descriptively called, this "dark continent" image of Africa as a mixture of desert and jungle, savage beasts and beastly savages, has persisted to such an extent that it has become over time the essential way in which most Americans have come to understand African realities.[4]

Since I was simultaneously intrigued and troubled by Malcolm X's statement about Africa, I began to ask how Americans had come to hold these views. In the case of young Malcolm Little, who thought of Africa in terms of jungles and tigers, it is logical to assume that he was simply giving life to a popular stereotype of the time. The newly made Tarzan films of the 1920s, which emphasized the exotic qualities of the African landscape and the simian characteristics of African people, were just beginning to be exploited fully by the

American mass media. Moreover, photographs of bare-breasted African women and bare-buttocked African men began to appear on the pages of many American magazines of the time.[5] But was there more to this misguided convention than just movies and magazines? Were there not other, earlier popular sources upon which these later manifestations were ultimately based? Was there not in fact a much broader cultural basis for these commonly accepted ideas about Africa? But how to proceed?

As the problem began to define itself, it became clear that Malcolm X's image of Africa as a land of "naked savages" and "steaming jungles" was neither exclusively a product of his time nor an idiosyncratic view of his own making. It was, to the contrary, bound up with an American tradition of writing about Africa that had begun prior to the clash of ideas between the young man and his father about the reality of Africa. Its roots lay with the earliest and one of the most significant sources of information about the continent: the recorded impressions of Americans who had actually travelled to Africa.[6] Firsthand descriptions of Africa written by Americans were profoundly influential in shaping American ideas of Africa. Because people form impressions of foreign lands based on what they read, particularly when they lack direct experience, the recorded observations of Americans in Africa in effect formed the cultural prism through which Africa was seen by a majority of Americans at home. As self-conscious attempts at organizing the complexity of the continent, their writings determined the reality of Africa. These American reports from Africa, in essence, *were* Africa.

Thus, to an extent not previously realized, a tradition of describing Africa was established in America, beginning with the opening decades of the nineteenth century and continuing throughout the late nineteenth and early twentieth centuries. During this latter period especially, the most detailed and widely circulated writings about Africa began to appear in America as more Americans travelled to the continent. Books about Africa were published regularly by D. Appleton, J. B. Lippincott, Harper and Brothers, Macmillan, A. C. McClurg, Charles Scribner's Sons, Houghton Mifflin, Fleming H. Revell, Arena Publishing, Dana Estes, Eaton and Mains, and Frederick A. Stokes, among others. Articles about Africa appeared frequently in the most popular periodicals of the time: *Missionary Review of the World, Century Magazine, Chautauquan, Our Day, Southern*

Workman, Scribner's Magazine, North American Review, National Geographic Magazine, Collier's Magazine, Atlantic Monthly, Harper's Weekly, World's Work, and *Arena.* Such accounts of Africa, moreover, were written not by a band of esoteric and relatively unknown travel writers but by some of America's most celebrated figures.

Among the more important American authors of books about Africa was Henry M. Stanley, a naturalized American of Welsh descent, whose two-volume work *Through the Dark Continent* was a best-selling book.[7] Theodore Roosevelt, a former U.S. President and former governor, wrote *African Game Trails,* probably the most famous hunting book written by an American. Originally published in 1910, the book sold well and was serialized in *National Geographic Magazine.*[8] Richard Harding Davis, an American writer of note and a Fellow of the Royal Geographical Society who wrote frequently about Africa, authored *The Congo and Coasts of Africa* in 1907. Paul Belloni Du Chaillu, a naturalized American of French extraction, was not only the first non-African to discover the African gorilla but also an important author who compiled an impressive list of publications on Africa. A writer of great skill and popularity, Stewart Edward White published three books about the continent: *African Camp Fires* (1913), *The Land of Footprints* (1913), and *The Rediscovered Country* (1915). Finally, Mark Twain's observations about South Africa were made a part of his widely read travel book, *Following the Equator,* published in 1897.[9]

Writing about Africa was not the exclusive domain of famous men. Many American women, either independently or as the companions of men, journeyed to Africa and wrote about their experiences there. Caroline Kirkland, for example, the American author of *Some African Highways: A Journey of Two American Women to Uganda and the Transvaal* (1908), established herself as a bona fide African traveller. The daughter of Major Joseph Kirkland of Chicago, a former literary editor of the *Chicago Tribune,* and the sister of Ethel Kirkland Ennis, wife of George Ennis, judge of the Uganda Protectorate, Kirkland made an extensive trip throughout eastern and southern Africa. Because of her substantial work in East Africa, Mary French-Sheldon became a recognized authority on the customs and beliefs of East African peoples, most notably the Masai. Even though she was never accorded the title of anthropologist or geographer in her lifetime, French-Sheldon's writings for the general public and for scholarly associations made her an important observer of African life. Her most significant full-length work, *Sultan to Sultan: Adventures Among the Masai and Other Tribes of East Africa*, was published in Boston in 1892.[10]

This study, then, is an attempt to discover the origins and subsequent development of an American tradition of viewing Africa by examining the experiences of those Americans who had actually journeyed to Africa. It is not a history of African-American relations, although the subjects of colonization, commercial exploitation, and American missionary activity in Africa are not ignored. Nor is it a history of the American contribution to the discovery of Africa, although it does deal with the American presence on the continent as well. Rather, it is an examination of how Africa and Africans—both the land and its peoples—were seen by Americans in Africa and ultimately of how their descriptions shaped American ideas about the continent in a very particular way. Thus the central focus of my efforts is on discovering how Americans in their writings created a language of discourse about Africa and Africans.

While my initial interest in the problem was directed at understanding the substance of American writings for the kinds of explanations of Africa they contained, analyzing primary descriptions of the continent also illustrated the methodological process by which a group of people perceive and understand an alien environment. It became evident that American perceptions of Africa were as much shaped by expectations and predispositions about it, that is, by what Americans wanted from Africa and by what they expected it to be, as they were by the actual characteristics of the continent and its peoples. What was initially assumed to be an objective recording of facts about an unfamiliar place was very often the product of a culturally defined point of view. In addition, the past experiences of Americans who wrote about Africa played a critical role in shaping their understanding, evaluation, and ultimate description of the continent. In one instance, for example, some Americans likened parts of eastern and southeastern Africa to the western sections of America they previously had known.

Assumptions such as these about the nature of environmental perception not only guide the present work but also take on added significance, since they are consistent with a major line of reasoning that has been developing about the nature of our ability to understand the world.[11] In recent years a number of investigators from various disciplines have supported the idea that the reality of a given time is a humanly or socially created one. As cognitive animals, people are viewed as symbolizing creatures, constantly engaged in a never-ending struggle to better understand their world. In order to make sense out of the complexity that confronts them, people attempt to break up reality by creating patterns that give order to chaos and sense to their world. These artificial constructs, paradigms, or models, as they are called, set the form for their inquiry and establish the context in which a group of people think and act about the world around them. Individuals, the argument concludes, rarely encounter objective reality but view the world through the assumptions, expectations, and predispositions they have about it.[12]

In the case of Americans in Africa, a taxonomy of reality was established in order to comprehend how Americans perceived, organized, structured, and evaluated the world of Africa. Of major concern is an analysis of the cognitive categories that Americans used in order to describe the complexity of the African continent—both to themselves and to others. By viewing the confrontation between Americans and Africa within a problem-solving context in which many Americans were confronted with the very real problem of making sense of Africa, an attempt is made to show how Americans imaginatively dealt with the task of translating their experiences in Africa into explanations of Africa. The prospect of writing at some length on that subject, however, presented a number of additional choices and decisions that had to be made about the overall structure of the study.

Since the process of interaction between Americans and Africa is necessarily complex, and perception a multidimensional phenomenon, the present work is organized thematically rather than chronologically around American evaluations of the natural, built, symbolic, and cultural environments of Africa. *Natural environment*, as used here, denotes vegetation and wildlife and includes weather, climate, and all other physical processes and characteristics of Africa. It is different from the *built environment*, a term employed to suggest physical structures erected and designed elements of the landscape executed in Africa. A *symbolic environment*, in further distinction, is a landscape charged with a particular cultural meaning, such that complicated ideas about it can be compressed into a limited number of specific concepts. A symbolic environment is evocative of something larger than itself. Finally, the term *cultural environment* is used to indicate any place or series of places where people or groups of people manifest various aspects of their culture.

It should be pointed out that this approach develops themes that are to some extent arbitrary, but they are not capricious; in fact, these categories represent an attempt to break down the complexity of the American experience in Africa, just as Americans who had travelled to the continent sought to provide explanations for what they had seen. In addition, there is great value in such an arrangement if the topics are well chosen. Since my intent is not to relate events in terms of movement or simultaneous development, but to explore components of American perceptions of the African environment, a topical format is appropriate here. There is, however, a temporal structure to the investigation, and changes and modifications in perception are noted when significant.

In Chapter 1, the long view is taken in which the idea of Africa is placed within the context of Western thought, beginning with the ancient Greeks, to the nineteenth century. In Chapter 2, a number of topics involving Americans in Africa are considered: When did Americans begin to travel to Africa? Why did they go there and where did they travel? A discussion of American racial attitudes, as cultural predictors of American responses to Africa and Africans, is introduced. An examination of American reactions to the natural environment of Africa is undertaken in Chapter 3. What were considered the outstanding geographical and topographical features of the continent? Were there comparisons to be made between parts of Africa and sections of America? In Chapter 4, I analyze how Americans described and evaluated selected aspects of Africa's built environment. What were the characteristics of African farms and cities? How did they differ from American ones? What influence did Europeans and Americans have on designing the look of the African landscape?

Chapter 5 demonstrates how Africa came to be thought of as a commercial wilderness, a continent symbolic of the economically undeveloped parts of the world where Western civilization had made very few advances. Chapter 6 examines American responses to Africans and their cultures, as seen through the eyes of American missionaries. Why were Africans in such need of redemption? What was so exotic and different about their world? Chapter 7 reveals how commentary about Africa and Africans—on a regular basis—was incorporated into selected kinds of secondary publications in the United States, especially geography schoolbooks, children's literature, American travel books, the Afro-American press, and the work of black American scholars. The concluding chapter, Chapter 8, deals with two important topics: the impact of descriptions of Africa on the lives of Afro-Americans and the legacy of such a tradition of reporting Africa.

Unlike its organization, the overall chronology was a matter more easily decided upon. A certain intellectual compulsiveness provided the initial motivation for going back to the time when Americans first set foot upon the shores of Africa in the eighteenth century. This urge was overly ambitious and virtually impossible to satisfy because of the scarcity of early extant sources. As a result the work finds its chronological center around that century-long period of time when the most important data were obtained—from the opening decades of the nineteenth century to the start of the twentieth, but in particular (and more important) during the late nineteenth and early twentieth centuries. It was during this latter time especially, unlike any other era, that a large number of Americans began to travel to Africa and to comment upon their experiences in detail. The study concludes around the post-World War I period, when the idea of Africa as the "dark continent" became an established part of American thinking about Africa.

In tracing the earliest antecedents for Malcolm X's vision of Africa, several different types of sources, varying both in quality and utility, were examined. Americans who travelled to Africa were eager to write about their experiences, although not all made sense of them. Like the British and Portuguese travellers who had gone to Africa before them, Americans recorded their reactions to the continent most frequently in travel narratives and periodical literature, less so in personal correspondences, and sometimes in official United States government documents. Despite the variety and the sheer number of items that were available for inspection, and notwithstanding the related problem of deciphering exactly what the sources meant, the most popular and widely disseminated material about Africa published in America has been examined.

Brief mention should also be made about the impetus for the

present undertaking. Toward the end of a two-year residence in the highlands of northeastern Ethiopia, I became interested in the problem of how individuals react to unfamiliar places. In Ethiopia it was apparent that there had been a great deal of mutual misunderstanding between Americans and Ethiopians. While some Ethiopians were familiar with particular facets of American life, many held a number of misconceptions as well. Was America still that Wild West frontier country, the land of the eternal cowboy, as many Ethiopians believed? Equally disturbing, however, was the fact that many Americans thought of Africa in a manner not unlike that of Malcolm X. Because an obvious problem in cross-cultural understanding existed, upon my return to the United States it seemed that an analysis of American perceptions of Africa might be useful for an uncomplicated reason. By exposing the light of analysis to the origins and subsequent development of an American tradition of seeing Africa as the "dark continent," such a process might be understood and confronted. For Americans who seek to understand Africa, this kind of revelation is necessary. But even more, for Americans of African descent who seek clarification and illumination about one important and misunderstood aspect of their cultural heritage, it is essential.

Finally, I would like to consider my present effort an extension of past works in culture studies. In recent years the modification of accepted modes of perception and conception in the experience of radically different environments has constituted something of a major theme. Henry Nash Smith's *Virgin Land: The American West as Symbol and Myth* (1950) quickly comes to mind as a classic example of this type, while Cushing Strout's *The American Image of the Old World* (1963) is a fine study in cultural cross-fertilization. But in concentrating solely either on the American scene, as Smith does, or on the relationship between America and Europe, as Strout does, studies of American perceptions of what has been termed the "third world" have been largely ignored. In light of this fact, and because they have shared a common past for so long, the connection between America and Africa is a topic that deserves scrutiny.

Notes

1. Malcolm X, *The Autobiography of Malcolm X* (New York: Grove Press, 1966), p. 7. For the view of Africa held by Malcolm X's father, a

follower of Marcus Garvey, see John Henrik Clarke, ed., *Marcus Garvey and the Vision of Africa* (New York: Vintage Books, 1974).

2. Melville J. Herskovits, "The Image of Africa in the United States," *Journal of Human Relations* 10 (Winter and Spring, 1962), 236–45; United States National Commission for UNESCO, Eighth National Conference, *Africa and the United States: Images and Realities*, Boston, October 22–26, 1961.

3. Samuel P. Verner, *Pioneering in Central Africa* (Richmond, Va.: Presbyterian Committee of Publication, 1903), p. 473; and Samuel P. Verner, "The White Man's Zone in Africa," *World's Work* 13 (November, 1906), 8227.

4. Although it is true that some Americans, like W.E.B. Du Bois or Franz Boas, possessed a specialized knowledge of Africa that ran counter to this popular view, most Americans, both black and white, have held a pejorative view of Africa as the "dark continent." For a comprehensive discussion of Afro-American knowledge of Africa, see George Shepperson, "The Afro-American Contribution to African Studies," *Journal of American Studies* 8, no. 3 (1975), 281–301. For a survey of the pervasiveness of a negative view of Africa in America, see Harold R. Isaacs, *The New World of Negro Americans* (New York: John Day Co., 1963).

5. I am thinking here about the most popular "window on the world" for Americans, *National Geographic Magazine*, about which little has been written concerning its importance as a transmitter of worldwide cultural views.

6. A fine historical survey of American interest in Africa can be found in Edward H. McKinley, *The Lure of Africa: American Interests in Tropical Africa, 1919–1939* (Indianapolis and New York: Bobbs–Merrill Co., 1974). And for the British experience, Philip D. Curtin, *The Image of Africa: British Ideas and Action, 1780–1850* (Madison: University of Wisconsin Press, 1964).

7. See Frank Luther Mott, *Golden Multitudes: The Story of Best Sellers in the United States* (New York: Macmillan Co., 1947), p. 322. Mott incorrectly lists *In Darkest Africa*.

8. John Tebbel, *A History of Book Publishing in the United States*, 3 vols. (New York: R. R. Bowker Co., 1975), 2:654.

9. See Mark Twain, *Following the Equator: A Journey Around the World* (Hartford, Conn.: American Publishing Co., 1897). See also Coleman Parsons, "Mark Twain: Traveler in South Africa," *Mississippi Quarterly* 29 (Winter 1975–1976), 3–41.

10. Sometimes known as "Bé Bé Bwana," French-Sheldon also wrote "Customs Among the Natives of East Africa, from Teita to Kilimegalia, with Special Reference to Their Women and Children," *Journal of the Anthropological Institute* 21 (1892), 358–90.

11. These ideas and much more are most fully developed in Yi-Fu Tuan, *Topophilia: A Study of Environmental Perception, Attitudes, and Values* (Englewood Cliffs, N.J.: Prentice-Hall, 1974).

12. Among the most notable, Peter L. Berger and Thomas Luckmann, *The Social Construction of Reality* (New York: Doubleday and Co., 1966), and Thomas Kuhn, *The Structure of Scientific Revolutions* (Chicago: University of Chicago Press, 1970).

Acknowledgments

I would like to thank a number of people for their helpful criticisms and gracious support, particularly Edward Griffin, Yi-Fu Tuan, and Henry Louis Gates, Jr. I acknowledge my gratitude to George Shepperson of the University of Edinburgh, who encouraged me to pursue the topic by the personal example of his own scholarship. I thank also the staffs of the University of Minnesota Libraries, especially Erika Linke and Marcia Pankake, the University of Maryland Libraries, especially Betty Baehr, and the Library of Congress for their resourcefulness in locating many hard-to-find items. Numerous other library staffs, but in particular the generous people at the University of North Carolina, Howard University, Duke University, the University of Wisconsin, and Yale University, who freely lent their materials, are thanked for their spirit of cooperativeness. One way of looking at the somewhat unsettling experience of being a visiting professor early in academic life is that I was able to meet a number of extraordinary people quickly: at the University of Florida, Ronald Foreman, Samuel Hill, and Julian Pleasants; at Rutgers, David Oshinsky; and at Franklin and Marshall College, Sanford Pinsker, Jeffrey Steinbrink, and Joseph Voelker. Because of what they have either said or written I thank the following remarkable group of people: John Blassingame, Carl Bode, James Borchert, William

xxviii   Acknowledgments

Cohen, Philip Curtin, David Brion Davis, William Ferris, Eugene Genovese, John Fraser Hart, Neil Isaacs, J. B. Jackson, Winthrop Jordan, Peirce Lewis, David Lowenthal, Philip Porter, Robert Stepto, Gene Wise, Peter Wood, and Wilbur Zelinsky. I am also grateful to Pearl Leopard and Katie Helene, who typed the manuscript several times, and Mary O'Neil, who checked the accuracy of the proof. My son, Michael, helped in the preparation of the maps. A portion of this work originally appeared in the *Journal of American Studies*. Financial assistance was provided from the research funds of the University of Minnesota, while additional support—financial, as well as psychological and emotional—was provided by my wife Mary.

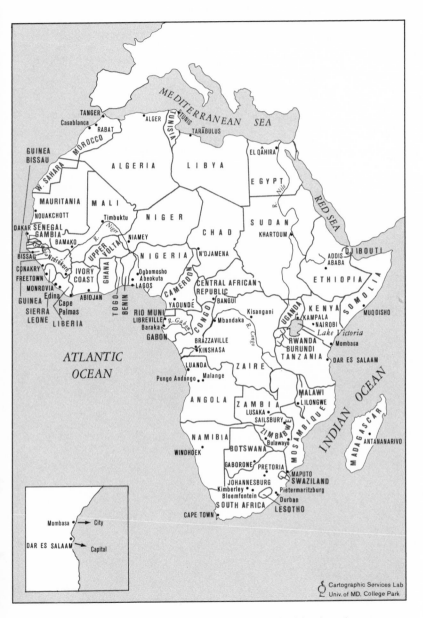

Map 1. Countries of Africa, with locations visited by Americans.

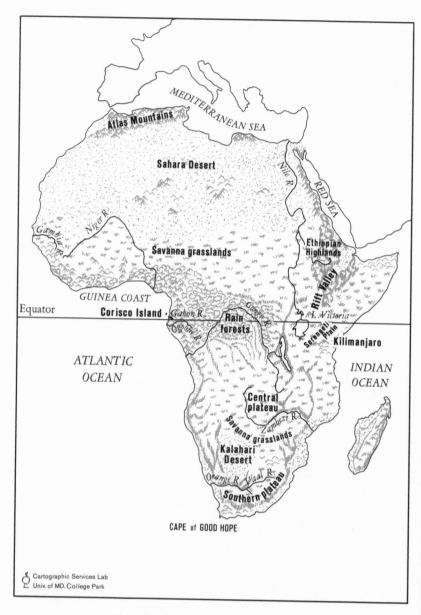

Map. 2.   The physical regions of Africa.

Cartographic Services Lab
Univ. of MD. College Park

Dark Continent

1

Africa and the West

When Americans began to publish detailed reports of their impressions of Africa and its inhabitants, beginning in the early nineteenth century, they did so, in one sense, from the perspective of fresh experience. As colonists, missionaries, or commercial agents, they attempted to answer questions in their writings about the nature of Africa which strangers to new lands have always asked: How is this country similar to our own land? What is the climate like? What are the important geographical characteristics of this region? What about the people? How are they like or unlike us? There is a feeling of first encounter with a wholly untested environment. It is important to remember, however, that in another sense the experiences of Americans in Africa are part of an encompassing tradition of evaluating Africa and Africans. From the writings of ancient Greece and Rome, to the books about Africa published during Europe's Middle Ages, to the many accounts of the continent that began to appear in Elizabethan England, the explanations of things African put forth by Americans complement, modify, and intersect the thoughts of others who had written about Africa before them. Although it is impossible to trace exact correlations between the writings of Americans and other descriptions of Africa, American reports about Africa can be placed within the context of previous narratives of the continent, which they both repeat and extend.

The great geographers of the classical world were the Greeks, and one person in particular was preeminent.[1] Although his knowledge of Africa was never extensive or complete at any one time, Herodotus was familiar with the northern coasts of Africa, as were many of his contemporaries. However, Herodotus knew little about Africa's interior. The Sahara desert formed the limit of his understanding. The existence of the Nile River was known to him, but its sources were altogether mysterious. Nevertheless, a lack of information did not prevent Herodotus from formulating a theory on the subject of the origins of the Nile, in which he presented in the form of a story a curious view into the interior of Africa.

According to the tale, five young Nasamonians, a Libyan people, had set out to explore the desert area south of Libya. After travelling through familiar terrain for some time, the Libyans entered the desert proper. There they journeyed for many days until they came upon an unexpected grove of fruit trees. As they began to help themselves to the fruit, they were approached by a band of strange men. In Herodotus's words, the young men "were suddenly surprised and taken short by a company of little dwarfs, far under the common pitch and stature of men, whose tongue the gentlemen knew not, neither was their speech understood of them."[2] The five Nasamonians were taken prisoner and herded through a stretch of marshland. Finally they reached the city of their captors, where all the residents were skilled in magic and where a river inhabited by crocodiles flowed.

There is no reason to reject Herodotus's story as being entirely fabulous since there is a degree of credibility to it. In travelling south from Libya, it is conceivable that the five young Nasamonians actually did reach the Niger River. And yet there is an extreme tone of vagueness about the tale, even though it must have been cherished as being authentic since it was written by a celebrated scholar. The adventures of a handful of Libyans were not the only report of Africa written by Herodotus. On another occasion, he wrote about a group of people he called "Macrobian Ethiopians," individuals evidently regarded by Herodotus as the most remote inhabitants of Africa. Like his previous story, it too was a nebulous tale of exotic people. These "Ethiopians," in contrast to the "little dwarfs" of before, were a tall race of handsome African men who lived, on the average, to be 120 years old in a land of abundant gold where the dead were buried not in coffins but in pillars of transparent crystal. The Macrobians existed on a diet of meat and milk, and they bathed in a magical fountain that was the chief source of their health and longevity.

Although Herodotus's writings about Africa were highly speculative and imaginative, they were exceeded in both regards by a second classical commentary on Africa: the work of Pliny the Elder. Caius Plinius Secundus's *Natural History* is an extraordinary mixture of truth, myth, and fantasy. It is also a digest of over two thousand books read by Pliny, from which he collected approximately twenty thousand facts considered worthy of notice. Like the literary technique of Herodotus, Pliny introduced the subject of Africa by telling a tale, in this case the story of two officers who journeyed to the "Great Swamp," an area south of "Fashoda." Although writing speculative accounts about the interior of Africa was a common practice among the educated men of Alexandria, in Pliny's *Natural History* there emerged a bizarre African world, a region populated by strange beasts and weird men who lived together in a land of burning heat.

There were, for example, Ethiopians with extraordinary human forms. Some had neither "nose nor nostrils," but just "all face"; others had no lips; some had no tongues and were therefore unable to speak. Some people breathed through a small hole in their heads and were thereby forced to drink through a straw. Others, called "Arimaspi" by Pliny, had only one eye, which was situated squarely on their foreheads. Some Africans who were eight feet tall lived with elephants, while others preferred the company of lions. There were people who looked more like dogs, and Africans who were entirely naked. Others had no heads: their mouths and eyes were implanted in their breasts. Finally, in a world literally turned upside down, there were many Africans who walked about, not on their feet, but on their hands. In Pliny's words,

> There be found both men and beasts of strange and monstrous shapes, considering the agility of the sun's fierce heat, so strong and powerful in those countries, which is able to frame bodies artificially of sundry proportions, and to imprint and grave in them divers forms. Certes, reported it is, that far within the country eastward there are a kind

of people without any nose at all on their face, having their visage all plain and flat. Others again without any upper lip, and some tongueless. Moreover, there is a kind of them that want a mouth, framed apart their nostrils: and at one and the same hole, and no more, taketh in breath, receiveth drink by drawing it in with an oaten straw, yea, and after the same manner feed themselves with the grains of oats, growing of their own accord without man's labour and tillage for their only food. And others there may be, who instead of speech and words, make signs, as well with nodding their heads, as moving their other members.[3]

A final perspective on Africa from the ancient world was provided by Ptolemy, a Greek born in Egypt, who wrote in Alexandria about the middle of the second century A.D. Ptolemy's work generally lacks the speculative twists and turns characteristic of the writings of Herodotus and Pliny.[4] Ptolemy tried to be the exact scientist and was successful in at least one case. He referred to the people living northeast of the Nile as the Mastitae and their town as Maste. This statement is a probable reference to the Masai peoples of Kenya. Yet the most interesting part of Ptolemy's work was not his view of northeastern Africa but his view of the southern end of the continent. Ptolemy theorized that southern Africa was linked to southern Asia, and that the "Dead Sea," now known as the Indian Ocean, was nothing more than a somewhat larger Mediterranean sea. Moreover, southern Africa, in being connected to southern Asia, stretched westward into the ocean for an unknown distance. Ptolemy not only enlarged the inhabitable world of his time, but his ideas were so popular and convincing that they remained at the center of a question asked by curious Europeans in the Middle Ages: Was it possible to sail around this mysterious continent of Africa? Only in 1498 was the answer provided by Vasco da Gama, who rounded the Cape of Good Hope, finally reaching India by sea.

Classical accounts of Africa such as these contained a combination of gross speculation and some fact. Allusions to Africa and Africans were scattered and brief since information was inadequate for comprehensive analysis. Although there was a lack of detailed knowledge about the continent, there was still a substitution of fantasy for fact which was pointedly antagonistic. When reference was made to Africa and its inhabitants, for example, emphasis was placed on the strange and the exotic. This proclivity suggests that ancient writers felt a need to create a chasm, one that separated their own civilized world from the primitive domain of their subjects. The implications were obvious: Africans lacked the accepted forms of civilization, ethics, and social organization. In contrast, they were a cruel and promiscuous race of people, freaks who were more akin to animals than humans. In essence, nature without restraint was monstrous in Africa. The continent exemplified the world's unrestrained primitive areas, which civilized lands, like Greece and Rome, must never become.

From the classical world of Herodotus, Pliny, and Ptolemy, a pattern of thought about Africa and Africans emerged, forming the basis for an approach to the continent and its inhabitants that persisted well into the Middle Ages. At that time, in addition to classical writings about Africa, a small number of Europeans who were able to read Arabic had at their disposal a number of books about the continent prepared by Muslim scholars living in Spain, Sicily, and the Middle East. While European merchants who regularly traded in North Africa with Arabs retold stories about the African kingdoms of the Western Sudan, the writings of Arabic travellers and geographers were being translated into European languages, with two authors in particular being especially noteworthy: Abdullah al-Bakri, a Muslim from Granada, Spain, and Muhammad ibn-Battūta, who visited the kingdom of Mali in 1352. Their writings are distinguished for their accuracy and consequently were of great value to the interested European reader, since they had direct knowledge of the places and the peoples about which they wrote. Thus, long before they explored the coast of West Africa for themselves, Europeans had access to reports about the kingdoms of the Western Sudan. Unfortunately, the work of al-Bakri and ibn-Battūta existed alongside many literary efforts of a kind that suggested something else entirely about Africa.

Travellers' tales were a popular form of entertainment in the Middle Ages, and one of the most widely read books about Africa was the *Travels of Sir John Mandeville*. Written as a fictitious account, it appeared for the first time in the fourteenth century. The reason for its popularity was linked to the nature of its subject matter. The work was rife with strange tales about wild animals and oddly shaped people who inhabited the interior of Africa. In addition, it contained stories about which every reader in the Middle Ages might have dreamed: rivers flowing with precious stones, there for the taking, in a kingdom of marvelous dimensions. The people of Africa were referred to as "Moors," and Africa was described as a land of extreme climatic changes. There were, in fact, water wells in parts of Africa that were so hot during the day and so cold at night that no person could drink from them. But in one passage a striking description of the people of Africa was given:

> In that country be folk that have but one foot and they go so blue that it is marvellous. And the foot is so large that it shadoweth all the body against the sun when they lie down to rest. In a certain island to the south live folk of strange build that have no heads, and their eyes be in their shoulders. And their mouth is crooked as a horseshoe, and that is in the midst of their breast. And in another isle be folk that have the face all flat, all plain without nose and without mouth, but they have two small holes all around instead of their eyes, and their mouth is flat also without lips.[5]

Besides the similarity between Mandeville's description of Africans and the characterization offered by Pliny the Elder, the judgments implied in both cases were also equally clear: nature takes on a hideous look in an African landscape of chaotic proportions.

A second tale about Africa popular in the Middle Ages centered around the figure of Prester John, supposedly a powerful Christian king who lived somewhere in Africa. The belief that a Christian kingdom existed beyond the geographical limits of Persia and Armenia, somewhere beyond the territory of the infidel Mohammedans in the Orient, was widely circulated in Europe during the twelfth century.[6] The story supported the hope that Christianity existed in the unknown world beyond Islam. The presence of Prester John had a special appeal for Christian Europe, since the idea of a mighty king arose precisely when the wish for such an ally against the infidels of Islam was strongest. However, no direct contact with Prester John had ever been made, nor had any positive proof of his existence been established until the appearance in Europe of a letter. Allegedly written by the Christian king, the letter stated that Prester John's rule was supreme and his military power unsurpassed. In a realm of wondrous proportions, a river ran, studded with emeralds, sapphires, topazes, and other precious stones, and a royal palace stood, made from ebony, gold, crystal, ivory, and onyx. The letter proved to be a forgery, fabricated by some unknown author. Unlike any other single piece of writing, however, it was widely circulated throughout Europe. Thousands of copies were made which were translated from the original Latin into the vernacular languages of medieval Europe.

As the letter passed through the hands of different translators, the original content was so distorted that it eventually became a compendium of the most popular myths, marvels, and fables of the Middle Ages. The embellished letter, for example, told of ants as big as foxes, having the skins of panthers, the wings of sea locusts, and the tusks of forest boars. In Prester John's kingdom, there were unicorns so ferocious that they could kill lions. Strange serpents, amazons, and centaurs lived here, and even "horned men, who have but one eye in front and three or four in back." The priest-king recruited cannibals as soldiers, granting them permission "to eat our enemies, so that of a thousand foes not one remains who is not devoured and consumed." The letter prudently stated, in closing, that the cannibals were quickly sent home after fighting, since, "if we let them stay longer with us, they would eat us all."[7] Through the efforts of Prester John and his unknown collaborators, another fabulous tale about Africans was added to the already increasing abundance of speculative writing about the continent.

At about the same time that the mythical Prester John was being revered in Europe, the Portuguese were beginning to make actual contact with real Africans. They arrived in the kingdom of the Kongo in the 1480s. As proof of the popularity of Prester John, however, the Portuguese in fact had hoped that Kongo might adjoin the mythical kingdom of Prester John. Their involvement in Kongo, nonetheless, and then with the West African kingdom of Benin in the fifteenth century, provided some revealing descriptions about African life. As the coastline of West Africa was further explored, information supplied by the Portuguese increased throughout the sixteenth century, when it was eventually supplemented with the publication of Leo Africanus's *History and Description of Africa*.[8]

A Moor from Spain, Joannes Leo Africanus travelled to the Western Sudan as a diplomat. In 1518 he was captured by pirates in the Mediterranean and was sold in Italy as a slave. There he came to the notice of Pope Leo X, who subsequently freed him. Although written in defective Italian, his *History* provided a firsthand account of the empires of the interior of West Africa and is still a valuable commentary on the region, as his careful description of the city of Timbuktu reveals:

> Tombuto is situate within twelve miles of a certaine branch of Niger, all the houses whereof are now changed into cottages built of chalke, and covered with thatch. Howbeit there is a most stately temple to be seene, the wals whereof are made of stone and lime; and a princely palace also built by a most excellent workeman of Granada. Here are many shops of artificers, and merchants, and especially of such as weave linen and cotton cloth. And hither do the Barbarie-merchants bring cloth of Europe.... The inhabitants, and especially strangers there residing, are exceeding rich, insomuch, that the king that now is, married both his daughters unto rich merchants.... Corne, cattle, milke and butter this region yeeldeth in great abundance: but salt is verie scarce heere; for it is brought hither by land from Tegaza, which is five hundred miles distant.[9]

According to the author, the king of Timbuktu was exceedingly rich; he conducted his court in regal splendor and was attended by a great army. Doctors, judges, priests, and other learned people could be found throughout the city. Books and manuscripts were readily available. The citizens were good-natured and often sang and danced in the streets:

> The rich King of Tombuto hath many plates and scepters of gold, some whereof weigh 1300 poundes: and he keepes a magnificent and well furnished court.... He hath alwaies three thousand horsemen, and a great number of footmen that shoot poysoned arrowes, attending upon him. They have often skirmishes with those that refuse to pay tribute, and so many as they take, they sell unto the merchants of Tombuto.... Here are great store of doctors, judges, priests, and other learned men, that are bountifully maintained at the kings cost and charges. And hither are brought divers manuscripts or written bookes out of Barbarie, which are sold for more money then any other merchandize. The coine of Tombuto is of gold without any stampe or superscription: but in matters of final value they use certaine shels brought hither out of the kingdome of Persia, fower hundred of which shels are worth a ducate.... The inhabitants are people of a gentle and cherefull disposition, and spend a great part of the night in singing and dancing through all the streets of the citie: they keepe great store

of men and women-slaves, and their towne is much in danger of fire: at my second being there halfe the town almost was burnt in five hours space.[10]

Timbuktu's only deficiency, according to Leo Africanus, was its lack of gardens and orchards.

Complementing the work of Leo Africanus on Africa was Richard Hakluyt's *The Principal Navigations, Voyages, Traffiques and Discoveries of the English Nation*. Appearing in 1589, the publication was a compilation of travel accounts, many of which dealt specifically with Africa and Africans. For example, in one narrative, Africa was portrayed as a "golden land" of great abundance where ivory and gold were plentiful.[11] The continent, however, was also described as an alien environment: the weather, vegetation, animal life, and people were unlike anything known in Europe. The west coast of Africa was intensely hot; the winds and rains were violent at times.[12] The sea near the coasts was treacherous, and the inland rivers were terrifying. Great detail was given to Africa's animals in Hakluyt's work, particularly the elephant, because of its shape and size, and the crocodile, because of its sinister appearance.[13] Although Hakluyt's volumes contained much accurate information, the overall impression conveyed to the reading public of Europe was that in Africa nature was too awesome—and too disturbing.

Through the writings of the Portuguese, Leo Africanus, Richard Hakluyt, and many others, a substantial body of information about Africa began to appear in Europe by the beginning of the sixteenth century. It existed, nonetheless, side by side with popular tales about the more fabulous dimensions of the continent. Detailed accounts of Timbuktu vied with portrayals of legendary monsters and deformed human beings, and the task of separating fact from fiction was a real problem, and one which was not easily resolved. By the latter part of the sixteenth century in England, ancient sources, legendary tales, and contemporary travel narratives had become mixed together.[14] In 1555, William Watermann's *The Fardle of Fashions*, a translation of Johan Boemus's *Omnium gentium mores* (1520), became a popular source on Africa.[15] Watermann drew freely upon Herodotus's writings about Africa and other ancient authorities, including Pliny the Elder. But he supplemented the older tales with more recent works, including the fictitious account of Africa attributed to Sir John Mandeville. Watermann presented the people of Africa to the people of Europe as licentious brutes. Wandering about the interior parts of the continent, free from care, they feasted on plentiful amounts of meat, while almost all the men revelled with a willing supply of dark-skinned, promiscuous women.

A year later, in 1556, *A Summary of the Antiquities and Wonders of the World...Out of the Sixteen First Books of...Pliny* was published, in which the most exotic portrayals of Africans made by Pliny were catalogued:

> Of the Ethiopians there are divers forms and kinds of men. Some there are toward the east that have neither nose nor nostrils, but the face all full. Others that have no upper lip, they are without tongues, and they speak by signs, and they have but a little hole to take their breath at, by which they drink with an oaten straw. There are some called Syrbote that are eight foot high, they live with the chase of elephants. In a part of Affricke be people call Ptoemphane, for their king they have a dog, at whose fancy they are governed...Toward the west there is a people call Arimaspi, that hath but one eye in their foreheads, they are in the desert and wild country. The people called Agriphagi live with the flesh of panthers and lions: and the people called Anthropomphagi which we call cannibals, live with human flesh. The Cinamolgi, their heads are almost like the heads of dogs....In Libie which is at the end of the Ethiopes, there are people differing from the common order of others, they have among them no names and they curse the sun for his great heat, by the which they are all black saving their teeth and a little the palm of their hands, and they never dream....Others called Gramantes, they make no marriages, but all women are common. Gamphasantes they go all naked. Blemmyis a people so called, they have no heads, but have their mouth and their eyes in their breasts. And others there are that go more by training of their hands than with their feet.[16]

Descriptions such as this imbedded in the popular mind the idea of Africans as a grotesque race of people, a notion that found wide acceptance in Europe by the middle of the sixteenth century.

During the seventeenth century, European contact with Africa expanded. At the start of the century, the Dutch, Danes, French, and English competed among themselves for trade with West Africa. In search of gold, Richard Jobson visited Gambia in 1620, during which time he described in detail a town he called "Setico":

The towne was built round, after the manner of a Circle, whereof the front of the houses, did not containe any great thicknesse, but as we may say, the breedth of a reasonable faire street, joyning their houses or walles of their yards and barnes close together, the diameter whereof, that is from the North, to the South, or likewise from any one point to his opposite, we did conceive to be neere an English mile, within which Circute was much Cattle, especially store of Asses, whereby it may be conjectured, that they contrived their towne in that sort, to keepe out the ravening beasts and securing those Cattle they had about them.... [17]

Jobson's remarks were typical of other firsthand observations resulting from direct contact with Africa and Africans; and while it can be said that almost every European visitor to Africa provided some new bit of information about the continent, the writings of Willem Bosman, who reached Elmina on Africa's western coast in 1688, constituted an additional perspective on Africa rendered by a newly arrived European.

Bosman was a Dutchman employed by the Dutch West India Company who became one of the company's most important commercial agents. As a resident of Africa's west coast, he offered a number of opinions about the African peoples of the area with whom he traded. Bosman was tolerant and sensitive and attempted to treat Africans as equal partners in trade. Yet on many occasions he thought that their unfamiliar customs and religious practices were "foolish and ridiculous." [18] He claimed that many Africans were lazy, given to idleness, and often reluctant to work; he believed that they were neither attentive nor intelligent. When Africans were young, according to Bosman, they were ugly, and when old, they were frightening. Bosman saw some Africans in a more favorable light—especially those with whom he needed to do business—but his view of almost everyone else was far from being without bias. His writings, nonetheless, like those of Richard Jobson, significantly increased the amount of factual information Europeans were beginning to accumulate about Africa. By 1700, then, a number of travel accounts had been published in Europe about the African coastal areas by individuals who had actually journeyed there. The interior of the continent was still very much unknown, and mapmakers of the time, sometimes to fill up space, populated the interior of the continent with those mythical objects that had become so much a part of the European image of Africa.

But in 1772 a Scottish explorer named James Bruce travelled to Ethiopia, reaching what he believed to be the source of the Nile. His exploits in Ethiopia were widely published, and his travels added considerable knowledge about the Nile in particular and East Africa in general. In 1778, Sir Joseph Banks founded the Association for Promoting the Discovery of the Interior Parts of Africa, and with the explorer Mungo Park's first expedition to the Niger in 1785, the systematic reconnoitering of Africa by Europeans began. By the latter part of the eighteenth century, intense scientific interest was directed toward Africa, reflecting a sustained curiosity about the geography, the animal and plant life, and especially the people of the continent. Moreover, the great exploration of Africa was initiated only a short time afterward. At the start of the nineteenth century, knowledge of the interior of the continent was scattered: the courses and sources of the great African rivers—the Niger, Nile, Congo, and Zambesi— were still unknown. By 1885, in contrast, the continent had been crossed from east to west, the extent of the Sahara had been charted, and the major rivers of Africa had been followed and mapped. Increased exploration, financed by organizations with scientific aims or by governments interested in commerce and the suppression of the slave trade, was undertaken very often by solitary discoverers, individuals who left a recorded legacy of their experiences in Africa.

Despite a considerable expanse of time, extending from the classical world of Greece and Rome well into the nineteenth century, there is a pattern to this tradition of reporting Africa that can be traced and interpreted. Generally, the African narratives written, published, and disseminated by travellers from the West indicated directly or implied obtusely that Africans lacked civilization, or any redeeming type of social organization. As a race, they were promiscuous and cruel, and their behavior was more akin to beasts than to people, an idea advanced by portraying Africans as having less than human form. Africa, in addition, was seen as a mirror image of what Greece, Rome, or Europe should never be: a land where nature had gone wild, where chaos and anarchy reigned, where people were deformed both in body and spirit, and where gross excesses of behavior were not the exception but the rule.

As contacts between Europe and Africa became greater, beginning in the eighteenth century, knowledge of Africa and Africans increased. Although monsters no longer filled the pages of reports from Africa, as they had at an earlier time, a negative prejudice toward the primitive replaced a fascination with the grotesquely fabulous, and with an equally distorting effect. At this time, moreover, the cumulative effect of past descriptions of the continent tended to influence subsequent evaluations. In short, a cultural formula of expression became the accepted form of analysis for dealing with Africa. The nature of this prejudgment not only prevented adequate observation by non-Africans but also hindered careful description of what was to be observed. Accurate information about Africa began to accumulate, but the complexity of the task of cultural analysis—a problem for any white-skinned European who faced a dark-skinned African for the very first time—was a difficult one. The major defining features of these eighteenth-century accounts of Africa rendered by Europeans were cultural parochialism, negative prejudice toward the primitive, and cultural stasis.[19]

With the rise of more educated travellers to Africa in the nineteenth century, a desire for accuracy increased. Although new patterns of scientific inquiry surfaced, even the best of them were limited and crude, and remnants of the old form of analysis, parochialism, prejudice, and stasis remained and were supplemented by an expanding body of theory about the nature of race. As a result, European and American travellers to Africa were better with descriptions of geography than of people. Topography was more susceptible to accurate appraisal. The physical was easier to analyze than the cultural or human for an important reason: Cultural differences of necessity involved moral judgments, and any moral judgment involved stressing certain aspects of a culture while suppressing others.

Although American descriptions of Africa in particular did not increase measurably until the late nineteenth and early twentieth centuries, they became a part of this earlier tradition of reporting Africa, a heritage founded upon patterns of belief nurtured by fact, exaggeration, distortion, and ignorance. But as a prelude to our analysis of American perceptions of Africa, a number of introductory questions about the nature of American activity on the continent need to be raised. When, we might ask, did Americans begin to travel to Africa in numbers sufficient to measure? Why would Americans want to travel to Africa in the first place? Since Americans who travelled to Africa could not possibly traverse all the continent because of its vast size, with what parts did they become familiar? And what of the racial attitudes that Americans carried with them to the continent? Answers to these preliminary questions are essential for understanding the American experience in Africa, but taken in sequence they also provide a point of departure for discussing what might be conveniently termed "America in Africa."

Notes

1. See E. H. Bunbury, *A History of Ancient Geography Among the Greeks and Romans from the Earliest Ages till the Fall of the Roman Empire*, 2 vols. (New York: Dover Publications, 1959) and H.K.W. Kumm, "Africa as Known to Greek and Roman Geographers," *Scottish Geographical Magazine* 42 (January 1, 1962), 11–22.

2. Bunbury, *History of Ancient Geography*, 1:269.

3. *Selections from the History of the World Commonly Called the Natural History of C. Plinius Secundus*, trans. Philemon Holland and ed. Paul Turner (Carbondale: Southern Illinois University Press, 1962), p. 66.

4. Bunbury, *History of Ancient Geography*, 2:633.

5. *Mandeville's Travels*, ed. M. C. Seymour (London: Oxford University Press, 1968), pp. 121–22.

6. See John K. Wright, *The Geographical Lore of the Time of the Crusades: A Study in the History of Medieval Science in Western Europe* (New York: American Geographical Society, 1925), pp. 283–86.

7. Henri Baudet, *Paradise on Earth: Some Thoughts on European Images of Non-European Man*, trans. Elizabeth Wenthold (New Haven: Yale University Press, 1965), pp. 16–17.

8. Joannes Leo Africanus, *A Geographical History of Africa*, trans. John Pory (London, 1600; reprint, Amsterdam: Da Capo Press, 1969).

9. Ibid., p. 287.

10. Ibid., p. 288.

11. "The Voyage of M. Thomas Windam to Guinea and the Kingdom of Benin, Anno 1553," in Richard Hakluyt, *The Principal Navigations, Voyages, Traffiques and Discoveries of the English Nation*, 8 vols. (London: J. M. Dent and Sons, 1927), 4:41.

12. "The Voyage of M. John Lok to Guinea, Anno 1544," in Hakluyt, *Principal Navigations*, 4:60–61.

13. Ibid., pp. 55–58.

14. Eldred D. Jones, *The Elizabethan Image of Africa* (Charlottesville: University Press of Virginia, 1977), p. 1.

15. Ibid., p. 6.

16. As cited in ibid., pp. 5–6.

17. Richard Jobson, *The Golden Trade; or, A Discovery of the River Gambra, and the Golden Trade of the Aethiopians* (London: Penguin Press, 1932), pp. 89–90.

18. See generally Willem Bosman, *A New and Accurate Description of the Coast of Guinea, Divided into the Gold, the Slave, and the Ivory Coasts...*, trans. from the Dutch (London: J. Knapton, D. Midwinter, 1721), pp. 121–36.

19. I follow closely here Katherine George, "The Civilized West Looks at Primitive Africa: 1400–1800," *Isis* 49 (1958), 62–72.

2

America in Africa

America's involvement with Africa has varied in intensity and purpose from the seventeenth century to the present, from its initial complicity in the Atlantic slave trade to current efforts to come to terms with Africa's strategic importance in global affairs.[1] When the adventurous and ambitious traders from Holland deposited their cargo of twenty African slaves on the shores of Jamestown, Virginia, in 1619, a relationship of unforeseen significance between America and Africa was dramatically established.[2] Although the connection began as an economic one—a desire to carry on a trade in human beings and material goods—the ties that have bound America to Africa have become increasingly more varied through the centuries. From the slaves and rum of a former time, American interests in Africa have come to include such diverse phenomena as the ideology of Pan-Africanism or, more recently, the political fate of Africa's emerging nations.[3] However, the African presence in America was established when the first slaves from Africa arrived in colonial Virginia in the early part of the seventeenth century, and though tentatively begun, the consequence of people from Africa being in America quickly became evident, as the recorded history of that period makes clear.[4]

The importance of Americans in Africa at a similar time, in contrast, is not as easily discoverable. Unlike the seafaring Portuguese who had managed to work their way down the western coasts of Africa, establishing commercial posts there by the end of the fifteenth century, prior to the nineteenth century the American presence in Africa was limited in scope to scattered attempts at commerce.[5] Even though some Christians in seventeenth- and eighteenth-century America, individuals like Cotton Mather and Anthony Benezet, had expressed a genuine interest in the spiritual welfare of Africa, the trade in rum, brandy, and tobacco and the search for whales, together with the commerce in slaves, initially placed colonial Americans on African shores.[6] As enterprising Yankee merchants began to seek out new markets to exploit, and as the demand for the labor of Africans grew, American relations with Africa expanded. Acquisitive trading families like the Beekmans of New York or the Moses Browns of Rhode Island dispatched ships to Africa in order to establish lucrative commercial ties with the continent.

The significance of Americans in Africa during this early time did not increase proportionately to the rise in trade. This seemingly paradoxical situation can be attributed to the very character of their travel. Americans confined themselves to the coastal fringes of Africa because they considered the interior of the continent to be impenetrable for non-Africans, and their visits were sporadic and infrequent. Americans who sailed to Africa, moreover, did so for very short periods of time, and their primary interests lay not in settlement or discovery but in trade and profit. Until the beginning of the nineteenth century, their contacts with Africa can best be understood as short-term business trips. However, involvement in Africa became greater as the nature of the relationship changed. Because of increased exploration and discovery, undertaken mainly by European explorers who helped open up Africa to the outside world, Americans became more active on the continent as more of it became known to them. By the early part of the nineteenth century they had begun to make their presence in Africa evident for several reasons.

Initially, Americans journeyed to Africa in order to colonize parts of West Africa for America's emancipated slaves. As a result of a successful effort to abolish slavery in the United States, the fate of these newly freed slaves and their place in American society became a pressing social issue. Resettlement in Africa was seen as a possible solution, and in response to the problem a number of colonization groups were organized in the United States between 1816 and 1865. The most active attempts at translating ideas of relocation into workable schemes of settlement were those of the American Colonization Society, the Maryland Colonization Society, the Mississippi Colonization Society, and the American Colonization Society of Pennsylvania.[7]

There were individual efforts at settlement in Africa as well. For example, Paul Cuffe, a successful New England merchant, visited Sierra Leone several times during the early nineteenth century.[8] Martin Delany, the antebellum abolitionist, editor, and physician, reconnoitered a section of the valley surrounding the Niger River in 1859–1860 with Robert Campbell, a Jamaica-born chemist. They did so not only to make a "Topographical, Geological and Geographical Examination" of the region, but also to find out how suitable the area might be for future settlement by black Americans.[9] Bishop Henry M. Turner of the African Methodist Episcopal Church attempted to acquire a portion of the continent, however small, in the late nineteenth century, so that individuals who wished to escape America's racial turmoil might find sanctuary in Africa.[10] While specific approaches to particular colonization plans differed from one group to another, and from one individual to another, depending on the support available to each organization and the energy of its leaders, the collective aim of all colonization efforts was ultimately the same: to establish viable settlements in Africa.

A second reason for going to Africa was centered around the belief that Africans were in desperate need of spiritual salvation. Although the English were the first to contribute to the growth of the foreign missionary movement with the organization of a system of missions by the Methodists in 1787, the idea of sending missionaries to Africa was favorably received in America. Samuel Hopkins of Newport, Rhode Island, originally proposed in 1770 to train a number of emancipated slaves for service as missionaries in Africa. Although he was unsuccessful, and despite this initial setback, the American missionary movement eventually prospered through the efforts of zealous people like Hopkins, who hoped to convert the "wayward" people of the world, including Africans, to the doctrines of Christianity. In addition, as part of a general religious revival associated with the Enlightenment in Europe in the eighteenth century, the role of missionaries as foreign agents of Christianity was expanded throughout the nineteenth century.[11] Many Americans who were both intensely Christian and fervently Protestant wished to convert to Christianity dark-skinned "heathens," wherever they might be. Their proselytizing efforts were directed toward North and South America, China, Japan, the Sandwich Islands, and also the "pagan" population of Africa.[12]

American religious groups established missionary stations and placed missionaries throughout Africa. The following missionary societies, together with the dates of their entry into Africa, were organized in the first half of the nineteenth century: the American Baptist Missionary Union (1822); the Missionary Society of the Methodist Episcopal Church (1833); the American Board of Commissioners for Foreign Missions (1833); the Domestic and Foreign Missionary Society of the Protestant Episcopal Church (1836); the Board of Foreign Missions of the Presbyterian Church, North (1842); and the Foreign Missions Board, Southern Baptist Convention (1850). To this list can be added societies established in the latter half of the century: the Board of Foreign Missions of the United Presbyterian Church (1854); the Christian Missionary Alliance (1887); and the Executive Committee for Foreign Missions of the Presbyterian Church, South (1891). Less active groups included the Gospel Missionary Union (1894), the Africa Inland Missions (1895), and the Peniel Missionary Society (1895).[13]

Although the prospect of turning fallen Africans into upright Christians was a task that occupied the energies of missionaries, other Americans were attracted to Africa for reasons that had less to do with saving souls and more to do with filling pocketbooks. American traders and merchants, in search of new markets and potential sources of raw materials, were attracted by Africa's supposedly undeveloped state. Though their trade with Africa never became significant, like their European counterparts, Americans believed that great material gain could be amassed by exploiting portions of the continent. The idea had a compelling ring to it, especially as the commercial horizons of the United States began to broaden during the nineteenth century.[14] Africa was economically attractive not so much because of its present state but because of its future promise.

Samuel P. Verner's commentary in this regard is revealing:

At Victoria Falls, there will be another Buffalo; near the southern end of Tanganika will be a city as large as Detroit, one-third of whose inhabitants will be whites. Stanleyville, the present metropolis of the center of the Congo, will be a black St. Louis. On the shores of Lake Albert, there will be an African Cleveland. Khartoum will rival Memphis; and Cairo and Alexandria together will have the present population of New York. Somewhere in the highlands of Abyssinia, on the Blue Nile, there will have arisen the African Pittsburg; a black New Orleans, somewhere about the lower Niger, will be shipping palm oil to its prototype across the Atlantic.[15]

Verner's vision of Africa was typically American: the continent was prized not for what it presently was but for what it might eventually be. In addition, with the discovery of gold and diamonds in the southern part of Africa in the 1850s and 1860s, Americans reasoned that if such treasures signalled Africa's actual bounty, then surely the future held much more.[16] If the continent's fertile acreage produced so many tons of coffee, barrels of palm oil, and cords of wood with the labor of untutored Africans, then with American aid could not Africa be coaxed into giving up even more of its resources?

To colonize, to Christianize, and to commercialize were the principal reasons Americans travelled to Africa. Being in Africa, however, was also part of the structure of a more complex story, a matter not simply of advocating colonies, Christ, or commerce, but of fostering "civilization" and everything embraced by that powerful word. Writing in 1860, Charles W. Thomas, a chaplain for the United States African Squadron, a naval unit that patrolled the coasts of Africa to inhibit the export of slaves, noted:

Civilization is advancing even in Africa. The roar of cannon, the plunging of heavy anchors, the rush of the paddle-wheel, have disturbed the gambols of the hippopotami, and the river-horse no longer rolls in the lower floods of the Gambia. The lion, the leopard, and the stately elephant are disappearing from its banks; the mimicking parrot has already carried the echoes of the steam-whistle into the deep forests of the interior—the voice of a bird telling the dawn of a coming day—and after them shall follow, with slow but steady tread, the heralds of religion and the sons of trade. The march of humanity is "onward!" Progress is inevitable....[17]

Americans journeyed to Africa for aims other than spreading "civilization" to the "unenlightened," however; they came for more narrowly focused, less lofty reasons as well.

American scientists were intrigued by Africa's animal and plant life because they knew so little about it. As we have seen, from the time of the ancient Greeks, Africa had been considered a continent of special dimensions, a land thought to be inhabited by unusual animals and covered by exotic vegetation. During the Middle Ages, curious Europeans wondered what lay beyond Africa's coasts. They debated Africa's true nature and speculated about people who were dwarfs, beasts that resembled people, and a tropical luxuriance that defied accurate description. In commenting upon that period, one American recalled that Africa had been portrayed as "the abode of griffins, dragons, rocs, headless men, and other strange monsters."[18] However, in order to dispel some of the mystery surrounding the continent in their own time, America's scientific community undertook a number of expeditions to Africa during the late nineteenth and early twentieth centuries.

The United States Scientific Expedition sailed for the west coast of Africa in 1889 in order to follow a solar eclipse. It was successful in its astronomical efforts, but the expedition also collected specimens of African plant life. In 1913, the American Biological Expedition to Africa was organized, while the National American Government Expedition was begun a year later. Yet the most heralded of all organized scientific excursions to Africa was the Smithsonian Institution Expedition of 1909, whose purpose was common enough: to collect several species of birds, mammals, reptiles, and big game peculiar to Africa, to be displayed at the National Museum in Washington, D.C. But what gave this African safari an illustrious quality was the notoriety of the participants involved: former President Theodore Roosevelt; Edmund Heller, the noted taxidermist; J. Alden Loring, a well-known naturalist; and F. C. Selous, the famous hunter.[19]

Artistic motives complemented scientific reasons for travelling to Africa. The continent, some American writers felt, offered an extraordinarily creative milieu. For the established literary figure, and for the aspiring writer as well, adventure and intrigue seemed to be natural parts of the African scene. They equated Africa with unprecedented physical danger, a setting in which their heroes and heroines could battle savage, beast, or almost anything in between.

Africa provided dramatic contexts and untold story possibilities for a number of American writers, especially those who wrote explicitly for children. Thomas W. Knox wrote *The Boy Travellers on the Congo: Adventures of Two Youths in a Journey with Henry M. Stanley (Through the Dark Continent)* in 1888. William James Morrison chronicled the daring exploits of an American boy in *Willie Wyld: Lost in the Jungles of Africa* (1912), while Herbert Strang told his youthful audience about *Fighting on the Congo: The Story of an American Boy Among the Rubber Slaves* (1906).

Finally, Americans were drawn to Africa for the psychological benefits to be gained by being there. Particularly during the late nineteenth and early twentieth centuries, Africa appeared as an exciting alternative to civilization.[20] In contrast to the complexity of living in an increasingly industrialized and urbanized America, Africa was seen as a chance to leave behind the frustrations of civilized life and to test one's courage. Poultney Bigelow, an American journalist and author, remarked that as a boy he was thrilled by playing "Indians and pirates" but that as a man adventure was to be found in "exploring dangerous countries" like Africa.[21] John McCutcheon, an award-winning cartoonist for the *Chicago Tribune*, felt that except for wars, which were all too "few and far between" for him, lion hunting in Africa was "about the only thing left" for testing his potential for heroism:

> Africa! What a picture it conjured up in my fancy! Then, as even now, it symbolized a world of adventurous possibilities; and in my boyhood fancy, it lay away off there—somewhere—vaguely—beyond mountains and deserts and oceans, a vast, mysterious, unknown land, that swarmed with inviting dangers and alluring romance.[22]

For at least one segment of American society, travelling to Africa was motivated by "the boyish desire to be a hero."[23]

Africa was also a test of character. As he wrote to an English friend, a trip to Africa in 1909 was a way of managing defeat for Theodore Roosevelt.[24] Just a year before he had been unsuccessful in his bid for the presidency. In Africa he hoped to renew himself as leader of the Smithsonian Institution Expedition, just as during an earlier time in his life Roosevelt had sought refuge from personal and political pressures in the unspoiled lands of the western Dakotas.[25] Roosevelt, moreover, believed that there was something morally uplifting in experiencing Africa firsthand. For someone who measured life in terms of swagger and swearing—as Roosevelt did—a "vigorous manliness" was nurtured by being in direct contact with a demanding environment and by engaging in the acts of hunting and killing wild animals.

Journeying to Africa, then, was bound up with a number of specific aims. It involved settling colonies, establishing missionary outposts, and broadening commercial horizons. On a lesser scale, it included writers, scientists, and those who desired adventure and escape. Although the impetus for travel, like the common body of water separating America from Africa, ebbed and flowed over time, the question remains: In what regions and places in Africa was the American presence most strongly evident?

Geographically, Americans concentrated their efforts in only certain parts of the continent.[26] In West Africa, they were particularly active on the coast along a thin ribbon of hot, humid land separating the ocean from the uplands of the interior. Because of a high incidence of death due to malaria and other diseases among non-Africans, this region was sometimes referred to as a "white man's grave." Americans travelled throughout the Sherbo district of Sierra Leone; to Monrovia, Cape Mount, Edina, Bexley, Bassa Cove, and Cape Palmas in Liberia; to the area adjacent to Abeokuta in Nigeria; to Cameroon, and to Corisco Island in Equatorial Guinea; to the region surrounding the bay of the Gabon River in Gabon; and to Pungo Andongo, Malange, and Luanda in Angola.

Increased exploration moved other Americans away from the coastal fringes of the continent and placed them in selected parts of the grassy uplands and rain forests of the interior. Paul Belloni Du Chaillu, for example, penetrated the interior of west central Africa, starting from the Gabon River, and then moved eastward, while Henry M. Stanley explored a route carved out by the force of the Congo River. Throughout *In Darkest Africa*, Stanley called parts of Central Africa the "lower world of vegetation" where "eternal interlaced branches" covered the forest terrain.[27] Today it is an area that includes the countries of Zaire and Congo and such cities as Kisangani (Stanleyville), Mbandaka (Coquilhatville), Brazzaville, and Kinshasa (Léopoldville).

In eastern and southeastern Africa, Americans confined their travels to a three-thousand-mile strip of the African continent running northeastward from Cape Town to Nairobi. Of all the sections of Africa in which Americans travelled, it is the most topographically diverse. The region contains great stretches of desert in the south, with mountains, lakes, and valleys in the east. The eastern part of the continent was once proclaimed a "white man's land" by Americans and Europeans because a temperate climate made settlement and travel both possible and desirable.[28] The area includes the present-day countries of South Africa, Zimbabwe, Zambia, Malawi, Tanzania, Uganda, and Kenya and such cities as Cape Town, Kimberley, and Pretoria in South Africa; Bulawayo and Salisbury in Zimbabwe; and Mombasa and Nairobi in Kenya, to name the most prominent.

Although Americans were active in many geographically diverse parts of the continent, it is clear that they did not traverse the entire length and breadth of Africa. They were restricted to selected areas of the continent by the demands placed upon them by the African environment, by their own individual motivation and disposition toward exploration, discovery, and settlement, and by the freedom allowed to them by the actions and decisions of various African peoples. Nonetheless, American perceptions of Africa were accurate and reliable when describing the physical characteristics of the parts of Africa in which they travelled: topography, variations in climate, and generally the appearance of the natural environment. But judgments and evaluations made by Americans about Africans—their creative acts, the form of their social organization, and the moral and ethical foundations of their cultures—were interpreted through the cultural apparatus that Americans brought with them. In particular, American responses to Africans were influenced by a body of racial thought about the dark-skinned people of the world that had been developing in America and Europe throughout the nineteenth century.

During the nineteenth century, theories about race emerged as a main current in American thought.[29] Such ideas posited the innate or permanent inferiority of dark-skinned peoples of the world generally, and a doctrine of black inferiority in America in particular. Since black people were seen as threats to order and stability, they needed to be controlled, studied, and made more predictable. The threat of race war and insurrection was never really distant. A sense of cultural inferiority subordinated blacks to whites, and skin color, as a permanent sign of origin, precluded social equality. As whites sought to consolidate their positions of power in American society, one way of ensuring their status was by defining blacks as subhuman. This system, of course, depended on the idea that whites were, in theory, superior to blacks in all ways possible.

The case against black people in America was advanced by showing that their African ancestors had failed to develop a fully civilized way of life. If Africans could not do it in their homeland, then how could their progeny possibly be expected to do any better in America? Proslavery writings, for example, depicted Africa as a land of unrestraint, cannibalism, and debauchery. The physiological and anatomical differences between whites and blacks were obvious for all to see in Africa. Did not Africans, the ancestors of black Americans, more resemble apes than humans? Could this surely not be a good explanation for their supposed mental and physical inferiority? Had not Africans actually failed to raise themselves above these animal creatures? As part of the indictment, science became the apologizing rationale for racial subordination. The races of mankind, according to those who believed in polygenesis, had been separately created as distinct and unequal, and not simply as varieties of the same species. This idea was at variance with, and replaced, an older theory of monogenesis, which claimed that all races were of the same species and that diversity could be attributed to differences found in the environment.[30] Blacks were not akin to whites, but separate from them.

By the late nineteenth century, in the aftermath of Charles Darwin's publication of *On the Origin of Species*, a theory of evolution became the most prominent scientific pronouncement on race. Although Darwin's work focused on movement toward higher forms of life derived from the conflict and competition of varieties and species in the natural world, "survival of the fittest," the phrase by which the theory became popularly known, appealed to many who saw some races being favored over others. It suggested the eventual disappearance of the "inferior races," especially those that were considered poorly adapted for the emerging industrial order or ill-suited to take part in the progressive development of Western civilization. Blacks stood far below nonblacks in the capacity for survival, since they had shown no racial progress or intellectual development. The notion of permanent black inferiority proved to be a beguiling scientific hypothesis. Having had their character formed in Africa, the result was obvious: it was a legacy of inefficiency and chaos, the perfect distortion of what Americans of the period held sacred—progress, efficiency, sexual restraint, and moral rectitude.

Racial degeneracy and the possibility of extinction provided a basis for antiblack propaganda during the late nineteenth and early twentieth centuries. The depiction of blacks as "beastlike" was derived, in part, from portrayals of Africa. American blacks, like African blacks, could be bloodthirsty, vicious, and murderous. Ruled by sexual passion, they needed to be controlled by being segregated and disfranchised. Moreover, anti-imperialists of the time stressed that annexation of foreign territory would mean extending the flag to inferior races.[31] Although there was no actual annexation of territory in Africa by Americans, the argument provided a racist rationale for intervention in the affairs of African peoples. Americans, in good conscience, could take up the "white man's burden" of uplifting the inferior peoples of the world, a proposition that supported the missionary and commercial spirit of the time. Economic exploitation, if done benevolently, served as a justification for expansion, since mankind would be uplifted in the process. People could be elevated, even those in Africa. All they needed was the tutelage of Americans to achieve at least some sense of limited improvement.

Thus, despite some divergent opinion from Americans, especially reform-minded abolitionists who spoke out against racism, there was a consensus among most white Americans about certain assumptions about black-white relations: namely, that blacks were not only different from whites in the ways they looked, thought, and acted, but that those differences accounted for their being defined as intellectually and emotionally inferior. These differences, in addition, were either permanent in nature or subject to change only by a slow process of development or evolution. Consequently, the future of black people in America was either subordination or elimination.[32]

The story of Americans in Africa, however, is not just the story of racial attitudes formed in America being transplanted to a new setting. It also includes the knowledge of Africa and Africans that Americans gained by being in Africa, the discoveries they made about Africans that were at variance with their preconceived notions, and how their understanding of Africa was changed as a result of their experiences.

Notes

1. For a survey of American relations with Africa, see Clarence C. Clendenen and Peter Duignan, *Americans in Black Africa up to 1865* (Stanford, Calif.: Hoover Institution on War, Revolution, and Peace, Stanford University, 1964); Clarence Clendenen, Robert Collins, and Peter Duignan, *Americans in Africa 1865–1900* (Stanford, Calif.: Hoover Institution on War, Revolution, and Peace, Stanford University, 1966).

2. See David Brion Davis, *The Problem of Slavery in Western Culture* (Ithaca, N.Y.: Cornell University Press, 1966); Eugene D. Genovese, *Roll, Jordan, Roll: The World the Slaves Made* (New York: Pantheon, 1974); Winthrop Jordan, *White over Black: American Attitudes Toward the Negro, 1550–1812* (Chapel Hill: University of North Carolina Press, 1968).

3. For an interesting aspect of Pan-Africanism, see Kenneth James King, *Pan-Africanism and Education: A Study of Race, Philanthropy, and Education in the Southern States of America and East Africa* (New York: Oxford University Press, 1971); and Edward W. Chester, *Clash of Titans: Africa and United States Foreign Policy* (Maryknoll, N.Y.: Orbis Books, 1974); Rupert Emerson, "The Character of American Interests in Africa," in Walter Goldschmidt, ed., *The United States and Africa* (New York: Frederick A. Praeger, 1963).

4. For a discussion of the demography of the slave trade, see Philip D. Curtin, *The Atlantic Slave Trade* (Madison: University of Wisconsin Press, 1969).

5. Lawrence Cabot Howard, "American Involvement in Africa South of the Sahara, 1800–1860" (Ph.D. diss., Harvard University, 1956); Russell Warren Howe, *Along the Afric Shore: An Historic Review of Two Centuries of United States–African Relations* (New York: Barnes and Noble, 1975); Eric Rosenthal, *Stars and Stripes in Africa* (London: George Routledge and Sons, 1938).

6. For a discussion of American commercial ties at a later time, see George E. Brooks, Jr., *Yankee Traders, Old Coasters and African Middlemen: A History of American Legitimate Trade with West Africa in the Nineteenth Century* (Boston: Boston University Press, 1970).

7. P. J. Staudenraus, *The African Colonization Movement* (New York: Columbia University Press, 1961).

8. See Paul Cuffe, *A Brief Account of the Settlement and Present Situation of the Colony of Sierra Leone in Africa* (New York: Samuel Wood, 1812). Also Sheldon H. Harris, "An American's Impressions of Sierra Leone in 1811," *Journal of Negro History* 47 (January, 1962), 35–41.

9. M. R. Delany, *Official Report of the Niger Valley Exploring Party* (New York: T. Hamilton, 1861), p. 12; and A.H.M. Kirk-Greene, "America

in the Niger Valley: A Colonization Centenary," *Phylon* 23 (Fall, 1962), 225–39.

10. Edwin S. Redkey, *Black Exodus: Black Nationalist and Back-to-Africa Movements, 1890–1910* (New Haven: Yale University Press, 1969); and Sterling Stuckey, *The Ideological Origins of Black Nationalism* (Boston: Beacon Press, 1972).

11. A point made throughout Charles Pelham Groves, *The Planting of Christianity in Africa*, 4 vols. (London: Lutterworth Press, 1948–1958).

12. For attempts at saving the Chinese, for example, see Stuart Creighton Miller, *The Unwelcome Immigrant: The American Image of the Chinese, 1785–1882* (Berkeley: University of California Press, 1969).

13. This material was collected from the following sources: Harlan P. Beach, *A Geography and Atlas of Protestant Missions*, 2 vols. (New York: Student Volunteer Movement for Foreign Missions, 1901–1903); Henry Otis Dwight, "The Distribution of Missionary Forces in Africa," *Missionary Review of the World*, n.s. 18 (August, 1905), 590–96; Frederic Perry Noble, *The Redemption of Africa: A Story of Civilization*, 2 vols. (Chicago: Fleming H. Revell Co., 1899); and J. Leighton Wilson, *Western Africa: Its History, Condition, and Prospects* (New York: Harper and Brothers, 1856).

14. See Brooks, *Yankee Traders, Old Coasters and African Middlemen*; and also George E. Brooks and Frances K. Talbot, "The Providence Exploring and Trading Company's Expedition to the Niger River in 1832–1833," *American Neptune* 35 (1975), 77–96.

15. Samuel P. Verner, "Africa Fifty Years Hence," *World's Work* 13 (April, 1907), 8733. Samuel Phillips Verner (1873–1943) was the son of a former comptroller general of South Carolina and an 1892 graduate of the University of South Carolina. He was appointed business manager for the Mission Board of the Southern Presbyterian Church in 1895. See also his *Pioneering in Central Africa* (Richmond, Va.: Presbyterian Committee of Publication, 1903).

16. Thomas J. Noer, *Briton, Boer, and Yankee: The United States and South Africa, 1870–1914* (Kent, Ohio: Kent State University Press, 1979).

17. Charles W. Thomas, *Adventures and Observations on the West Coast of Africa, and Its Islands* (New York: Derby and Jackson, 1860), p. 225.

18. A. H. Godbey, *Stanley in Africa: The Paladin of the Nineteenth Century* (Chicago: Donohue Brothers, 1902), p. 21.

19. See Joseph L. Gardner, *Departing Glory: Theodore Roosevelt as Ex-President* (New York: Charles Scribner's Sons, 1973), esp. chap. 7, "Through Darkest Africa," pp. 107–37.

20. See Robert H. Wiebe, *The Search for Order, 1877–1920* (New York: Hill and Wang, 1967), esp. pp. 44–75.

21. Poultney Bigelow, *White Man's Africa* (New York: Harper and Brothers, 1900), p. 219.

22. John T. McCutcheon, *In Africa: Hunting Adventures in the Big Game Country* (Indianapolis: Bobbs-Merrill Co., 1910), pp. 1–2.

23. Stewart Edward White, *The Land of the Footprints* (Garden City, N.Y.: Doubleday, Page and Co., 1913), p. 5.

24. As quoted in Gardner, *Departing Glory*, pp. 107-37.

25. Michael McCarthy, "Africa and the American West," *Journal of American Studies* 11 (August, 1977), 187–201.

26. See F. Dixey, "African Landscape," *Geographical Review* 34 (1944), 457–65; and also William A. Hance, *The Geography of Modern Africa* (New York and London: Columbia University Press, 1975).

27. These observations about Africa and more can be found in Stanley's principal works: *Coomassie and Magdala; The Story of Two British Campaigns in Africa* (London: Sampson Low, 1874); *The Congo and the Founding of Its Free State; A Story of Work and Exploration*, 2 vols. (New York: Harper and Brothers, 1885); *How I Found Livingstone; Travels, Adventures, and Discoveries in Central Africa* (New York: Charles Scribner's Sons, 1899); *In Darkest Africa*, 2 vols. (New York: Charles Scribner's Sons, 1890); *Through the Dark Continent*, 2 vols. (New York: Harper and Brothers, 1879); and *Through South Africa* (London: Sampson Low, 1898).

28. See George Shepperson, "The United States and East Africa," *Phylon* 13 (1952), 25–34; Robert A. Huttenback, *Racism and Empire: White Settlers and Colored Immigrants in the British Self-Governing Colonies, 1830–1910* (Ithaca, N.Y.: Cornell University Press, 1976); Elspeth Huxley, *White Man's Country: Lord Delamere and the Making of Kenya*, 2 vols. (London: Chatto and Windus, 1935); and David Killingray, *A Plague of Europeans: Westerners in Africa Since the Fifteenth Century* (Baltimore, Md.: Penguin Books, 1974).

29. George W. Stocking, Jr., *Race, Culture and Evolution: Essays in the History of Anthropology* (New York: Free Press, 1968), pp. 42–132.

30. John S. Haller, *Outcasts from Evolution: Scientific Attitudes of Racial Inferiority, 1859–1900* (Urbana: University of Illinois Press, 1971), pp. 70–79.

31. Rubin Francis Weston, *Racism in U.S. Imperialism: The Influence of Racial Assumptions on American Foreign Policy, 1893–1946* (Columbia: University of South Carolina Press, 1972), pp. 4–55.

32. George M. Fredrickson, *The Black Image in the White Mind: The Debate on Afro-American Character and Destiny, 1817–1914* (New York: Harper and Row, 1971), pp. 320–21.

3

The African Scene

In 1860, upon his return to the United States, Charles Thomas recorded his impressions of a recent trip to West Africa, and as visitors to new lands often do, he described the places and the people he had encountered. Although there were many subjects to write about, Thomas was most impressed by West Africa's scenic beauty, because it was a revelation for which he had been wholly unprepared. He spent a good deal of time describing the colors of the vegetation; he noted the pleasurable effects he experienced while watching ocean waves break in upon nearby beaches. It was an African scene, he wrote movingly, that both stimulated his mind and excited his senses.[1] But as the novelty of the region began to fade into a more recognizable familiarity with the passage of time, Thomas's view of West Africa changed. He became more anxious as his knowledge of the area increased. He was alarmed by the gradual loss of strength he felt in the African heat and frightened by the presence of poisonous snakes and insects. He was shaken, moreover, by the realization that he might succumb—one day—to the ravages of tropical fever. He felt that the coastal environment of West Africa, an area which encompassed for him Sierra Leone and Liberia, was capable of testing both his mental and physical well-being. What had been initially a source of beauty and pleasure for him subsequently became a place of danger, disease, and possible death.

Charles Thomas's reaction to West Africa was similar to the experiences of other Americans who, like him, also found the region to be a land of apparent contradiction. It attracted and then repelled them; it was the source of delight and then the occasion for concern. For the newly arrived, the area's surprising beauty produced great expectations about the appearance of Africa, yet its exacting environment suggested hard times for the uninitiated. Observations like these, however, were not confined to selected areas of West Africa. The diversity of Africa's natural environment, in other parts of the continent, provoked a variety of responses as well. There was, besides the coastal area that Thomas visited, a great deal written about the interior sections of the continent. The rivers, valleys, mountains, and forests of Central Africa appeared to be wondrous in design because they were all so new, different, and unexpected, while sections of eastern and southeastern Africa, in contrast, fascinated other Americans because they resembled parts of western America they knew so well. Despite the fact that evaluations of Africa's natural environment varied both in quality and completeness, their overall usefulness in assessing the origins of a particular view of Africa that was popular in America is clear: it was through these recorded accounts that Africa came to be understood in America as a land of exotic natural dimensions.[2]

Consider, for example, how descriptions of Africa's natural environment have been made an essential element in recent portrayals of the continent. In Malcolm X's youth, as we have seen, the most commonly accepted views included depictions of Africa as a land of "burning sands," fever, and oppressive climatic conditions. It was a place thought to be composed solely of jungle terrain, with dense vegetation covering vast portions of a continent populated almost exclusively by animals. Obviously these views are oversimplified compressions of a complex array of data, but such impressions, over time, became equated with the very reality of the continent, and therein lies their importance.[3] However, an analysis of the natural environment of Africa, or more concisely, the African scene, as reported by Americans might fall prey to generalization were it not for the fact that American perceptions of Africa can be precisely classified.[4] They can be traced to particular periods of time when they first occurred with noticeable frequency. They can be linked to certain groups of Americans who first assumed the burden of explaining certain parts of Africa to the American public. And finally, the motivation for evaluating and describing Africa from a special point of view can be determined as well. It is possible, then, to move from a series of individual experiences to more generally articulated cultural explanations of the African continent.[5]

To trace the roots of America's popular vision of Africa as a strangely exotic land to descriptions of Africa's natural environment, however, is essentially to understand the nature of American contacts with the continent as evolving in three distinct phases.[6] Beginning in the early nineteenth century and continuing through the 1850s, West Africa was the focal point of American travel undertaken by colonists and missionaries. Individuals like Ephraim Bacon, who were interested in encouraging settlement in West Africa, compiled detailed accounts of the region for use by potential émigrés, as well as for consumption by a more general audience in America. During the 1860s and 1870s, two naturalized Americans, Henry Morton Stanley and Paul Belloni Du Chaillu, above all others, were responsible for making Central Africa known to the American reading public. As explorers, their aim was to tell the world of their discoveries, but as writers their common goal was to sell books, a task accomplished by devoting sufficient space to sensational descriptions of the rain forests of Central Africa. Finally, during the late nineteenth and early twentieth centuries, Americans travelled to eastern and southeastern sections of the continent in increasing numbers to pursue their interests in hunting "big game." Their recorded impressions of experiences while on "African safari" were extensive and did much to promote the popular idea that Africa was indeed the world's zoo. Their writings, together with earlier impressions of West and Central Africa, thus form the chronological and spatial framework through which American perceptions of the African scene, in greater detail, can be viewed.

When American missionaries and colonists left behind the familiar shores of the United States for the unknown coasts of West Africa in the early part of the nineteenth century, the voyage across the Atlantic was a significant event in shaping their initial impressions of West Africa. At that time, sailing to Africa was an experience involving great anxiety. Under uneventful circumstances, a voyage from New Bedford, Massachusetts, or New York City to Monrovia,

Liberia, or Freetown, Sierra Leone, involved at least one month's travel. With few exceptions, Americans described how the rough Atlantic seas exacted many sleepless nights. In addition, they wrote extensive accounts about the problems of seasickness, discontent, and boredom aboard ship, and of being confronted by an undistinguished seascape that offered them little diversity from the hardships of the voyage, as this brief passage summarizes: "Days and nights of 'close hauled' sailing, angry seas, closed ports, wet decks, fearful pitching, terrific rolling; billious headaches, desponding hearts, sour looks, cross answers; ennui, nausea, and general discontent...."[7]

As they disembarked from the ships that carried them to West Africa, however, the contrast between the monotony of the sea and the variety of the land became evident. The West African coast elicited a number of responses from the newly arrived missionaries and colonists from America. Seen through the filter of novelty, the colors of the flora, the odor of the earth, and even the strength of the wind left indelible marks.[8] The American missionary William G. Crocker was so shocked by the splendor of the West African coast that he caught himself staring at one particular vista in Monrovia. Crocker was born in the coastal town of Newburyport, Massachusetts, in 1805 and died in Monrovia in 1844, having spent just over six years in Liberia for the American Baptist Board of Foreign Missions. But Newburyport was no match for Monrovia, Crocker thought, and his intention was to record as much of the scene as possible, with such precision that no one could ever doubt his word about West Africa's scenic beauty.[9] David Francis Bacon, the author of *Wanderings on the Seas and Shores of Africa*, a popular book published in New York City in 1843, did the same:

The hues and shading of the land, the direction and power of the light, the feeling of the air, and the general indescribable sense of the whole scene—were all new. I had now been long enough free from the effects of the voyage to appreciate everything without exaggeration; but every sight and tone, and the very odor of the earth and the breeze, and all the impressions of the scene—were rich with conceptions as novel as those of another life. The songs of new birds were in my ear; the light and shade of a new clime passed in striking change before me, as I moved smoothly along; the objects of every sense, and the ideas suggested by them, seemed all new and strange.[10]

Positive impressions of West Africa's natural environment involved categorizing the hills, ridges, mountains, and slopes of the region according to their size, form, and outline. J. Leighton Wilson, an American missionary from South Carolina and a graduate of Princeton University, noted that their proximity to the sea presented an interesting contrast to the flatness of the shore; in another instance, James Washington Lugenbeel, a physician and commercial agent in Liberia for the United States government, believed that the many hills surrounding Monrovia gave the area a truly unmatched topographical appearance.[11] Farther down the coast, the magnificence of the mountains near Gabon were praised because of their size, shape, and the fact that they rose straight from the ocean floor, where they stretched far back into the interior of the country.

The richness of the vegetation in West Africa was also a shock to many American observers. They remarked how parts of West Africa appeared to be forever green, and frequently resorted to the word "lushness" to describe the region, believing that West Africa's natural growth had a way of never really dying out.[12] For R. M. Johnson in particular, whose book *Liberia As It Is* was widely consulted in Philadelphia during the mid-nineteenth century, the density of the Liberian countryside was so overwhelming that he believed the country was a part of the world where nature took no rest.[13] Similarly, Thomas Jefferson Bowen, a missionary for the Southern Baptist Convention, in analyzing his own reactions, stated:

> One of the first things that attracts the attention of a new comer to Africa, is the greenness and density of the vegetation. A person who has never been in the tropics can form no just conception of its luxuriance. The hill sides and the banks of streams often present the appearance of solid walls of leaves and flowers. The grass on the prairies is from eight to twelve feet in height, and so thickly set as to be almost impervious.[14]

The surprise, wonder, and excitement that was associated with the natural environment of West Africa produced euphoric feelings in Americans. Liberia and Sierra Leone were not just stretches of arid coast; they were inviting places in which to be, and many Americans thought that the beauty of the region was so overpowering that it might in turn convince others to come to West Africa as well.[15]

Nonetheless, as Americans became more familiar with West Africa with the passage of time, their reactions to the area changed, a shift in perception that can be gauged by examining the modifications they made to their original responses. After living along the West African coast for any extended period, they often referred to the area as a "land of contradictions." What had once appeared to them to be a paradise on earth was tempered by descriptions of "mingled beauty." The vistas that were so inviting from a distance upon closer inspection became nothing more than clumps of bushes or assortments of obnoxious weeds.[16] The writings of Robert Nassau illustrate this point well. As a missionary for the Presbyterian Board of Foreign Missions, Nassau had left for Africa in 1861 and did not return permanently to the United States until 1912. He had spent over thirty years on Corisco in Equatorial Guinea, an island fifty miles north of the equator, where he captured in verse the essence of what other residents of West Africa believed to be true:

> To view, the scene is beautiful
> —And charms surpassingly;
> But, Pestilence and Fear are There,
> —And Death lies treacherously.
> Beneath those leaves an Asp can hide.
> —There's Poison in that flower.[17]

But what could account for such a change in perspective, as Nassau's poem suggests? Why did initial aesthetic responses give way to more carefully constructed evaluations in the writings of Americans?

Although West Africa was initially appealing, the region imposed a number of difficulties on non-African outsiders who intended to establish permanent settlements on the continent. Discussions of survival subsequently formed a central theme, as the numerous travel narratives and magazine articles published for the reading public in America reveal. From the early part of the nineteenth century to about 1850, statements made by colonists and missionaries about the region mirrored their changing perceptions of it. As they became more aware of their surroundings, and as their understanding of the area became more complex, considerations of beauty were supplanted by strategies for survival. This change reflected their common aims for being in Africa. Their primary task was not to describe nature but to survive in it, and while the physical dimensions of the region set the context for what could possibly be described, motivation and purpose determined what would be the two principal concerns of their reports: climate and fever.

West Africa was an exacting environment for which accommodations had to be made, and books and articles written by Americans were filled with any number of questions: Was there anything unusual about the climate of this particular region that should be noted? Was it suitable for settlement? Was there enough water? What about crops, and what kinds could be grown? Although there were some who believed that the climate of West Africa was no more oppressive than New England in the summer, West Africa was clearly a different experience for the majority of Americans because death, they thought, might result from prolonged exposure. Consequently, they paid close attention to clothing and diet. Direct contact with the "dews" of the night was to be avoided. A good mental attitude was an important asset, since an overly morbid fear about the climate could be deadly in itself. A hopeful disposition rather than depression and despondency was absolutely indispensable for good health.[18] Death, however, struck many, and others enjoyed no good health at all.

While the climate of West Africa was a constantly discussed topic because it could be directly felt, equally important from the point of view of Americans in Africa was the prevalence of "tropical fever" because it too was a danger to both mind and body.[19] Discussions of climate were inextricably linked to the subject of fever, since for a time one was considered the result of the other. Malaria was discovered later to be the cause of so much illness and death, but graphically sketched accounts of "tropical fever" became a literary staple of American reports from West Africa. A typical description of a set of fever symptoms, for example, included loss of appetite, distressed liver, impaired digestion, prolonged weakness, and sudden chilliness. Vomiting and delirium accompanied the more advanced stages of the affliction, and death was not uncommon:

> This sickness indicates its approach by headache, pains in the back, loss of appetite, and more or less gastric derangement, and rapidly develops into bilious remittent fever. This sometimes yields to a mild medical treatment, and the patient, if young and of good constitution, without further initiating physical penalties is prepared to endure

ordinary exposure to his adopted climate. Generally, however, this disease assumes the tertiary, or other forms of intermittent fever, accompanied by bilious vomiting, furred tongue, a dull expression of the eye, and in the febrile paroxysms intense headache and delirium. This is the African fever. It sometimes passes into the inflammatory type, and death follows from the congestion of some vital organ.[20]

The motivation of American missionaries and colonists was to prepare people for the hardships of life in West Africa. Although they praised the countryside for its obvious natural beauty, they also felt a duty to make any potential immigrant to Africa aware of the hardships to be suffered in the region. American missionaries, in particular, had a special reason for describing West Africa in such a vivid manner.[21] As instruments to test their faith and their commitment to the "unredeemed," repeated descriptions of Africa's climate and fever served them well. By exploiting the nature of the demands placed upon them, they succeeded not only in focusing attention on their work but also in making the burden they carried seem so enormous, they created a view of West Africa for the reading public in America that emphasized only the most exotic and dreaded aspects of the West African scene. If, however, the work of colonists and missionaries can be considered narrowly focused, then the writings of Paul Belloni Du Chaillu and Henry Morton Stanley achieved a level of notoriety for their descriptions of Central Africa that have remained unsurpassed, even to this day.

Beginning in the 1860s and 1870s, American reports about Central Africa were largely the efforts of two naturalized Americans, Paul Belloni Du Chaillu and Henry Morton Stanley, who were influential in focusing international attention on this section of Africa. As writers, Du Chaillu and Stanley were well received, and though Du Chaillu is less well known today than Stanley, both were celebrated figures in their own time for their writings about Africa. Du Chaillu was born in France, but came to the United States in the early 1850s. Before that time, however, Du Chaillu had spent several years in Africa near the bay of the Gabon River, a few miles north of the equator, where he had lived with his father, a French commercial agent who traded in the region. Sponsored by the Philadelphia Academy of Science to explore the west-central part of the continent, he returned to Africa in 1855.

Du Chaillu is credited with being the first non-African to discover and write about the African gorilla that inhabited the equatorial rain forest of the continent, a fact recounted in his two most important books, *Explorations and Adventures in Equatorial Africa; With Accounts of the Manners and Customs of the People, and of the Chase of the Gorilla, the Crocodile, Leopard, Elephant, Hippopotamus, and Other Animals* (1861), and *A Journey to Ashango-Land: and Further Penetration Into Equatorial Africa* (1867). In 1863, Du Chaillu travelled throughout the equatorial rain forest, where he discovered "pygmies," an event detailed in *The Country of the Dwarfs* (1872). Du Chaillu was a corresponding member of the American Ethnological Society, the Geographical and Statistical Society of New York, and the Boston Society of Natural History.

Henry Morton Stanley, like Du Chaillu, became synonymous with Africa. Of Welsh background, his entire life was anything but ordinary. He was born John Rowlands in Wales on June 1, 1841, and shipped out as a cabin boy for New Orleans at an early age. In 1859 he was befriended by a local Louisiana merchant whose name he subsequently assumed. After travelling throughout various parts of the western United States in 1866, he eventually became a staff reporter for the *New York Herald*. The paper's owner, James Gordon Bennett, commissioned Stanley in 1869 to find Dr. Livingstone, the famous British missionary-explorer who had been presumed lost somewhere in Africa. During the 1870s, Stanley's search for Livingstone, reports of which were front-page items for the *New York Herald*, created sustained interest in Africa. At a later time, Stanley crossed the African continent from east to west. His expeditions opened up portions of central and eastern Africa to European and American merchants. He traversed the course of the Congo River through Central Africa, compiling extensive notes about his experiences in the equatorial rain forest. Although late in life he assumed British citizenship, at the time of his explorations in Africa he considered himself an American. His most popular books are two-volume works, *Through the Dark Continent* (1879) and *In Darkest Africa* (1890).

As writers, explorers, and travellers, both Du Chaillu and Stanley helped to reveal the "dark continent" to the reading publics of Europe and America. At the time of their entry into Central Africa, however, neither person understood the dimensions of the region.

Because it was, after all, a part of the continent about which little was known in the mid-nineteenth century, estimating the actual size of the region was a major priority. Du Chaillu believed that most of Central Africa was covered with jungle, beginning near the coast in Gabon and stretching almost indefinitely into the interior.[22] Stanley, who was less sure, pointed out that even though the groves of Central Park, New York, or the wooded grounds of Windsor, England, were extensive, they were actually miniscule in comparison to the forested area of Central Africa, and like Du Chaillu, Stanley too wondered whether or not Central Africa was all forest terrain.[23]

Uncertainty about scale was not their only concern. What made this section of Africa so frightening for them was the intimidating combination of smells, sounds, and sights. Much of the area was damp with dew so great that it covered large portions of the forest, freely working its way down vines and branches, where it fell indiscriminately upon the unsuspecting traveller. Decaying vegetation gave the area a pungent smell, while the cacophony of jungle sounds worked upon the sensibilities of the uninitiated. As Stanley recalled:

> We, accustomed to rapid marching, had to stand in our places minutes at a time waiting patiently for an advance of a few yards, after which would come another halt, and another short advance to be again halted. And all this time the trees kept shedding their dew upon us like rain in great round drops. Every leaf seemed weeping. Down the boles and branches, creepers and vegetable cords, the moisture trickled and fell on us. Overhead the wide-spreading branches, in many interlaced strata, each branch heavy with broad thick leaves, absolutely shut out the daylight. We knew not whether it was a sunshiny day or a dull, foggy, gloomy day; for we marched in a feeble solemn twilight, such as you may experience in temperate climes an hour after sunset. The path soon became a stiff clayey paste, and at every step we splashed water over the legs of those in front, and on either side of us.[24]

Along another stretch of forest, Stanley recalled again:

> We had certainly seen forests before, but this scene was an epoch in our lives ever to be remembered for its bitterness; the gloom enhanced the dismal misery of our life; the slopping moisture, the unhealthy reeking atmosphere, and the monotony of the scenes; nothing but the

eternal interlaced branches, the tall aspiring stems, rising from a tangle through which we had to burrow and crawl like wild animals, on hands and feet.[25]

As Stanley's statement indicates, travel in the jungle was a demanding experience. Tropical vegetation grew to heights in excess of twenty feet, and as both Du Chaillu and Stanley discovered, hacking at vines and bushes, one foot at a time, proved to be the only effective means of negotiating the terrain. Even if the way were clear, tracks in the forest were difficult to follow and paths that were once well marked quickly disappeared in the undergrowth. Adding confusion to an already exacting experience, darkness abounded in an environment where little sunlight could filter through the canopy of trees, and a sense of orientation was difficult to achieve where the rhythm of a day was marked by neither sunrise nor sunset. When both men referred to the African rain forest as "a great prison of foliage," it was a recognition of the real possibility of being overwhelmed by their surroundings.

The combined effect of the jungle's smells, sounds, and sights produced feelings of melancholy and gloom, but they were not the only forces with which Du Chaillu and Stanley had to contend. The animals of Central Africa were a threat to human life. As Du Chaillu and Stanley often remarked, the possibility of being attacked was constant, and death might be easily met by crossing the wrong path or by making a wrong turn. However, the gorilla was an animal especially feared by them.[26] Running on its hind legs, slightly bent forward, the gorilla in many ways resembled a human being. But it was a powerfully built animal of immense size, almost six feet tall, with muscular chest and well-developed arms.[27] It had fanlike teeth, which it clearly displayed when provoked, a "hellish expression of face," "ferocious" eyes, and "projecting eye-brows."[28]

No one captured the essential drama surrounding the gorilla better than Du Chaillu. As an explorer and a writer, he added a particular note of terror to the natural environment of Central Africa through his numerous portrayals of gorillas, as this incident reveals:

At six a.m. again on the march. My men were tired with the exertions of yesterday, for we had been wet all day, so, to keep them up to the speed, I led the column myself. We were soon buried again in the shades of the forest. It was a wild, desolate district, and I marched along in anything but a cheerful mood, thinking of the hard task I had imposed upon myself in attempting to cross Africa. I was going along, a little ahead of my party, when my reverie was suddenly disturbed by a loud crashing and rustling in the trees just before me. Thinking it might be a flock of monkeys feeding on some wild fruit-tree, I looked up, peered through the thick foliage, and was thoroughly roused by seeing on a large tree a whole group of gorillas.[29]

And in an even more dramatic context, Du Chaillu relates:

We stood therefore in silence, guns in hand. The gorilla looked at us for a minute or so out of his evil gray eyes, then beat his breast with his gigantic arms, gave another howl of defiance, and advanced upon us.

Again he stopped, now not more than fifteen yards away. Still Malaouen said, "Not yet."

Then again an advance upon us. Now he was not twelve yards off. I could see plainly the ferocious face of the monstrous ape. It was working with rage; his huge teeth were ground against each other so that we could hear the sound; the skin of the forehead was moved rapidly back and forth, and gave a truly devilish expression to the hideous face; once more he gave out a roar which seemed to shake the woods like thunder, and, looking us in the eyes and beating his breast, advanced again. This time he came within eight yards of us before he stopped. My breath was coming short with excitement as I watched the huge beast. Malaouen said only "Steady," as he came up.

When he stopped, Malaouen said, "Now." And before he could utter the roar for which he was opening his mouth, three musket balls were in his body. He fell dead almost without a struggle.[30]

If the gorilla was a devil, as Du Chaillu claimed, then the forest region of Central Africa was a hell on earth. In fact, the analogy of forest-as-hell seemed to summarize best the experiences of both Du Chaillu and Stanley. As a parting gesture of defiance, just prior to leaving the region, Stanley related how his party shook their clenched fists at the jungle they had come to hate:

"Aye, friends, it is true. By the mercy of God we are well nigh the end of our prison and dungeon!" They held their hands far out yearningly towards the superb land, and each looked up to the bright blue heaven in grateful worship, and after they had gazed as though fascinated, they recovered themselves with a deep sigh, and as they turned their heads, lo! the sable forest heaved away to the infinity of the west, and they shook their clenched hands at it with gestures of defiance and hate. Feverish from sudden exaltation, they apostrophised it for its cruelty to themselves and their kinsmen; they compared it to Hell, they accused it of the murder of one hundred of their comrades, they called it the wilderness of fungi and wood-beans; but the great forest which lay vast as a continent before them, and drowsy, like a great beast, with monstrous fur thinly veiled by vaporous exhaltations, answered not a word, but rested in its infinite sullenness, remorseless and implacable as ever.[31]

It had managed to torment him, driving him to a state of near delirium. It had killed many of his companions, and in return it had shown little remorse for the pain it had inflicted. The jungle had proven its power to push people to their physical and psychological limits.

Although Central Africa comprised only one part of the African continent, its geographical size belied its cultural significance. Du Chaillu and Stanley were successful in conveying the emotional and imaginative content of the region. Their subject matter was not only inherently exotic, but their style of presentation also emphasized mystery and danger, making their writings an important part of the American image of Africa. The impact of their work, moreover, is clearly illustrated in the attitudes of Americans who subsequently visited Africa. During the late nineteenth and early twentieth centuries especially, Americans who had the time, money, and the desire to do so travelled to eastern and southeastern Africa to hunt, explore, and generally to be adventurous. Since they lacked firsthand knowledge of the continent, they relied upon others for information about Africa. But at the time of their departure for Africa, the most popular sources were not about their intended destinations in eastern and southeastern Africa: they were the works of Du Chaillu and Stanley, whose descriptions of Central Africa were widely read and consulted. As a consequence, most American travellers who arrived on the continent during the late nineteenth and early twentieth centuries came with certain preconceived notions about what all of Africa should be like, predicated on descriptions of other selected areas.

Eastern and southeastern Africa did not meet their expectations, since there existed a basic incongruence between actual Africa and imagined Africa, between what the eastern and southeastern sections of Africa were actually like and what those parts of Africa were supposed to be. The common reaction of Americans to the topography of the region was utter surprise. It was difficult for them to reconcile the discrepancy between what they had expected to see, based on their reading of Du Chaillu and Stanley, and what they actually saw, based on their own experiences. Everything was not jungle. Sections of Uganda and Kenya, for example, contained open savannas, rolling hills, and high plateaus.

A typical reaction to the natural environment of the region was made by E. Alexander Powell. Powell was born in 1879 and attended Oberlin College but left at the outbreak of the Boer War in an attempt to join the British army in South Africa. Later in life, he became an official at the American consulate in Egypt, a Fellow of the Royal Geographical Society, and a respected author and traveller with three books about Africa to his credit: *The Last Frontier: The White Man's War for Civilisation in Africa* (1912); *Beyond the Utmost Purple Rim: Abyssinia, Somaliland, Kenya Colony, Zanzibar, the Comoros, Madagascar* (1925); and *The Map That Is Half Unrolled: Equatorial Africa from the Indian Ocean to the Atlantic* (1925). From 1909 to 1911 he was made special correspondent for *Everybody's Magazine*, at which time he travelled throughout Sudan, Kenya, Mozambique, and Rhodesia. However, it was during one of his many journeys by train through the fertile foothills of Africa just north of Salisbury, Rhodesia, that he stopped, rubbed his eyes at the scene he had just observed, and remarked:

As you sit on the observation platform of your electric-lighted sleeping-car, anywhere along that section of the "Cape-to-Cairo" between Cape Town and the Zambesi, you rub your eyes incredulously as you watch the rolling, verdure-clad plains stretching away to the foot-hills of distant ranges, and you say to yourself, as you drink in the dry, champagne-like air, "There is some mistake; this cannot be Africa; surely I cannot be south of the LINE. Where are the impenetrable forests and the reeking jungles and the naked savages and the blistering heat of which I have always heard? This is not Africa; this is the American West." And the illusion is completed by the people, for the only natives you see are careless, happy, decently clad darkies who might have come straight from the levees of Vicksburg or New Orleans, while on every station platform are groups of fine, bronze-faced, up-standing fellows in corded riding-breeches and brown boots, their flannel shirts open at the neck, their broad-brimmed hats cocked rakishly—just such types, indeed, as were common beyond the Mississippi twenty years ago, before store clothes and the motor car had spoiled the picturesqueness of our own frontier.[32]

Surprise at the comparability of the topography of eastern and southeastern Africa to western America was the shared response of other Americans besides Powell.[33] Charles Richard Tjader led an expedition into British East Africa in 1906 for the American Museum of Natural History, finally returning to the United States in 1907, where he gave many illustrated lectures about his exploits. In his writings he likened parts of East Africa to sections of Oregon and northern California because of the abundant rainfall and mountainous ranges that were common to both.[34] Theodore Roosevelt, on another occasion, spoke to his fellow Americans about the unforeseen similarity he encountered in Africa. Upon his return from Kenya, he delivered an important address before the National Geographic Society in Washington, D.C., in 1911 in which he described the highland regions of East Africa.[35] He told the assembled audience how these parts of Africa reminded him of western America, particularly Wyoming, Colorado, New Mexico, and Arizona, a perception he reaffirmed at another time when he remarked:

In many ways it reminds one rather curiously of the great plains of the West, where they slope upward to the foot-hills of the Rockies. It is a white man's country. Although under the equator, the altitude is so high that the nights are cool, and the region as a whole is very healthy. I saw many children, of the Boer immigrants, of English settlers, even of American missionaries, and they looked sound and well. Of course there was no real identity in any feature; but again and again the landscape struck me by its general likeness to the cattle country I knew so well. As my horse shuffled forward, under the bright, hot sunlight, across the endless flats or gently rolling slopes of brown and withered grass, I might have been on the plains anywhere, from Texas to Montana; the hills were like our Western buttes....[36]

Two factors accounted for the comparisons between parts of Africa and America's West.[37] First, the most commonly held experience of those Americans who travelled to eastern and southeastern Africa was their firsthand knowledge of western America. Theodore Roosevelt was the most representative of this type of person: He had lived in the Dakota territory at various times and had displayed his knowledge of western America by writing *The Winning of the West* (1889–1896). There were, however, other less-illustrious Americans who knew western America as well as eastern and southeastern Africa. Poultney Bigelow, a journalist, author, editor, and a friend and classmate at the Yale Art School of one of the most famous artists of the American West, Frederic Remington, travelled across America in 1880, beginning in California, before journeying to Africa. Edgar Beecher Bronson, who memorialized his African adventures by writing *In Closed Territory* (1910), was also the author of such tales of the West as *Reminiscences of a Ranchman* (1908), a book based on his experiences in western America. Stewart Edward White, the author, mined gold in the Black Hills of South Dakota between 1895 and 1896 prior to sailing for Africa in the early part of the twentieth century.

A second reason for comparison was the predisposition of Americans who travelled to Africa expecting to see only jungles. When they saw that the topography of the region was different than expected and not the jungle terrain anticipated, they attempted to define it in terms that were familiar to them. Their descriptions of eastern and southeastern Africa were not only influenced by topography but were the result of the interaction of expectations, environment, and experience. Their past experiences were as important in determining their explanations of this part of the continent as were the physical characteristics of the landscape. Nonetheless, despite the fact that a section of Africa and a part of America could resemble each other was a startling revelation to be made, the most important—and memorable—result of their writings was the emphasis they gave to the region's wildlife population. Animals "in the wild," of course, were not restricted to any one part of the continent. Varieties of wildlife inhabited other sections of Africa as well. But the number and kinds of animals, many of them unique to Africa, endowed this region with its most striking feature and were characteristics about which American travellers frequently wrote.

One illustration, in particular, is revealing. In 1901 the Uganda

Railway reached the shores of Lake Victoria, an area that had been declared earlier a protectorate by the British and named British East Africa in 1895. The railway was completed in 1904, allowing travel from Mombasa, on the coast, to the temperate uplands, where the concentration of Africa's animal population was the greatest. While travelling through this region aboard the Uganda Railway, Caroline Kirkland, the American author of *Some African Highways*, was so overwhelmed by the very numbers of animals she saw on her trip that she likened the scene to a circus setting in reverse. Normally, a small number of circus animals would be confined behind bars to be viewed by a much larger audience of people. In Uganda, in contrast, the arrangement was just the opposite: A small number of people were confined to their cagelike trains while large herds of animals enjoyed the freedom of movement.[38]

Americans observed, described, and photographed the African lion, panther, leopard, giraffe, zebra, crocodile, rhinoceros, and hippopotamus in their native habitats. Pictures of animals filled the pages of *National Geographic*, and their photographs illustrated numerous travel accounts as well. Because so many animals were unique to Africa and therefore new to Americans, their size, color, and peculiar characteristics were duly recorded. In addition, African wildlife was also looked at in another way. By 1915, eastern and southeastern Africa had become synonymous with "big game," and big business flourished around tracking and killing animals. Many Americans had come to this part of Africa expressly for the purpose of bagging a lion or a leopard. As John Y. Filmore Blake, the American Commander of the British army's "Irish Brigade" in the South African War, observed while travelling in Tanzania, out there on the Serengeti Plain were many candidates for trophy rooms in America.[39]

Americans also wrote books about their African adventures which introduced to the reading public a new genre of travel literature: the African animal epic. So influential were these tales from Africa that they helped to define the continent as the world's zoo, a place where animals were more prominent and important than people. Intensity and drama were the hallmarks of these epics. According to the formula, the story usually begins as "the great white hunter," accompanied by a retinue of docile African porters, wanders deeper and deeper into the "bush" in search of game. The safari party advances for several days, until the hunter is startled by an unexpected movement. What could it be? The beat of his heart quickens, we are told, as the porters become more frightened by the sound. Suddenly, a lion appears, beyond a clump of trees, and as the distance between animal and hunter becomes less, the suspense increases. The animal begins its charge; the hunter raises his rifle, but only at the last possible moment does he pull the trigger, slowly, bringing the mighty animal down. The episode is predictably concluded by having the hunter place his foot atop the slain beast's head. From a literary perspective these tales deserve little comment, but from the point of view of evoking a particular sense of Africa, they are unsurpassed.

This genre was very popular. In 1896, William Astor Chanler published *Through Jungle and Desert; Travels in Eastern Africa*, a well-received book dedicated to Judge Charles P. Daly, then president of the American Geographical Society. Chanler was a native New Yorker, the holder of a master's degree from Harvard University, an honorary member of the Imperial and Royal Geographical Society of Vienna, and wealthy enough to finance his own expedition to East Africa for two years from 1892 to 1894. Thirteen years later, Theodore Roosevelt published the most widely read African safari narrative of its kind, *African Game Trails* (1909), an account of his expedition to East Africa on behalf of the Smithsonian Institution. There were many other attempts, less successfully executed, but the writings of Chanler and Roosevelt were able to convey, to a large reading audience, the distinct impression that danger and adventure were always close by because East Africa, as they defined it, was truly the land of the wild animal.[40]

As viewed by Americans, the African scene was as much the product of the continent's natural environment as it was the result of their expectations, assumptions, and motives. Although particular locales in Africa set the context for possible evaluation, Americans considered, selected, and emphasized only certain aspects. Their descriptions did not reflect the entire complexity of the continent's natural environment. In Liberia, for example, where permanent settlement was the desired aim, colonists and missionaries made passing references to the region's unexpected beauty, but they always paid careful attention in their writings to the climate and diseases of the region, two factors that threatened their survival. In Central Africa, emphasis was placed on graphically portraying the jungle environment in order to inform as well as to entertain. Du Chaillu and Stanley were explorers, and sharing their discoveries with the rest of the world was important to them. They were, however, also writers, highly conscious of a larger reading audience whose appetite for sensational accounts of daring exploits in exotic places was practically insatiable. Finally, in the eastern and southeastern sections of Africa, Americans described a region whose most prominent feature was not that it resembled the American West (although this was a startling discovery) but that "animals in the wild," creatures that could be observed, photographed, and hunted, gave this area its most memorable characteristic.

Africa, nevertheless, was more than American descriptions of it, and in a sense, these reports of the continent are deficient. However, the writings did demonstrate the potency of popular sources in creating the reality of a land, a process that might best be described from the point of view of one American who visited East Africa in the early part of the twentieth century. In 1913, the American writer and traveller Stewart Edward White attempted to explain it this way:

> Probably each of us has his mental picture that passes as a symbol rather than an idea of the different continents. This is usually a single picture—a deep river, with forest, hanging snaky vines, anacondas and monkeys for the east coast of South America, for example. It is built up in youth by chance reading and chance pictures, and does as well as a pink place on the map to stand for a part of the world concerning which we know nothing at all. As time goes on we extend, expand and modify this picture in light of what knowledge we may acquire.[41]

As people change, so also do their original observations, and as part of a lifelong process of education, White explained, their "first crude notions" become modified, depending on the acquisition of additional information.

To further illustrate his thesis, White then turned to Africa. By 1913 he reckoned that an unprecedented amount of material about Africa had become available in America. Yet much of it, he pointed out, emphasized only the most unusual aspects of Africa's natural environment or repeated certain sensational themes. Consequently, White felt that descriptions of the continent had given American readers the false impression that Africa was an "extra-human con-

HENRY WHITTEMORE
LIBRARY

STATE COLLEGE

tinent," a land that was understandable only in extraordinary terms or, in White's words, "a country impossible to be understood and gauged and savoured by the ordinary human mental equipment."[42] What White did not mention, however, was that the foundation for this false impression of Africa was not without context: It had been set down before, at specific times, for well-defined reasons, by particular Americans who had assumed the burden of explaining Africa both to themselves and to others.

The natural environment of Africa presented to the uninitiated American a world of surprising complexity. Its coastal beaches, tropical rain forests, and rolling green hills made it a land difficult to measure. Bold geographical contrasts placed mountains close to the sea, and sharp differences in climate rendered parts of Africa either oppressively hot or forever damp. In addition, Africa was a continent of expansive dimensions. Spectacular vistas could be found in Liberia and Sierra Leone, and the Congo River was a waterway of unsurpassed length and breadth that flowed through the heart of the continent. Nevertheless, as Americans who went there discovered, the African continent was more than the sum of the parts of its natural environment. It was also a designed landscape that had been worked on by indigenous African peoples as well as by transplanted Europeans, by the Hausa and Zulu as well as by the British and Dutch. It was to this aspect of the continent that Americans also turned their attention.

Notes

1. Charles W. Thomas, *Adventures and Observations on the West Coast of Africa, and Its Islands* (New York: Derby and Jackson, 1860), pp. 307–8.

2. See Melville J. Herskovits, "The Image of Africa in the United States, *Journal of Human Relations* 10 (Winter and Spring, 1962), 236–45; and also Farid Abolfathi, "The Americans' Image of Africa: An Exploratory Discussion," *Pan-Africanist* 3 (December, 1971), 37–38.

3. A valuable work on the formation of international stereotypes is still William Buchanan and Hadley Cantril, *How Nations See Each Other* (Urbana: University of Ilinois Press, 1953).

4. See Yi-Fu Tuan, *Topophilia: A Study of Environmental Perception, Attitudes, and Values* (Englewood Cliffs, N.J.: Prentice-Hall, 1974), esp. chaps. 7 and 8.

5. For a discussion of "image regions," see J. Wreford Watson and Timothy O'Riordan, *The American Environment: Perceptions and Policies* (London and New York: John Wiley, 1976), pp. 15–28.

6. For parts of that history, see Eric Rosenthal, *Stars and Stripes in Africa* (London: George Routledge and Sons, 1938).

7. Thomas, *Adventures*, p. 57.

8. Ephraim Bacon, *Abstract of a Journal Kept by E. Bacon, Assistant Agent of the United States, to Africa* (Philadelphia: Clark and Raser, 1824), p. 134.

9. R. B. Medbery, *Memoir of William G. Crocker* (Boston: Gould, Kendall, and Lincoln, 1848), p. 92. See also J. A. Carnes, *Journal of a Voyage from Boston to the West Coast of Africa: With a Full Description of the Manner of Trading With the Natives on the Coast* (Boston: John P. Jewett and Co., 1852), p. 81, who, in assessing the reason for his positive reaction to West Africa, stated: "Perhaps it was occasioned by those associations naturally formed in the mind on visiting any strange place in a foreign land. Every thing we see is new to us, and is therefore more strongly impressed on the mind than when we view those things that are familiar in our own country."

10. David Francis Bacon, *Wanderings on the Seas and Shores of Africa* (New York: Joseph W. Harrison, 1843), p. 134.

11. J. Leighton Wilson, *Western Africa: Its History, Condition, and Prospects* (New York: Harper and Brothers, 1856), p. 146; and J. W. Lugenbeel, *Sketches of Liberia: Comprising a Brief Account of the Geography, Climate, Productions, and Diseases of the Republic of Liberia* (Washington, D.C.: C. Alexander, 1850), p. 7.

12. George S. Brown, *Brown's Abridged Journal* (Troy, N.Y.: Prescott and Wilson, 1849), p. 52.

13. R. M. Johnson, *Liberia As It Is* (Philadelphia: Brown's Steam-Power Book and Job Printing Office, 1853), pp. 6–7.

14. Thomas Jefferson Bowen, *Central Africa: Adventures and Missionary Labors in Several Countries in the Interior of Africa, From 1849 to 1856* (Charleston, S.C.: Southern Baptist Publication Society, 1857), p. 256.

15. Melville B. Cox, *Remains of Melville B. Cox, Missionary to Liberia With a Memoir* (Boston: Light and Horton, 1835), p. 154.

16. Thomas, *Adventures*, pp. 288, 84.

17. Robert Hamill Nassau, *Africa: An Essay* (Philadelphia: Allen, Lane and Scott, 1911), p. 14.

18. See, generally, Henry A. Ford, *Observations on the Fevers of the West Coast of Africa* (New York: E. O. Jenkins, 1856).

19. Johnson, *Liberia*, p. 4.

20. Thomas, *Adventures*, pp. 144–45.

21. Samuel J. Whiton, *Glimpses of West Africa, with Sketches of Missionary*

Labor (Boston: American Tract Society, 1866), p. 27; and Lugenbeel, *Sketches*, p. 32.

22. Paul B. Du Chaillu, *A Journey to Ashango-Land: and Further Penetration Into Equatorial Africa* (New York: D. Appleton and Co., 1867), pp. 406, 419.

23. Henry M. Stanley, *How I Found Livingstone; Travels, Adventures, and Discoveries in Central Africa* (New York: Charles Scribner's Sons, 1899), pp. 322–23; and Henry M. Stanley, *In Darkest Africa*, 2 vols. (New York: Charles Scribner's Sons, 1890), 1:125.

24. Henry M. Stanley, *Through the Dark Continent*, 2 vols. (New York: Harper and Brothers, 1879), 1:130–31.

25. Ibid., 2:139.

26. Du Chaillu, *Journey to Ashango-Land*, p. 49.

27. Ibid., p. 411.

28. Ibid., pp. 50, 92.

29. Ibid., pp. 91–92.

30. Paul B. Du Chaillu, *Explorations and Adventures in Equatorial Africa* (New York: Harper and Brothers, 1861), p. 322.

31. Stanley, *In Darkest Africa*, 1:28.

32. E. Alexander Powell, "All Aboard for Cape Town!" *Outlook* 99 (November 25, 1911), 728.

33. Stewart Edward White, *African Camp Fires* (Garden City, N.Y.: Doubleday, Page and Co., 1913), p. 151.

34. See, generally, Charles Richard Tjader, *The Big Game of Africa* (New York: D. Appleton and Co., 1919).

35. Theodore Roosevelt, "Wild Man and Wild Beast in Africa," *National Geographic Magazine* 22 (January, 1911), 7.

36. Theodore Roosevelt, *African Game Trails: An Account of the African Wanderings of an American Hunter-Naturalist* (New York: Charles Scribner's Sons, 1910), pp. 27–28; and also Joseph L. Gardner, *Departing Glory: Theodore Roosevelt as Ex-President* (New York: Charles Scribner's Sons, 1973), esp. chap. 7, "Through Darkest Africa," pp. 107–37.

37. See George Shepperson, "The United States and East Africa," *Phylon* 13 (1st quarter, 1952), 25–34.

38. Caroline Kirkland, *Some African Highways: A Journey of Two American Women to Uganda and the Transvaal* (Boston: Dana Estes and Co., 1908), p. 209.

39. J.Y.F. Blake, *A West Pointer with the Boers* (Boston: Angel Guardian Press, 1903), p. 25.

40. J. Alden Loring, *African Adventure Stories* (New York: Charles Scribner's Sons, 1914), p. vii.

41. Stewart Edward White, *The Land of Footprints* (Garden City, N.Y.: Doubleday, Page and Co., 1913), pp. 6–7.

42. Ibid., p. 5.

4

The African
Landscape

Evaluating Africa's natural scene was only one element in the intricate process of understanding the continent. Making sense of Africa also meant decoding the imprint of culture upon the land, a task that involved interpreting the artifacts of human invention, as distinct from the designs of nature.[1] The problem was a difficult one for Americans, since it involved judging aspects of Africa's built environment: its rural landscape, its villages, towns, and cities, and the diversity of its architecture. In reading the African landscape as the product of human creativity, however, Americans in their writings essentially created two worlds on one continent. They bifurcated a continent of many elements into two distinct cultural landscapes. One landscape was African, the work of indigenous African peoples, while the other was Western, the product of non-African, European settlers. The landscape of Africans was considered static, backward, and a limited entity of primitive proportions, while in contrast, the landscape of Europeans embodied growth, progress, and was the ever-expanding result of modern ingenuity. The consequence of seeing Africa with such a double vision was that Americans effectively created two cultural domains in Africa: one African and the other European, separate and unequal.[2]

Distinctions based on considerations of location or time were not important in evaluating the landscape of Africans. What mattered most to Americans was defining the selected farm, house, or city as being either "African" or not. In the early part of the nineteenth century, for example, American missionaries in West Africa compiled rather detailed sketches of African villages. They noted their size (whether large or small), their shape (whether round or linear), their appearance (whether clean or dirty), and the type of materials used in construction (whether mud or stone). Americans in southern Africa during the late nineteenth century did the same. Yet in both cases, although the observers were separated by a considerable amount of time and space, their essential concern was in classifying a particular farm, house, or city as being either familiar, and Western, or unfamiliar and African. Differentiation was not an issue. Thus, devoid of a sense of difference and change, American analyses of the African characteristics of the continent's landscape had a synchronic quality about them.

The European landscape, by comparison, was clearly located where the influences of non-Africans had been the most noticeable. Although Europeans had settled elsewhere in Africa, they had made the greatest impact in eastern and southern Africa, and in particular in South Africa and Rhodesia. Called by some "white man's Africa," Americans compared this part of the continent to their own country:

> White Man's Africa is a very small portion of the great Dark Continent, stretching from the Cape of Good Hope for a thousand miles or so northeastward along the Indian Ocean. As compared to the whole continent, it reminds one of the thirteen united colonies of America in 1776. Here is the only section of Africa where the white man has established self-governing communities. This is the New England of Africa, whose enterprising sons are doggedly conquering the wilderness step by step, carrying with them Christianity and constitutional government. These pioneers, whether we call them English or Boer, have in their veins the blood of a common ancestry.[3]

Americans endowed this part of Africa with a sense of history, and since progress and change were its distinguishing characteristics, a sense of development over time was made an important element in American descriptions of the region. As Americans noted, even though Europeans had been in Africa since the seventeenth century, the most active period of growth in "white man's Africa" was during the late nineteenth and early twentieth centuries.

Writing in 1915, the year in which he published *Through Central Africa from Coast to Coast*, the American author James Barnes discussed the changes he noticed taking place in southeastern Africa. He remarked it was "a strange thing" that the "merest sign" of Western civilization could radically alter the face of Africa. He noted how a "single line of telegraph posts and barbed wire fencing" had transformed the open veldt, which had for centuries been "unchanged" into the "most modern of back pastures." He described in detail how the railroad had thoroughly commercialized "the most primitive of landscapes" in the region.[4] This part of Africa, he noted, was beginning to look less African and more Western, a vision of the two spheres of the designed environment of Africa which was shared, reaffirmed, and written about by many other Americans as well.

An element of the landscape of Africans that came in for extensive scrutiny was the farmland worked by Africans. To the American observer, accustomed to neatly separated parcels of land, the rural farms of Africa were ill defined. They lacked legible borders and were haphazardly planned. They were open and unfenced, and they stretched over almost limitless tracts of land. In the rural areas surrounding the cities of Monrovia and Nairobi, for example, Americans had difficulty making distinctions between natural growth and land readied for tillage. Boundaries separating one farm from another were often nonexistent, Americans noted, with continuous stretches of countryside running into more unbroken parcels of land. Rural African farms were chaotic because they lacked regular edges, and they seemed to be "half-neglected" since so much land appeared to be uncultivated. Why, Americans wondered, did the farms of indigenous African peoples look this way?

Several explanations were offered to account for the formless and unused look of the land. Americans believed, first of all, that the African environment was so naturally lush that humanly devised methods of agriculture were unnecessary. J. Leighton Wilson, a missionary for the American Board of Commissioners for Foreign Missions and a native of rural South Carolina, felt that the African environment had placed few demands upon the African.[5] Living an uncomplicated existence, the wants of the African were few, and whatever needs he had were quickly satisfied by an abundant and bountiful landscape. Wilson noted, for example, that vegetables thrived particularly well in Gabon, where he had established his mission station, and fruits were always available in large quantities. Since the African's survival did not demand it, nor did the environment upon which he depended require it, there were few incentives to use farmland productively.

A second theory stated that specific African methods of agriculture themselves were instrumental in shaping the look of the rural landscape. The absence of an appropriate technology contributed to the uncultivated appearance of the African farm. With amazement, Americans wrote about how Africans would go about the task of farming a large piece of land armed only with a small hoe. Even in the dry seasons, when the land was brittle, Africans cleared areas for cultivation with nothing more than an implement resembling a "heavy pruning knife." In attempting to cut through heavy vegetation and obstinate undergrowth in this manner, Americans reasoned that a difficult task was made an impossible one.

A third explanation advanced by Americans to account for the uncultivated appearance of African farmland involved the African practice of abandoning land even after a short period of cultivation. For Africans, surrendering a parcel of land was a natural response to Africa's ecology, and in the western and eastern parts of the continent, where the practice was traditionally followed, the custom served both the land and the farmer equally well. Where soil was either too fragile, thin, or delicate, farming could not possibly be maintained on a continuing basis. By cultivating the ground only intermittently, however, vegetation could eventually return, and by allowing time for replenishing the nutrients that had been removed, the earth was once again nourished. On a continent where land was generally abundant, the custom preserved the soil while producing few hardships for the farmer.

The practice, nonetheless, was generally misunderstood by Americans who held it accountable for the wasteful appearance of rural Africa. A case in point was the observations of Lewis Grout. As a missionary for the American Board of Commissioners for Foreign Missions stationed in Natal, South Africa, Grout lived for fifteen years among the Zulu peoples. Among his many accomplishments, he compiled a grammar of the Zulu language. Although he was a keen observer of Zulu customs as well, Grout believed that abandoning land was a wasteful practice. Within a brief period of time, he noted, unwanted vegetation could easily reclaim unoccupied land, and whatever cultivation existed might quickly be undone by the returning force of tropical growth. Because of such inattention, land was rendered useless, and without some form of daily management the soil was offered no protection from the corrosive effects of sun and heat. The earth became parched and arid, with unproductiveness and inadequate conservation the inevitable results.[6]

Finally, the unproductive look of the rural African landscape was tied to the physical separation of farmer and farm. Since it was not uncommon for workers and their land to be located some distance apart, farmers often lived in towns and villages far removed from the areas in which they worked. Such a custom, some Americans wrote, had disastrous consequences. How could farmers look after lands over which they exerted no immediate control? Would not a practice like this ensure neglect? How could farmers quickly attend to matters of urgency, such as the invasion of lands by unwanted animals or the destruction of crops by a sudden fire, if they were not nearby? Was not the division of cultivator and field a wasteful expenditure of time and energy?[7]

From an American viewpoint, an important part of the landscape of Africans resembled a chaotic mixture of trees, bushes, and undergrowth. The look of well-cultivated farmland was rare, and for Americans unaccustomed to African concepts of landownership or the selection of land, such practices were seen as having highly visible effects on the landscape. Samuel Whiton summarized the American perspective best:

> The native methods of farming are very simple and imperfect. The wants of the African in his heathen state are so few, and nature goes so far towards supplying them, that he has but little motive for exertion. The same spot of ground is cultivated only a year at a time, and then left to grow up to "bush." Each town or village has its farm, sometimes quite extensive, where the people raise their rice, cassava, sweet potatoes, and other food. The farms are often situated a long distance from the town. The land is first cleared up with hatchets and cutlasses, and afterwards burned over. Almost the only implement used in planting is a small hoe two or three inches in diameter.[8]

The appearance of the rural farms of Africa prompted speculation about how they might be changed. In some areas of the continent, where the influence of Western civilization was especially strong, the effect was noticeably evident: African farms, Americans thought, were much more orderly, and farming practices were much less wasteful. Nonetheless, most Americans agreed that any kind of agricultural reform could not be moved forward quickly, if at all. Caroline Kirkland, who had travelled throughout the rural parts of Kenya and Uganda in 1907, believed that the agricultural practices of Africans were too embedded to be changed rapidly.[9] Henry M. Stanley, in another instance, described in detail how an apparently rich piece of land in the Congo was not being properly used by the "natives":

> Here was a valley stretching four miles east and west, and about eight miles north and south, left with the richest soil to its own wild growth of grass—which in civilisation would have been a most valuable meadow for the rearing of cattle—invested as it was by dense forests, darkening the horizon at all points of the compass, and folded in by tree-clad ridges.[10]

Americans, Stanley further explained, would have put the land to even more extensive use by chopping it up into smaller lots to be sold speculatively or by introducing modern farming techniques.

In a final case, Julian Ralph cited the example of the "Kaffirs," a derogatory term used by non-Africans to refer to the Bantu-speaking peoples of South Africa. Ralph was an American journalist, born in New York City in 1853. For most of his adult life, he was London correspondent for the *New York Herald* and the *Brooklyn Eagle*. During the South African War of 1899–1902, he represented London's *Daily Mail*, eventually accompanying the British general Lord Roberts on his victorious march to Bloemfontein. In 1898, Ralph was made a member of the Royal Geographical Society. Ralph's importance, however, comes from his attempt to demonstrate how ineffective the Kaffirs were in designing their own environment. To do so he pointed out that although millions of Kaffirs had inhabited different parts of South Africa, because their seminomadic existence precluded permanent settlement, they had left "no mark on the landscape." [11] What good would sound agricultural practices be to a people who led such a shiftless existence?

Besides their farms, a second element in the landscape of Africans that was evaluated by Americans was Africa's rural villages. There is, however, some uncertainty in assessing precisely which African settlements Americans were describing. Their writings, unfortunately, lacked a desired specificity, making location a problem. Nonetheless, it is reasonable to assume that these settlements were in regions of Africa where Americans frequently travelled and lived: in Sierra Leone, Liberia, Nigeria, Cameroon, Gabon, Angola, Congo, Kenya, Tanzania, Rhodesia, and South Africa; and more specifically, in those areas surrounding such large urban centers as Freetown, Monrovia, Abeokuta, and Luanda in West Africa; and Nairobi, Salisbury, Bulawayo, Johannesburg, and Cape Town in eastern and southeastern Africa.

Some villages settled by Africans were more confusing to Americans in their appearance than others. Villages that were neither permanent sites nor fixed places but settlements of frequent change were especially puzzling. The Masai peoples of Kenya and Tanzania favored this kind of village life since it allowed them to travel with the seasons, throughout the high plains, in order to tend their cattle. Within a short period of time, a once-active settlement might become nothing more than an abandoned piece of land devoid of people. Americans who had come to East Africa to hunt and travel wondered what might account for such a bizarre arrangement among the Masai. Was it the lack of durable construction materials? Were the villages of the Masai especially vulnerable to destructive insects? Was there some "superstitious" prohibition that required the Masai to constantly move about? There was no consensus about an answer among Americans, only agreement that it was a truly primitive custom.

A second category of settlement was the established villages that had grown up around trade routes or markets. Commentary on this subject was extensive because the distinctions between African villages and the small towns of America were obvious. Americans commonly came upon an African village that was circular in design, a shape that was needed for security purposes or because the designed environment presented an African view of reality dictated by social, economic, or religious needs. In contrast, excluding the isolated American farmstead, most American towns were either linear, quadrangular, or rectangular in shape, reflecting a different set of design ideas. African villages, moreover, had an earthen look about them, since they were built from indigenous natural materials, while in America a composite of varying shapes and tones was achieved through the use of painted wood, clapboarding, brick, and stone. Finally, where an American town might have any number of structures of different shapes and sizes—a small wooden house here and a large brick church building there—an African village, at least to the American eye, lacked architectural diversity.

These variances were noted carefully by Samuel J. Whiton. An American missionary, Whiton had spent a number of years in West Africa travelling about the coastal areas of Liberia and Sierra Leone, sometimes venturing into the interior. However, early in his stay in Africa, upon viewing an African village for the very first time, he remarked that the settlement was more than unusual; it was, he wrote, in "perfect contrast" to the small towns and villages in America.[12] Of course not all African villages were the same. The settlements of the Masai of East Africa differed sharply from the villages of the Zulu of South Africa. Some African towns were made up of temporary shelters of little design, lean-tos constructed from sticks and leaves, or crudely fashioned mud houses. The farm villages of the Luba peoples, scattered across the grasslands and woodlands of present-day southeastern Zaire, were unlike the sun-dried brick towns of the Dogon peoples of Mali. However, on numerous occasions Americans spent considerable time describing in detail one noticeable aspect of these settlements because it seemed to be the perfect physical symbol of the "primitiveness" of the African landscape.

As it was called, the "native hut" reflected the rudimentary building skills of Africans. Conelike in shape, it was a structure of unusual form. Typically, a hut was fabricated from natural materials, with grass, reeds, and sticks being the most usual. Walls were made of mud, while bamboo leaves were used for roofs. Bare earth floors were sometimes covered with boards split from logs; windows consisted of crude holes punched through a wall, and a front door was the exception. Moreover, the functional aspects of the hut's interior were at variance with what was familiar to Americans. Activities that might command separate facilities in an American house were carried on in a single room. Since it lacked partitions, the interior space of an African hut served many functions: preparing food and making clothes, entertaining guests and conducting business, educating the young and caring for the old. Constant interaction among members of the same household was the rule. American missionaries, in particular, saw this spatial arrangement as a hindrance to morality and health. Without some privacy, they asked, would not "licentiousness" easily follow? And without adequate room, would not dirt and disease be persistent problems? When Americans wished to portray succinctly the primitive nature of life in Africa, descriptions, photographs, and sketches of the "native hut" were made an integral part of any narrative about Africa.

There was some recognition, nonetheless, that this kind of dwelling was well suited to Africa. It provided warmth and coolness; it made good use of readily available materials; and, on occasion, these small houses with thatched roofs, surrounded by an abundant foliage, charmed the American traveller, especially individuals from large, congested cities. In their design and construction Americans saw reflections of a simpler way of life. J. A. Carnes reported:

> Here, within the enclosure of these rude and humble dwellings, that our proud race look upon with contempt, the simple, unsophisticated sons and daughters of Africa laid themselves down on mats of their own manufacture, to that sweet repose unknown to many a pampered citizen of a wealthy metropolis, either in Europe, or our own boasted republic.[13]

There were other elements in the landscape of Africans that went unanalyzed either because they were not recognized by Americans or because Americans considered them unimportant. Since only the most pronounced aspects were scrutinized, there was scant attention paid to marketplaces, roads, paths, fences, and barns. If, however, the African landscape contained rural features unnoticed by Americans, then the extended commentary given African urban areas, in contrast, more than compensated for this deficiency.

African cities seemed complex and confusing because they were antithetical in design and conception to comparable areas in America. Of particular note was the manner in which an African city was planned. In contrast to the urban areas of America, African cities reflected a peculiar sense of order. Narrow, "crooked" streets were unsettling to Americans, making visual connections between points in a city impossible. Winding paths and roads moved the newcomer around in ever-widening circles. Because streets signified no clear direction, they promoted confusion, and because they lacked clear beginnings and ends, disorientation prevailed. Lacking paved streets and covered sidewalks, African cities were dirty; without illumination, they were dark; and for want of public spaces, they appeared to be crowded. There was an "air of intricate bewilderment" about these places, making them more akin to the older, more baroque cities of Europe rather than anything to be found in America.

Most Americans believed that the disorder of intricate streets and serpentine paths was symptomatic of a primitive state of civic development, a point well made by Horatio Bridge. Bridge was an officer in the United States Navy and a member of the African Squadron, a small contingent of American vessels that patrolled the west coast of Africa in order to prohibit the export of slaves. During his travels, Bridge had visited the Madeira and Canary Islands off the coast of Morocco, and Liberia and Sierra Leone as well. From his own experiences in Monrovia and Freetown especially, he concluded that the "promiscuously" designed cities of Africa, as he called them, were clear signs of the absence of "civilizing" influences.[14]

Unfortunately, Americans in Africa, like Bridge, made only passing reference to the ancient cities of Africa: Kumbi, Timbuktu, and Gao in the west and Meroe, Kilwa, and Zimbabwe in the east. They did, however, leave rather extensive accounts of their visits to other African settlements which reflected their bewilderment concerning this aspect of the landscape of Africans. To illustrate, consider the following case. Benjamin J. K. Anderson was an American-Liberian. In response to the interests of the president of Liberia, D. B. Warner, to learn more about the region beyond Liberia's borders, Anderson left Monrovia on February 14, 1868. His aim was to penetrate as far as possible into the interior of the continent. He returned to Monrovia in March, 1869, thirteen months later. The record of his trip was published in 1870 as *Narrative of a Journey to Musardu, the Capital of the Western Mandingoes*. As his report so clearly indicates, Anderson was literally turned around by what he encountered in Musardu, the present-day city of N'Zérékoré located approximately 175 miles northeast of Monrovia in Guinea. He was not especially perplexed by the size of the city: its fifteen hundred houses and seven thousand residents made it a city that was not particularly grand. Anderson had known larger cities in America, such as Boston and New York. The real source of distress, however, was his inability to find his way about a city of no apparent plan. Houses were haphazardly sited along randomly placed streets. Main thoroughfares were without obvious direction. Small paths and even walls indiscriminately intersected important streets at several points. On one occasion, without a sense of direction, he walked for hours throughout the city, lost and confused in a strange place.

A similar fate befell Anderson's interpreter and companion, an individual who was also new to the city. After a long and dusty trip, Anderson's friend felt the need to wash, and having found some suitable water in one part of the town, he bathed and then prepared to set out for his temporary residence, located in another section of the city. But to his dismay, his clothes had been stolen while washing, and for a time, the interpreter wandered about the city without them. Not until a sympathetic resident of the city guided him on his way, pointing him in the right direction, did he finally reach his intended destination. In defense of his friend, Anderson blamed the plan of the city for the confusion and obvious embarrassment:

> It is very perplexing on the first entrance of a stranger to find his way in these towns; for the houses seem to be dropped by accident into their places, rather than placed after any organized method. Chancellor, my interpreter, though well accustomed to these kinds of towns, was not at all assured for his own whereabouts. A woman gave him water to bathe; after he had performed his ablutions, he found himself naked, lost, and ashamed to ask where he was. He wandered over the town with the vessel in his hand, until someone, guessing the truth, brought him home. One does not lose his way on account of the size of these towns, but on account of the manner in which the houses are sprinkled about. You can march up to your house without knowing it, so completely does similarity and confusion repeat itself.[15]

In a city without clear reference points, where all the houses looked the same and all streets were entangled, experiences of this kind, Anderson argued, were inevitable.

Similar episodes about strange African cities were often recounted by Americans. However, the experience of the American missionary Thomas Jefferson Bowen was unique for the intensity his story conveyed. Born in Georgia in 1814, Bowen explored the Niger valley several times and wrote two books about Africa: *Central Africa: Adventures and Missionary Labors in Several Countries in the Interior of Africa, From 1849 to 1856,* and *Meroke; or, Missionary Life in Africa.* In 1853 he established a missionary station in Nigeria at Ogbomosho, north of Abeokuta, the capital city of the Yoruba people. In 1858 the Smithsonian Institution published his monumental study, *Grammar and Dictionary of the Yoruba Language.* Although Bowen expressed a familiarity with the area, he vividly recalled a frightful experience he had had in the Nigerian city of Abeokuta.

On that occasion, Bowen suffered doubly. As he recalled, he felt physically oppressed by the narrow, crooked paths of the city, and he longed for the comforting feel of spacious streets and avenues. He remembered how he had been forced at one point to wander through unknown lanes, courts, and small passageways, not knowing where he was heading. In addition, he described how the confusing nature of the city had played havoc with his mind. In one instance, he became claustrophobic, panic-stricken, and anxious, and felt confined, on all sides, by the clay walls of the houses:

> You pass on with rough solid clay walls close by on each side, and the eaves of the low thatched roofs almost brushing you in the face, till at last, weary of monotony and filth, you turn about to retrace your steps, and discover that you are lost in a net work of interminable alleys.[16]

So overwhelming was Bowen's experience that he became totally befuddled, and in attempting to recover his tracks and find his way, he discovered he was hopelessly lost, once again.

The experience of Bowen and Anderson and the many other Americans who wrote about different segments of a landscape fashioned by Africans is instructive. Irrespective of whether they were farms, villages, or cities, Americans attempted to classify them depending on how close, or how distant, they were from their own preferred cultural norm.[17] To do so, Americans needed to judge the creativity of Africans according to canons of taste and a hierarchy of design developed elsewhere in America. Beginning with the most "primitive" and culminating with the most "modern," Americans assumed movement toward a higher degree of civilization. But as the following commentary suggests, Africans had achieved very little according to the standards of the West:

> The African has never reached in fact, until the settlement of Liberia,

a higher rank than a king of Dahomey, or the inventor of the last fashionable grisgris to prevent the devil from stealing sugar-plums. No philosopher among them has caught sight of the mysteries of nature; no poet has illustrated heaven or earth, or the life of man; no statesman has done any thing to lighten or brighten the links of human policy. In fact, if all that negroes of all generations have ever done, were to be obliterated from recollection forever, the world would lose no great truth, no profitable art, no exemplary form of life. The loss of all that is African would offer no memorable deduction from any thing but the earth's black catalogue of crimes. Africa is guilty of slavery under which she suffered; for her people made it as well as suffered it.[18]

In describing the African landscape, Americans not only considered what was African, but they also considered the landscape designed by Europeans, which was clearly different to them, and in no better place were the distinctions between the African's lack of creativity and the European's capacity for ingenuity more evident than in the European cities of Africa. Pietermaritzburg, for example, the capital of the Natal province of South Africa, was declared a "cosmopolitan" city, an oasis of "civilization," which reflected a sense of prosperity generated by non-Africans. Named for two *Voortrekker* heroes, Pier Retief and Gert Maritz, it was no ordinary "outpost of civilization." A substantial-looking cast-iron bridge marked the entrance to the city, while other signs of Western technology were so evident everywhere that Lewis Grout, who had lived in the Natal province for fifteen years, described the area with a good deal of specificity:

Leaving the seaport town, we may take an *omnibus* in the morning, and, after a ride of fifty-four miles, find ourselves at night in the city of Maritzburg, the capital of the colony. In shape and size, this is a regular quadrangle, nearly a mile wide and about a mile and half in length with a population of about two thousand inhabitants. On approaching the city, we cross a cast-iron bridge, which has been thrown over the Little Bushman's river at a cost of more than two thousand pounds sterling. Near the bridge, is a large and valuable grist mill, which is driven by water taken by a canal from the river. The streets of the city are wide, and intersect each other at right angles. Along the side of almost every street there is a stream of running water, from which the inhabitants derive an abundant supply.[19]

Toward the center of town, generous vistas gave the city a spacious feeling, while a large open square dominated its center. Named "Market Square," it functioned as a commodity exchange where goods from the surrounding countryside were received. The city, moreover, contained a number of important structures that endowed it with a distinct "civilized" look. Located near the square were the city's most important buildings. There were several finely designed government houses for the legislature, courts of law, several banks, and a board-of-trade building. As a missionary, Grout proudly noted the Dutch Reformed churches and the structures of other Protestant denominations.

The South African city of Durban also provided the landscape of Europeans with an urban definition. Located on the coast, facing the Indian Ocean, and less than fifty miles from Pietermaritzburg, Durban was a city of considerable appeal. It offered the American traveller unexpected conveniences: Hotels rivalled those of America, and a flourishing banking community affirmed the city's growing financial power, prestige, and economic status. Steepled churches gave Durban's skyline the familiar look of many an American city. For Frank Vincent, it was difficult to believe that he was actually in "savage Africa" (as he called it) amid so many visible signs of Western civilization.[20] Vincent, who was one of many Americans who visited South Africa during the late nineteenth century, was born in Brooklyn, New York. In his time he was known as a traveller, collector, and author, and in 1895 he published *Actual Africa, or the Coming Continent. A Tour of Exploration.* Even though Vincent knew the delights of such big cities as New York and Philadelphia, Durban was still a surprise for him. It reflected, he thought, a high degree of civic development, and its design and scale were symptomatic of the advance of Western civilization in this part of the continent.

However, among the European cities of Africa—which included Bulawayo, Pretoria, and Johannesburg—one city attracted the most attention and commentary. Even to the casual observer, Cape Town, South Africa, was unique. By the late nineteenth century, a well-managed municipal government had made clean streets and excellent roads a civic virtue. American-made electric cars transported people about the city, and an efficient telephone and telegraph service linked Cape Town to London and New York, making it more like the city of Chicago than any place in Africa.[21] Skyscrapers, like the building that housed the Equitable Life Insurance Company of New York, had altered the contours of the city's skyline and were complemented by other architecturally diverse buildings. William Taylor, who lived in Africa for thirty-three years and was known as the Missionary Bishop of Africa of the Methodist Episcopal Church, remarked about how in Cape Town large amounts of land had been set aside for cultural, governmental, and recreational uses. To meet the needs of an expanding population, a library, a college, several hospitals, a railway station, public offices, and a House of Parliament had been erected within the city's limits, reflecting an assortment of different architectural styles.[22] The symmetrical composition of the city's Georgian buildings gave Cape Town a formal look, and the steeply pitched roofs and gingerbread trim of the Gothic revival was evident in its churches, while the mansard roof and patterned slate tiles of the Second Empire style defined both public buildings and private residences.

Outside the city, the "charming suburbs," as they were called, were prized because of their proximity to the sea and the ordered tranquility of their setting. Landscaped gardens, tree-shaded streets, covered streams, picturesque hedges, and many large houses built in the distinctive Dutch style were found here:

> Cape Town is not only a healthy place to live in, but is surrounded by most charming suburbs, combining land and sea. There is an excellent railway service in and out of the capital, and pretty much the whole Cape society lives out of town, somewhere about the base of the mysterious Table Mountain. The roads in all directions are of a character to make a cyclist delirious with joy; and though I rode and drove about a great deal over them, I cannot recall a single stretch which was unlovely. There are huge trees; massive stone bridges arching over pretty streamlets; farm-houses of a Dutch pattern, with thatched roofs and whitewashed walls, looking exceedingly comfortable among garden shrubbery.[23]

In addition, many houses were made of either brick or stone, covered by gable roofs, while gambrel roofs were not uncommon. For an American like William Harvey Brown, just seeing such sights in and around Cape Town forced him to revise his vision of Africa as a "wild-half-explored country."[24]

William Harvey Brown was born in Des Moines, Iowa, in 1862

and was educated at the University of Kansas, where he received a bachelor of science degree. Because of his scientific training in biology, he was employed by the Smithsonian Institution to travel to South Africa to collect samples of indigenous flora and fauna, which earned him the nickname "Curio" Brown. He was a member of the "Pioneer Column" of 1890 in the South African War and served as mayor of Salisbury, Rhodesia, from 1909 to 1910. Although Brown had made extensive trips throughout South Africa, Cape Town for him was a uniquely modern city. However, since city life in South Africa was so unlike the more "primitive" parts of the continent, considerable effort was expended in describing this "new world," or the larger society of Europeanized Africa.[25] For example, it was pointed out that private clubs "studded" the landscape, equalling the best establishments of Europe.[26] In Rhodesia in particular, "sporting clubs" formed a significant part of the area's social life, helping to establish important social and economic bonds. Within these clubs, information was exchanged, deals were made, and power was solidified. In reflecting on this "simple social system," E. Alexander Powell remarked about how the "progressive prairie towns" of America, instead of having the saloon and the dance hall, might have benefitted from establishing similar types of clubs.[27]

The landscape of South Africa contained a degree of elegance that separated it sharply from the primitiveness of the African bush. Men and women in fashionable attire gave Cape Town a sophisticated ambiance. Violins and cellos were played at society balls, while talk of theater and opera and of sailing and motoring was more common than discussions of animals or crops:

> The next scene is at the Mount Nelson Hotel. It is dinner time. A grand dining-hall, sparkling with plate and crystal, and set with snowy table linen, contains sixty or seventy persons in ultra-fashionable attire. The ladies are in décolleté dresses, and gems flash upon their necks and bodices. Musicians play to them from a gallery at one end of the hall, and Swiss waiters serve them with the delicacies of the London market, brought here in refrigerators by the ships of the Castle line.... The talk is of the opera, the play, the day's drive or sail.[28]

Unlike American perceptions of the static nature of the landscape of Africans, Americans singled out a number of non-Africans who were engaged in transforming certain parts of "white man's Africa." In Salisbury, Rhodesia, an American who had bought a hotel, thinking that different forms of amusement should be made a part of life in the city, constructed a number of theaters. The owner pointed proudly to one particular theater that was built on the very spot where only a short time before African chiefs had carried out their "savage" rites. Americans cited this development as a sure sign of progress. In another example, one enterprising American had designed, built, and marketed a unique item: "sectional houses," as he called them, made from corrugated metal. E. Alexander Powell recalled both cases:

> Another American, starting business as a hotel-keeper in Salisbury, soon perceived that the people were ripe for some form of amusement other than that provided by the cricket fields and saloons; so he built a string of cinematograph and vaudeville theatres combined, and to-day, on the very spot where Lobenguela's medicine-men performed their bloody rites a dozen years ago, you can hear the whir of the moving-picture machine and see on the canvas screen a military review at Aldershot or a bathing scene at Asbury Park. Still another American whom I met has increased the thickness of his wallet by supplying prospectors and settlers with sectional houses which are easily portable and can be erected in an hour. Taking the circular, conical-roofed hut of the Matabele as his model, he evolved an affair of corrugated iron which combines simplicity, portability, and practicability with a low price, so that to-day, as you travel through Rhodesia, you will see these American-made imitations of Kaffir huts dotting the veldt.[29]

But unlike the traditional "native hut" of the African, this later-day copy was considered an innovative part of a newly developing landscape.

Whether implicitly or explicitly, the landscapes of Africans and Europeans were constantly juxtaposed. Since they were so dissimilar in form and content to the American observer, comparison and contrast seemed a ready way of highlighting the important characteristics of each. In one particular instance, however, the differences seemed especially evident. On a clear day, Julian Ralph left Cape Town on foot, walking toward Table Mountain, the flat-topped natural elevation that slopes out behind the city. As he began to climb higher, he was able to see in all directions. To his left, Ralph noted, the desert stretched far into the distance, almost endlessly into vacant space devoid of crowds and bustling activity. To his right, toward Cape Town, there was, in contrast, something quite remarkable: large numbers of brick, stone, and clapboard houses and cottages, some covered with slate or metal roofs, several shaded by trees, and many surrounded by lush gardens and spacious lawns. Ralph then remarked about how the landscape of Cape Town was "like a tatter of dreamland," rising so near the desert. It was miraculous in itself, representing the accomplishment and creativity of Europeans in Africa. The desert, however, Ralph suggested, was without any signs of "civilization" and life—and that, he reminded his readers, was indicative of the primitive, backward, and unchanging nature of the landscape of Africans.[30]

Toward the close of the nineteenth century, there were many indications that parts of Africa were changing rapidly. Caroline Kirkland urged others to visit Africa quickly before "the extraordinary panorama has changed; before the wild animals have retired to remote regions; before missionaries have clad the savages in custom-made trousers and petticoats; before Cook is escorting chattering flocks of New England schoolma'ams to the whilom lairs and jungles of fierce savagery."[31] She might have added that the real forces changing Africa were the railroad and new means of communication. In making parts of southeastern Africa more accessible, the railroad encouraged more European emigrants to settle in eastern and southeastern Africa.[32] Charles Chaillé-Long, a native of Princess Anne, Somerset County, Maryland, noted that with the introduction of a sophisticated communication system in South Africa in the late nineteenth century, the spirit of civilization in the form of trade and commerce was clearly flourishing.[33]

Although the railroad, telegraph, and telephone were efficient examples of modern technology, they also made visible imprints on the African landscape as railroad tracks and telegraph poles worked their way across parts of the continent. But for most Americans in Africa, railroads, telegraphs, and telephones were associated only with the work of Europeans and were representative of growth, progress, and the spirit of Western ingenuity. The landscape of Africans, in contrast, was without any redeeming qualities, as evidenced by the farms, cities, and houses created by Africans. Thus, in their descriptions of the designed environment of Africa, Americans created two cultural landscapes for the reading public in America to consider: a changing, superior, European one and an unaltered, inferior, African one. The distinction was evident to all who read the American accounts of "life" in Africa—of the hut being overshadowed by the skyscraper, or the traditional African village being replaced by the modern city. It was, however, a division of the African landscape that not only had practical consequences, but far-reaching symbolic implications as well.

Notes

1. For the many definitions of culture, see A. L. Kroeber and Clyde Kluckhohn, eds., *Culture: A Critical Review of Concepts and Definitions* (New York: Vintage Books, 1963).

2. For a discussion of landscapes generally, see D. W. Meinig, ed., *The Interpretation of Ordinary Landscapes* (New York: Oxford University Press, 1979). See also F. Dixey, "African Landscape," *Geographical Review* 34 (1944), 457–65.

3. Poultney Bigelow, *White Man's Africa* (New York: Harper and Brothers, 1900), p. v.

4. James Barnes, *Through Central Africa from Coast to Coast* (New York: D. Appleton and Co., 1915), p. 72.

5. J. Leighton Wilson, *Western Africa: Its History, Condition, and Prospects* (New York: Harper and Brothers, 1856), p. 285.

6. Lewis Grout, *Zulu-Land; or, Life Among the Zulu-Kafirs of Natal and Zululand, South Africa* (Philadelphia: Presbyterian Publication Committee, 1864), pp. 33–34. See also Lewis Grout, *The Isizulu: A Grammar of the Zulu Language* (London: Trübner and Co., 1859); and *Autobiography of the Rev. Lewis Grout* (Brattleboro, Vt.: Clapp and Jones, 1905).

7. Samuel J. Whiton, *Glimpses of West Africa, With Sketches of Missionary Labor* (Boston: American Tract Society, 1866), p. 30.

8. Ibid., pp. 30–31.

9. Caroline Kirkland, *Some African Highways: A Journey of Two American Women to Uganda and the Transvaal* (Boston: Dana Estes and Co., 1908), p. 219.

10. Henry M. Stanley, *How I Found Livingstone; Travels, Adventures, and Discoveries in Central Africa* (New York: Charles Scribner's Sons, 1899), p. 76.

11. Julian Ralph, *Towards Pretoria: A Record of the War Between Briton and Boer to the Relief of Kimberly* (New York: Frederick A. Stokes Co., 1900), p. 78.

12. Whiton, *Glimpses*, p. 58.

13. J. A. Carnes, *Journal and Voyage From Boston to the West Coast of Africa* (Boston: John P. Jewett and Co., 1852), p. 283.

14. Horatio Bridge, *Journal of an African Cruiser*, ed. Nathaniel Hawthorne (New York: George P. Putnam and Co., 1853), p. 137.

15. Benjamin Anderson, *Narrative of a Journey to Musardu, the Capital of the Western Mandingoes* (New York: S. W. Green, 1870), pp. 66–67.

16. T. J. Bowen, *Central Africa: Adventures and Missionary Labors in Several Countries in the Interior of Africa, From 1849 to 1856* (Charleston, S.C.: Southern Baptist Publication Society, 1857), p. 295.

17. Henry M. Stanley, *Through the Dark Continent*, 2 vols. (New York: Harper and Brothers, 1879), 2:72.

18. Andrew H. Foote, *Africa and the American Flag* (New York: D. Appleton and Co., 1854), p. 207.

19. Grout, *Zulu-Land*, p. 336.

20. Frank Vincent, *Actual Africa, or the Coming Continent. A Tour of Exploration* (New York: D. Appleton and Co., 1895), p. 300.

21. Poultney Bigelow, *White Man's Africa* (New York: Harper and Brothers, 1900), p. 152.

22. William Taylor, *Christian Adventures in South Africa* (New York: Phillips and Hunt, 1881), pp. 26–27. See also J.Y.F. Blake, *A West Pointer with the Boers* (Boston: Angel Guardian Press, 1903), p. 14; and Jerome L. Babe, *The South African Diamond Fields* (New York: D. Wesley, 1872), p. 73.

23. Bigelow, *White Man's Africa*, p. 146.

24. Wiliam Harvey Brown, *On the South African Frontier: The Adventures and Observations of an American in Mashonaland and Matabeleland. . .* (New York: Charles Scribner's Sons, 1899), p. 38.

25. Levi Coppin, *Observations of Persons and Things in South Africa, 1900–1904* (Philadelphia: African Methodist Episcopal Book Concern, n.d.), p. 21.

26. Bigelow, *White Man's Africa*, p. 247.

27. E. Alexander Powell, *The Last Frontier: The White Man's War for Civilisation in Africa* (New York: Charles Scribner's Sons, 1912), p. 216; and also, Brown, *South African Frontier*, pp. 407–8.

28. Ralph, *Towards Pretoria*, p. 72.

29. Powell, *Last Frontier*, p. 218.

30. Ralph, *Towards Pretoria*, pp. 77–78.

31. Kirkland, *African Highways*, p. 35.

32. Stanley, *Through South Africa* (London: Sampson Low, 1898), p. 33; and also Thomas Stevens, *Scouting for Stanley in East Africa* (New York: Cassell Publishing Co., 1890), p. 209.

33. Charles Chaillé-Long, *Central Africa: Naked Truths of Naked People* (London: Sampson Low, 1876), p. 314. See also Powell, *Last Frontier*, p. 8; and Axel Lundeberg and Frederick Seymour, *The Great Roosevelt African Hunt and the Wild Animals of Africa* (New York: D. B. McCurdy, 1910), p. 61.

5

An African Wilderness

By the time young Malcolm Little had come to think of Africa as a land of monkeys, tigers, and jungles, African peoples had already worked out elaborate cultural systems of their own. They had devised religious creeds of theological sophistication and had created art, music, literature, and an impressive array of public and private artifacts to rival the best efforts of Europe and America.[1] The sculptures of Ife and Benin in West Africa represent one of the world's great art styles. Life-size portrait heads from Ife, the religious center of the Yoruba people, date from the twelfth century A.D. African music, moreover, is extremely complex. Although long dismissed as primitive, the drums, bells, flutes, and stringed instruments of Africa are capable of playing from five to twelve different rhythms simultaneously; Western classical music seldom employs more than two. Yet true to a vision dependent on both youth and ignorance, Malcolm Little made no mention of African accomplishments; the negative was connoted while the positive remained unacknowledged. To look solely to one individual for guidance about how Africa was seen by Americans would be overly restrictive, especially since other Americans evaluated Africa in terms that were similarly deficient.

Writing in the inaugural issue of *National Geographic Magazine* in 1889, Gardiner Hubbard, then president of the National Geographic

Society, stated that in general Africa had "never developed any high degree of civilization." Only when Africans had been brought into contact with Western civilization, Hubbard asserted, had they been able to make any sort of progress, and when this contact with the West was removed, Africans "deteriorated into barbarism." He further noted that, even as he wrote, a struggle was being waged in Africa "between civilization and barbarism," between progress and primitivism, between Europeans and Americans as the bearers of a superior way of life, and the "natives" of Africa and their elementary forms of social organization.[2] Hubbard's view of Africa as a continent without civilization of course was a reflection of his belief in both the racial superiority of the Anglo-Saxon and the benefits of Western civilization over all other kinds. But in light of Hubbard's statement, which attracted considerable attention in late nineteenth-century America, it is important to inquire more fully about how Africa came to symbolize the uncivilized, backward parts of the world.[3]

Antecedents can be traced to the experiences of Americans in Africa. In their travels throughout Liberia and Sierra Leone, Kenya and Zimbabwe, South Africa, and other parts of the continent, Americans were ready reporters of what they had seen. In particular, they wrote about the unfolding drama they were witnessing between Western progress and deep-seated primitivism. However, during the late nineteenth and early twentieth centuries especially, uncivilized— in one very important way—meant being undeveloped in an economic sense. In comparison to America, Africa was an embryonic continent, a land that needed to be modified, used, manipulated, and changed. Moreover, not only did Americans evaluate Africa in terms of what it was, but they also considered what the continent might be. Because it was a "passive" land, Africa required the uplifting hand of outside forces to exploit it commercially to the fullest. It might be undeveloped, but it was suitable for development; a continent that was "static" but capable of being progressive; a part of the world that was backward but had the potential for being moved forward. As a continent of obvious commercial potential, Americans remarked most about how little exploitation there had actually been.[4]

From impressions such as these, it is clear that the African world Americans confronted involved more than descriptions of what was literal and concrete. Although responses to Africa's natural scene, and evaluations of the continent's designed environment, formed an integral part of their writings, Americans sought to impose meaning upon Africa by defining the continent intellectually as well. Through their writings the African continent was transformed into a symbolic landscape, charged with cultural meaning, such that complicated ideas could be compressed into very specific concepts, allowing information about Africa to be transmitted from writer to reader in an economical and precise manner.[5] The concept of Africa as a symbol of undeveloped wilderness became a device for channelling the flow of information and a mechanism for interpreting seemingly unrelated events on the continent to the reading public of America, a nation that had only recently developed its own frontier wilderness areas. However, the reports coming out of Africa that described the continent as being economically undeveloped had a special clarity about them because they were cast within the context of two larger issues of the time: the political reality of European colonialism and the acquisitive spirit of American imperialism.

By the middle of the nineteenth century, European missionaries and entrepreneurs were urging further involvement in Africa. As their knowledge of the continent increased, so did their desire to interfere in the religious life of "pagan" Africans and to control the economic affairs of Africa. Not all Europeans were convinced that such involvement could be beneficial. Some religious leaders felt that there was little to be achieved from attempting to civilize Africans. They were considered to be unredeemable; and what could be extracted materially from a continent about which so little was known? The colonial domination of the continent was still several decades away, as Europe maintained knowledge of, and contacts with, the continent in only a peripheral way. Between 1876, however, when Leopold II of Belgium founded the International Association for the Exploration and Civilization of Central Africa, and 1912, when the French finally exerted dominance over Morocco by declaring it a protectorate, the major European powers had established their political influence in Africa; Liberia and Ethiopia were the only exceptions. Europe had attempted to carve up Africa as rapidly as possible, and the area south of the Sahara was the focus of their attention. Leopold II made an arrogant bid for empire in the Congo. Although the partition had already begun in fact, the Berlin West African Conference of 1884–1885, presided over by Bismarck and attended by all the major European powers and the United States, was held to recognize and legitimize each other's interests in Africa and to set the ground rules for imperialism.

The factors leading to the partition of Africa were many. Increased exploration in Africa by David Livingstone, Henry M. Stanley, and others had exposed more of the continent, thus making its penetration easier. European powers, in addition, were ready for imperial conquest. France, humiliated by its defeat and occupation by Prussia, wanted a colonial empire where victory would be easy and glorious. The newly united German empire, under its chancellor, Bismarck, needed new markets for its expanding industries and colonies for a growing population. Both England and Portugal, although long established on the African coasts, were determined to increase their domination over the interior parts of the continent. The recently established kingdom of Italy was interested in expanding its empire in almost any direction. Beginning in the late 1870s, then, when the commercial and political interests of several major European powers were directed toward Africa, to approximately the late 1890s, European nations effectively divided the continent among themselves.

A sense of the conquest of Africa can be measured by reference to the political map of Africa as it looked in the period prior to the Berlin Conference of 1884, and in 1914, when the colonization of Africa was completed. Before 1884, with the exception of two French trading stations in Senegal, European influences in Africa were entirely restricted to the coastal areas of the continent. The Portuguese had established themselves in Mozambique, present-day Angola, and Portuguese Guinea; the British in South Africa, Sierra Leone, Ghana, and Nigeria; the French in Gabon and Dahomey, and the Germans in Togoland. By 1914, in comparison, the four colonies of South Africa had united to form the Union of South Africa; the British had claimed dominance over Egypt, the Anglo-Egyptian Sudan, British East Africa, Nigeria, Gold Coast, Sierra Leone, and Gambia. The Portuguese continued in Mozambique, Angola, and Portuguese Guinea, while the French had established sovereignty over Algeria, Morocco, French West Africa, French Equatorial Africa, and Gabon. The Germans had laid claim to Togoland, Cameroon, South-West Africa, and German East Africa; the Italians were established in Libya, Eritrea, and Somalia; and the Congo Free State had been annexed by the Belgians.

Political leaders were generally supported by public opinion. People were enticed by the idea of colonial conquest and the prospect of increased empire and were convinced by the arguments used to justify intervention in Africa: the abolition of slavery, warfare, and other African atrocities through the introduction of commerce, Christianity, and Western civilization. However, the prime interest of Europe in Africa was economic exploitation. Although this does not deny the selfless work of individuals who had altruistic motives for being in Africa, the improvement of roads, the establishment of communication facilities, the controlling of diseases, the setting up of schools, and the introduction of new methods of agriculture were done to increase the value of their investments.[6]

In comparison with the European variety, American interests in Africa lacked the persistence exhibited by Europeans. Although American economic control in Africa never became great at any one time, Africa was seen as a continent of considerable commercial potential: as a supplier of raw materials, a market for finished goods, and a site for industrial and agricultural development. There was, however, opposition to the idea of expanding American interests to foreign countries, based in part on certain racial assumptions. Africans were unfit for self-improvement, the argument went, and incapable of development because they were racially dissimilar, innately inferior, and obviously subordinate. A vocal segment of American society, nevertheless, claimed that nations like the United States had an obligation to civilize inferior peoples. Motivated less by a desire for territory and more by purely economic considerations, many Americans were eager to take up the "white man's burden" in which the cultural differences between Americans and Africans played an influential part.

Since it was assumed that "people of color" were innately inferior, backward nations like Africa should not block the expansion of Western civilization. The pronouncements of Americans like John W. Burgess, Josiah Strong, and David Starr Jordan lent credence to the doctrine of white supremacy, and racial superiority was central to the idea of bestowing the blessings of civilization on those not capable of achieving them on their own. Racism provided one of the most influential forces for commercial adventurism in Africa, and since most Americans equated progress in Africa with white settlement, what to do with black Africans became a difficult problem. Furthermore, the racial assumptions of white Americans who travelled to Africa were based on their domestic racial experiences, and as a result of contact with the inferior peoples of America, namely, Indians and blacks, a pattern of thought emerged for dealing with similar peoples in other parts of the world.[7] But to create a sustained view for the reading public of America, one in which the word "Africa" was equated with being economically "uncivilized," required the promulgation of a number of specific explanations, some associated with race and some not, to account for the continent's being seen as "an African wilderness."

An immediate explanation for Africa's crude and undeveloped state involved discussions of its physical characteristics. Africa's lack of commercial development was explained by the restrictions of topography. In North Africa, the Sahara desert acted as a buffer, stretching more than three thousand miles, from the Atlantic Ocean to the Red Sea. This thousand-mile-wide band of windswept and stony desert was interrupted only sporadically by dry highlands and expanses of shifting sand. With the desert as a focal point, Americans saw the rapidly developing countries of Europe to the north, while to the south lay just the opposite: sub-Saharan Africa. The desert was a divisive force and a natural impediment not easily overcome, and for its ability to inhibit interaction between Africa and Europe, it was judged "more effective than a Chinese wall in guarding the whole continent to the South and keeping it in a state of continual isolation."[8] In addition, but to a lesser degree, the Atlas mountain range served as a barrier to development as well. With peaks rising to more than twelve thousand feet, the mountains cut off the commercial centers of Morocco and Algeria from the rest of Africa. Along the North African coast were the thriving cities of Casablanca, Tangier, and Algiers, while beyond the desert, to the south, was an uninhabited wasteland. Thus, the Atlas mountains, like the Sahara desert, were seen as another obstacle separating black Africa from the commercial capitals of the Mediterranean and the countries of Europe.

In East Africa, Thomas Stevens was one of many Americans who pondered the problems preventing the flow of trade in this part of the continent. Stevens arrived in East Africa through an unusual set of circumstances. In 1879, Henry M. Stanley had disappeared for some time into the African interior in his attempt to rescue Emin Pasha, the governor of Equatorial Egypt. Stevens, a reporter for the

New York World, a rival of Stanley's *New York Herald*, was sent by his paper to find Stanley. Stevens eventually located Stanley, but in the aftermath of his expedition Stevens articulated his impressions of the primitive state of East Africa's commercial life as well. In an important article published in *Scribner's Magazine* in 1890, Stevens linked the lack of commercial development in East Africa to the configuration of the continent's inland and coastal waterways. The presence of cataracts along the principal waterways and rivers of eastern Africa were, he felt, obstructive to trade. Because of difficulties in navigation, raw materials from the interior of the continent could not be quickly extracted, thereby stunting the growth of a commercial system connecting African ports with European and American centers of trade. Ships from these countries, conversely, were unable to penetrate Africa along its eastern shore. Without navigable rivers free of cataracts, waterfalls, and sharp fluctuations in depth, commercial enterprise could not possibly flourish.[9]

In Central Africa, a term used by Americans to designate the dense equatorial rain forest region of the Congo basin, an area that includes the present-day countries of Zaire and Congo, Americans defined the "primeval forest" as the source of the region's economic stagnation. Dense rain forests clogged the central lowlands of the basin-shaped nation of Zaire, while swamps, forests, and savannas dominated the topography of the Congo, making settlement difficult. The forests of Central Africa needed to be subdued, since uncleared land was considered useless land. Because the area lacked clearly defined limits, commerce could prosper only by altering the contours of the forest landscape. Where were the great cities, Americans asked, arising amid such tropical vegetation?[10]

The causes for West Africa's lack of development were twofold. The region's hot, humid climate and its history of disease, first of all, were important factors retarding economic growth. Sapped of energy by the heat, how could an individual work, and weakened by fever, how could industry and productivity be achieved? Second, the arrested commercial development of West Africa was tied to the shape of its coastline. Richard Harding Davis, a Fellow of the Royal Geographical Society and the American author of *The Congo and Coasts of Africa* (1907), felt that the beaches of West Africa were barriers to commerce and trade, making the construction of ports a precarious task.[11] Although explanations for Africa's apparent lack of development, derived from the physical nature of the continent, were convincing, Americans at home were presented with more cerebral reasons as well.

One such rationale was based on a loosely construed theory of history in which Africa was viewed as being hedged off from the rest of the world. In comparison to the all-changing activities of the West, Africa had remained, for centuries, outside the mainstream of progressive Western development. One had only to look to African societies, William Rainsford believed, for confirmation that no significant change had occurred on the continent for "thousands and thousands of years."[12] Except where non-African influences were clearly notable, Africa stood in timeless suspension. The West, in contrast, had been advancing toward "a higher and grander eminence"; societies were becoming more "modern" and efficient than previous ones.[13] While Africa was still "in the days of the Pharaohs and Herodotus and Ptolemy," the Western world had been engaged in the task of civilizing itself.[14] In effect, lacking history, Africa was without civilization, and since there had been "no native-born advancement" for thousands of years, the continent rested in "unalloyed barbarism."[15] Without cultural achievements of its own, without poetry and politics, and most of all, without any evidence of worthwhile commercial development, Africa's contribution to its own evolution had been extraordinarily insignificant.

Africa's materially deprived condition was also explained theologically. Since the continent possessed enormous economic potential, was it not divinely ordained to give the "very best land on earth" to those who could best exploit it, or as one American asked:

Has a wise providence prepared here another Canaan for our modern Israelites, to which they shall carry back the civilization and Christianity with which three generations of contact with the Anglo-Saxon race has impressed them, enlightening that pagan darkness, developing the wonderful riches of the country, and helping to make Africa again a potent factor in the world's affairs?[16]

For what other reason had Africa been concealed for so long? Had not the time come for so precious a possession to be appreciated, as Joseph H. Reading believed? As a commercial agent for the United States government in Central Africa, Reading had spent over fifteen years in Equatorial Africa. At one point he was both secretary and treasurer of the Gabon and Corisco Island missions of the Presbyterian Board of Foreign Missions. He published *The Ogowe Band; a Narrative of African Travel* in 1890, which documented his journey along the Ogooué River in Gabon, and in 1901 he authored *A Voyage Along the Western Coast or Newest Africa.* What was significant about his writings, however, was that Reading believed that "Providence" was guiding the development of Africa, just as it had done at one time in America. In fact, the task of "taming" Africa was even easier than settling North America, since more sophisticated means of exploitation were available to do so.[17]

Of the several explanations put forth by Americans to account for Africa's failure to develop economically, the most compelling theory was an ironic one: Africa's obvious material abundance. It was an observation derived from direct experience and immediate confrontation with the physical reality of Africa, and a belief predicated not on what the continent had failed to achieve but on what Africa actually already possessed: minerals that were untapped, forests that remained thick, and vast tracts of land that had been barely touched.[18]

Describing the abundance of Africa, however, had long been a part of American reports from Africa. In the early nineteenth century, American travellers in West Africa had made frequent references to the wealth of the continent, portraying the region as being among the richest in the world. Joshua Carnes, for example, noted how rumors about the availability of "solid lumps" of gold along the West African coast were freely circulating in America during this time.[19] Daniel Coker of Baltimore, Maryland, pictured the countryside of Sierra Leone as being "prolific beyond description."[20] Moreover, catalogues of West Africa's cornucopia, which were frequently compiled, mentioned abundant amounts of rosewood, teak, mahogany, hickory, and poplar trees; the almost "spontaneous growth" of sugar cane, mangoes, guavas, lemons, limes, coconuts, plantain, bananas, pineapples, and peaches; and orange and coffee trees so endowed that they were "breaking down" under the weight of their own produce.[21] But the natural opulence and "exuberant vegetation" of West Africa was perhaps captured best by an American missionary, George S. Brown, in a poem entitled "African Triumph."[22]

By contrasting the landscape of West Africa to the hills of New England, Brown writes:

American high-lands may boast of their green
Since a few months at longest, her collar is seen,
Then as many have pass'd through and very well know
That her beauty is soon changed by white frost and snow,
But our African Forest as thousands have seen,
Abounds with delightful, unchangeable green,
And her sweet smelling blossoms perfuming the air
As American high-lands at once would despair.

The flat "low lands" of the American Midwest are then compared to the moist clay and sandy "loam lands" of West Africa:

American low lands may talk of fine grass,
A few months at longest, her glory passed,
Then as many have witness'd while shiv'ring along,
Her turf dry, and frozen as hard as a stone.
But our African loam lands are dressed in stout grass,
Its constant green blooming forever doth last,
And her fatness and sweetness as many have said
Bids defiance to America, and waves her tall head.

In the second half of the poem, specific ways in which West Africa might even outdo America are taken up. However, the purpose of Brown's poem was to emphasize West Africa's ability to provide for potential settlers, and as Brown's comparison suggests, the abundance of West Africa was not the result of innovative farming techniques or special methods of agriculture. It was the product of natural growth in a bountiful environment.

Despite the many examples attesting to the abundance of West Africa, the most detailed statements articulated as proof of Africa's economically "uncivilized" condition were not those associated with the western portion of the continent during the first half of the nineteenth century. They were focused, rather, in the latter part of the century, on the material wealth of the Congo, an area strongly tied to the personal desires of Leopold II of Belgium and associated with the writings of three influential Americans.

As king of the Belgians, Leopold II had desired empire and wealth in Africa, and to achieve these ends he financed a large-scale expedition into the Congo river basin under the leadership of Henry M.

Stanley. After a series of covert financial maneuvers, Leopold not only claimed the entire area as a sovereign state but also promised, at the Berlin Conference of 1884–1885, the United States access to the Congo. Consequently, John Kasson, the American delegate to the conference, supported Leopold's claim. Known as the Congo Free State, the territory was thought to be the most materially promising part of Africa in terms of fertility and mineral resources.

In America, the writings of Henry M. Stanley, Samuel P. Verner, and Henry S. Sanford brought the Congo's richness to the attention of the reading public. While details of Stanley's life have already been noted, Verner and Sanford, though famous in their own time, are less well-known today for their involvement in the Congo. Samuel Phillips Verner, the son of a former comptroller general of the state of South Carolina and an 1892 graduate of the University of South Carolina, was sent to the Congo in 1895 as business manager for the Mission Board of the Southern Presbyterian Church. He spent eleven years in Africa and amassed the largest collection of ethnological specimens from the Congo ever seen in America, which he deposited with the Smithsonian Institution. In 1903 he was commissioned by the Louisiana Purchase Exposition to secure a group of Batwa "pygmies" for exhibition in America. Throughout his life, his special interest was in studying the relationship between Afro-Americans and Africans. His most important work on Africa, published in 1903, was *Pioneering in Central Africa*.

Henry Shelton Sanford, unlike Verner, was a career diplomat who had held government posts in St. Petersburg, Frankfurt, and Paris before becoming the United States minister to Belgium in 1861. In 1885 he represented the United States at the International Conference at Berlin. Because of his influence and prestige, the United States eventually recognized the flag of Leopold's newly formed "International Association for the Exploration and Civilization of Central Africa" as a friendly power. But in 1886 he organized what he called the "Sanford Exploring Expedition" to reconnoiter the Congo, and he was able to launch the first commercial steamer on the Congo River, *The Florida*, by having it transported piece by piece in sixty-pound parcels over a year's time on the heads of some two thousand African porters. As an advocate of further exploration in the region, he joined Stanley and Verner as one of the three most influential popularizers in America of the commercial exploitation of the Congo.

Of the three, Stanley was as familiar with America as he was with Africa, having spent considerable time in the United States and on the African continent, and to demonstrate just how abundant the Congo Free State was, he likened Central Africa to the central portions of America. The Congo and Mississippi rivers were obvious points of comparison since both were unusually large waterways. However, Stanley believed that the Congo was potentially superior for several reasons. The Congo River surpassed the Mississippi in length: it was 2,718 miles long, while the Mississippi ran about 2,350 miles. The Congo, in addition, was wider than the Mississippi and with greater concentrations of wildlife along its banks:

> The Congo is one and a half times larger than the Mississippi, and certainly from eight to ten times broader. You may take your choice of nearly a dozen channels, and you will see more beautiful vegetation on the Congo than on the American river. The latter lacks the palm and the calamus, while the former has a dozen varieties of the palm. Besides, it possesses herds of hippopotami, crocodiles innumerable; monkeys are gleefully romping on the islands and the main; elephants are standing sentry-like in the twilight of the dark forests by the river side; buffaloes red and black are grazing on the rich grass plains; there are flocks of ibis, black and white parrots, parroquets, and guinea-fowl.[23]

Moreover, Stanley believed that the Congo valley also outdid the Mississippi valley in the quality of crops. For example, the corn grown in the Congo region, he maintained, was far better than even the finest crops raised in Arkansas, Missouri, and Mississippi.

To sense the extent of the Congo's bounty, Stanley suggested that if the Congo region in 1880 were compared to the area surrounding the Mississippi when native American Indians held the land, just prior to its exploitation by "modern Americans," then the Congo indeed was "much more promising at the same stage of undevelopment."[24] Nothing in the Mississippi valley could equal the Congo's commercial promise, and yet in its present form Stanley felt the Congo was "a neglected waste," as reflected in an observation he made in 1882 about some land near Léopoldville:

> That broad low plain—from Kintamo south to the foot of Mabengu mountain—which forms the western shore of the Pool, is to me full

of promise and beauty. Even now it is almost idyllic in appearance, yet there is only the grass huts of Kintamo conspicuously in view; the rest is literally only a wilderness of grass, shrubs, and tree-foliage. But my mind, when I survey the view, always reverts to the possibilities of the future. It is like looking at the fair intelligent face of a promising child; we find nought in it but innocence, and we fondly imagine that we see the germs of a future great genius; perhaps a legislator, a savant, a warrior, or a poet. Supposing the rich fertile soil of that plain, well-watered as it is by many running streams, were cultivated, how it would reward the husbandman! How it would be bursting with fulness and plenty! In all the Mississippi valley there is no soil to equal it; yet there it lies a neglected waste. And perhaps for generations yet the prospect will possess the same idle slumbrous appearance it presents to-day.[25]

Many of Stanley's points were recast by Samuel Verner, who first expressed his views on the commercial exploitation of the Congo in 1901. Writing for *Forum* about the "development of Africa," he pointed out that since the exploration of Africa was nearly over, full-scale exploitation should begin.[26] Resources in the Congo were potentially staggering: diamonds, coal, petroleum, petrified gums, iron, gold, copper, lead, rubber, palm oil, timber, and guavas. He offered specific figures: After exploring the Congo-Zambesi region, he left convinced that the area contained over seven hundred thousand square miles of coal, while forty million dollars a year might be made from rubber production.[27] "There are," he stated, "millions of virgin acres as rich as any in the Mississippi valley" awaiting development.[28] In fact, by establishing trading stations in the Congo, America would have "the beginnings of what will be the Chicagos and Pittsburghs of the Orient."[29] The Congo, for Verner, was a part of Africa where the unutilized resources were so immense that a "boundless opportunity" existed for all American interests in the region.[30]

Although Verner's assessment of the material worth of the Congo was persuasively stated in other forms and at other times, the Congo's undeveloped state was also graphically sketched by a third American. As head of his own exploring expedition, Henry S. Sanford could barely contain his enthusiasm for the commercial prospects that lay before him. To him, the Congo offered new opportunities in two ways. First, it provided an area for the overflow from American markets, and second, since the Congo was obviously undeveloped, it contained plentiful amounts of raw materials.[31] "What a field for enterprise is here," he told readers of *Forum* magazine in 1890. "What an opening for our manufacturers among its fifty million of unclad inhabitants 'thirsting for trade.'"[32] As a part of the continent "surpassingly rich in vegetable and mineral values," the Congo displayed an array of potential wealth. It was a "wonderful abundance," a land of "unequalled richness," rivalling the most productive parts of America.[33]

However, as in the case of other undeveloped parts of the world, the Congo was of diminished value. In its present form it was only partially useful. It needed to be tamed, controlled, and transformed. What needed to be done was for the wealth of the Congo to be "brought out." This treasure of Africa could no longer remain concealed. Samuel Verner in particular reflected the sentiments of many others, both Americans and Europeans, when he wrote about the Congo,

> Here it lay—that dark mass of portentous immensity—land of fabled monsters, storied in the earliest records of mankind, the oldest and youngest continent of them all, preserved, as by a miracle, for the use of mankind at the very time when its power and progress are most capable of developing it; surely this is the day—dawn from on high to the darkness of its long slumbers, and the light of a new birth is at last streaming over it.[34]

Stanley, Verner, and Sanford were vigorous promoters of the idea of the Congo as an economically undeveloped territory, a land of vast commercial possibilities in need of exploitation. During the late nineteenth and early twentieth centuries, their accounts helped to shape a particular view of Africa as a virgin, embryonic, and passive land. Because of restrictions imposed upon it by topography, its lack of history, and the presence of divine intervention, it had been kept economically "uncivilized." One need only look to Africa's obvious material abundance for proof. There is, however, an important question to be asked involving the evaluation of the continent as "an African wilderness": What do these writings indicate about the perceived relationship between Africans and Africa? The implication, from the perspective of Americans in Africa, was clear, however: Africans lacked the ability to use their land wisely. Not only did

Americans deny the validity of a sense of African participation in the development of the continent, but they also affirmed the belief that the proper exploitation of Africa had begun only when non-Africans took control. Americans revealed this point of view in two interrelated ways: in their attitudes toward Africans and the continent's European population, and through expressions about their own place in Africa's future economic development.

A premise central to the development of Africa was the exploitation of Africans who were considered cheap labor but lacking motivation toward "industrious effort."[35] In their "native habitats" they were lazy and carefree.[36] They exerted little effort, it seemed, no matter what needed to be done:

> Of the future for the blacks in Africa it is difficult to speak. Pessimistic as it sounds, the present writer looks upon it as likely to be hopeless in the extreme. What has been said by earnest, hopeful, and sympathetic observers, diplomats and consuls, scientists, merchants, travellers, missionaries, concerning the natives of the West Coast, is equally applicable to those of the interior of the East Coast. They have no idea of business—for their bartering is not business—and no exchange of arts; the little they do of their own initiative in agriculture and stock-raising is not sufficient foundation upon which to erect an economic structure that is to survive.[37]

Joseph Reading made a similar observation about Africa and Africans:

> The truth is it is the richest land under the sun, and will soon be the greatest place in the world to make money. Africa possesses a vast labor supply which at present is running almost entirely to waste; this should be gathered up and carefully set to work, not only for its own good, but for the welfare of other lands and nations.[38]

Despite such misgivings about "native help," as it was called, Africans were needed. Though lazy, the argument went, they were "imitative and teachable"; and though prone to inactivity, if given the proper incentive and rewards Africans would perform satisfactorily.[39] If they were unskilled by Western standards, they were nonetheless "willing" and "obedient"; and since they remained "cheerful" under adverse conditions, they made an ideal labor force.[40] If Africans were placed under the "directive impulse of the white race," then the "regeneration of the continent" would proceed, with Africans supplying the muscle and their white masters providing the "brain."[41] It was essential that Africans be given directives, taught a number of commercially valuable skills, and develop such "habits of industry" as punctuality and discipline.[42] Since they could endure with ease the demands of the African environment, people "whose fathers never saw or heard of white men" needed to be trained as carpenters, masons, and pilots.[43]

In other instances, however, the role of Africans in the development of the continent was compared to the one played by native American Indians in the settlement of America. What better way to convey to the reading public in America a sense of the inadequacy of Africans than by comparing them to Indians? As a consequence, the meeting between non-Africans and Africans was often cast as a struggle between an assumed morally superior people and an inferior indigenous population, a situation reminiscent of the encounter between the settlers and Indians of America.[44] Arthur Donaldson Smith, for example, an American who led an expedition from Somaliland into Central Africa from 1894 to 1895 and who authored *Through Unknown African Countries* in 1897, believed that the strange appearance of the "native" peoples of both Africa and America was exactly similar. Were not their "barbaric" practices sure signs of savagery? And were not "savage" Africans like "savage" Indians in that clothing was as conspicuously absent from their bodies as were written laws from their systems of justice?[45]

The metamorphosis of black Africans into red Indians went beyond discussions of appearances and cultural similarities. Individuals like Smith believed that since the cultural life of "aboriginal" African peoples had placed them well behind the advance of Western civilization, a solution to the "native problem" in Africa was to confine Africans to designated parts of the continent, in a manner akin to the treatment of the American Indian. A policy of containment had the immediate effect of protecting non-Africans from the threat of Africans, and as Stanley argued, separation and segregation made Africa safe for Americans and Europeans who were "doggedly conquering the wilderness step by step."[46] In addition, the theme of "African-as-Indian" was further reinforced by the correspondences made between the "pioneers" of America and Africa.

Such a parallel was obvious to Theodore Roosevelt. While hunting in East Africa, he wrote to a friend about how the white settlers of East Africa reminded him of the very same people who had settled America. Both groups possessed qualities essential for survival in an untested environment: the ability to endure a spartan existence and the capacity to be persevering against hostile "natives." The European settlers of Africa reflected the same "rugged individualism" and self-reliant traits associated with pioneering Americans.[47] Edgar Beecher Bronson, who had written about his experiences in the American West, also recognized the affinity between the two groups. His writings essentially recorded the heroic exploits of American ranchmen in clearing the land and establishing communities. Africa, he thought, had similar people. The European pioneers of Africa, he wrote, were like the "hardy, tireless, [and] stout-hearted [settlers] to whom we are indebted for the winning of all North America from savagery."[48]

In the context of judging Africans inadequate for the task of transforming Africa by comparing them to native American Indians and Europeans in Africa to the pioneers of America, Americans did not preclude their own suitability for the task of opening up the continent. Rather, they drew freely upon selected aspects of America's collective history in order to advance the cause of Africa's exploitation and their place in it. Because Americans had once settled an undeveloped continent of their own, they believed that they could do in Africa what the "conquering Caucasian" had done in America.[49] Look to New England where the "heathen" had been "cheerfully expelled" by colonists who believed that "the earth belongs to those who make best use of it." For a nation of people who had crossed the Mississippi River, climbed the Rocky Mountains, and seized California and New Mexico, developing the backward parts of the world was a familiar enterprise. Had it not been essentially America's history?[50]

Likening Africans to Indians, and Europeans to the pioneers of America, and assessing their own role in the development of Africa involved the fusion of the historical process of settling America with an understanding of events in Africa. By interpreting new lands based on past familiar experiences, Americans connected one meaningful event to another and, in the process, saw parallels between circumstances in America and in Africa. Although there was no exact equation between the historical situations of the settlement of America and the history of colonization in Africa, there were obvious points of comparision to be made. In America's own brief history, a major theme had been how Americans had confronted the problems of settling and developing a wilderness land and pitting themselves against the hostile forces of an alien environment. The transformation of America from a wilderness landscape to a civilized nation had been one of the most enduring organizing concepts for understanding America's development and the characteristics of its people.

In Africa, a similar process had occurred. Throughout the nineteenth century, a general pattern of alienation of traditional African lands had taken place involving many disparate and uncoordinated events, culminating with the imposition of European colonialism. One series of events in particular, however, was singled out because the points of convergence seemed clear. It involved the highly visible movement of the South African Boers across the Transvaal into the agriculturally rich areas of the continent to the north.[51] Although the Dutch had settled at Cape Town as early as 1652, small groups of Dutch migrant farmers, or *trekboers*, gradually began to extend the frontiers of the Cape with the result that they often clashed with Africans as they moved into new territory. When the British, however, occupied South Africa in the first quarter of the nineteenth century, an increasingly large number of Boers moved northward in search of independence and land. In 1836 the "Great Trek" began, perhaps the greatest romantic event in Boer history, with several thousand Boer farmers and ranchers striking out inland over the *veld*, or plain. With their ox-wagons, horses, and rifles, they began to conquer the territory across the Orange and Vaal rivers, and as they pushed on, they battled the indigenous Zulu peoples of the region. Eventually the Boer pioneers succeeded in establishing a number of small, isolated rural settlements in their newly conquered territory.

In order to define the meaning of events in Africa intellectually for the reading public in America, individuals like Theodore Roosevelt or Poultney Bigelow used the story of the Boers, the British, and the Zulus for two reasons. Not only did the tale chronicle the revolt of a small group of "pioneers" against the superior forces of the British, but the story served as a convenient metaphor for highlighting the place to be occupied by Africans and non-Africans in the commercial development of Africa. In a role similar to the part played by the Indian population in America, Africans were seen as obstacles to, and not participants in, any future development of the continent.

In assessing the overall impact of such analogies, it might be well to remember that current views of reality are not past ones and that earlier concepts of place differ widely from present ones. Portraying Africans as Indians—when Africans were not seen as a source of labor—and Africa as a wilderness landscape was a means by which the African world was ordered and evaluated. It was the projection into a new situation of a series of attitudes and values that were formed in the more familiar setting of America. Defining Africa as a wilderness land for the reading public in America, moreover, was not solely dependent on comparison. By virtue of all the other information transmitted by Americans in Africa during the late nineteenth and early twentieth centuries, the word "Africa" became synonymous with being economically undeveloped. Because of topography and its lack of appropriate technology, coupled with the inability of Africans to exploit their land, Africa became a symbolic exemplar of the "primitive" parts of the world—a land that needed to be commercially exploited and developed, since it had "never developed any high degree of civilization," as Gardiner Hubbard had claimed in 1889.

An American who had written extensively about the commercial possibilities of Africa once remarked: "I hear the shrill sound of the whistle of the locomotive, which awakes within me an almost indescribable feeling," and "to hear its shrill notes in Africa, and on the banks of the mighty Congo, is indeed interesting and startling." As Charles Smith watched the movement of the railroad trains before him, he discovered himself "philosophizing on the possibilities of the future of Africa."[52] For an American like Smith who knew something of the history of his own country, understanding Africa as an undeveloped wilderness was a logical deduction from all he had seen on the continent. However, it also meant, as Smith discovered, coming to terms with the customs and behavior of Africans whose traditions and cultures differed substantially from his own.

Notes

1. Basil Davidson, *The African Genius: An Introduction to African Social and Cultural History* (Boston: Little, Brown and Co., 1969), pp. 160–67.

2. Gardiner G. Hubbard, "Africa, Its Past and Future," *National Geographic Magazine* 1 (April, 1889), 123–24.

3. On a closely related topic, see Kenneth E. Boulding, "National Images and International Systems," *Journal of Conflict Resolution* 3 (1959), 120–31.

4. Trade between Africa and America never did become great at any one time, but for a study of American commercial activity on the West Coast, see George E. Brooks, Jr., *Yankee Traders, Old Coasters and African Middlemen: A History of American Legitimate Trade with West Africa in the Nineteenth Century* (Boston: Boston University Press, 1970).

5. The best discussions of symbolization can be found in Edmund Leach, *Culture and Communication* (Cambridge: Cambridge University Press, 1976); and Victor Turner, *The Forest of Symbols* (Ithaca, N.Y.: Cornell University Press, 1967).

6. See Raymond Betts, ed., *The "Scramble" for Africa: Causes and Dimensions of Empire* (Boston: D. C. Heath and Co., 1966); and also John Scott Keltie, *The Partition of Africa* (London, 1893); and Sybil E. Crowe, *The Berlin West African Conference, 1884–1885* (London: Longmans, Green and Co., 1942).

7. Rubin F. Weston, *Racism in U.S. Imperialism* (Columbia: University of South Carolina Press, 1972), pp. 257–64.

8. John McKendree Springer, *The Heart of Central Africa: Mineral Wealth and Missionary Opportunity* (New York: Methodist Book Concern, 1909), p. 121.

9. Thomas Stevens, "African River and Lake Systems," *Scribner's Magazine* 8 (September, 1890), 335–42.

10. Even before the partition, Bowen stressed this point. See T. J. Bowen, *Central Africa: Adventures and Missionary Labors in Several Countries in the Interior of Africa, From 1849 to 1856* (Charleston, S.C.: Southern Baptist Publication Society, 1857), p. 326.

11. Richard Harding Davis, *The Congo and Coasts of Africa* (New York: Charles Scribner's Sons, 1907), p. 12.

12. William S. Rainsford, *The Land of the Lion* (London: William Heinemann, 1909), p. 202.

13. J. W. Buel, *Heroes of the Dark Continent* (Richmond, Va.: B. F. Johnson and Co., 1890), p. 35.

14. J. Scott Keltie, "About Africa," *Scribner's Magazine* 9 (February, 1891), 177–95.

15. Henry M. Stanley, "The Story of the Development of Africa," *Century Magazine* 51 (February, 1896), esp. 506.

16. Henry S. Sanford, "American Interests in Africa," *Forum* 9 (June, 1890), 428.

17. Joseph H. Reading, *A Voyage Along the Western Coast or Newest Africa* (Philadelphia: Reading and Co., 1901), pp. 18, 81.

18. Heli Chatelain, "Some Causes of the Retardation of African Progress," *Journal of American Folklore* 8 (July–September, 1895), 179; and also Henry M. Stanley, *The Congo and the Founding of Its Free State; A Story of Work and Exploration*, 2 vols. (New York: Harper and Brothers, 1885), 2:209.

19. J. A. Carnes, *Journal of a Voyage From Boston to the West Coast of Africa: With a Full Description of the Manner of Trading with the Natives on the Coast* (Boston: John P. Jewett and Co., 1852), p. 132; and also Charles W. Thomas, *Adventures and Observations on the West Coast of Africa, and Its Islands* (New York: Derby and Jackson, 1860), p. 209.

20. Daniel Coker, *Journal of Daniel Coker, A Descendant of Africa . . .* (Baltimore: Edward J. Coale, 1820), p. 44.

21. Armistead Miller, *Liberia Described; A Discourse Embracing a Description of the Climate, Soil, Productions, Animals, Missionary Work, Improvement, Etc., with a Full Description of the Acclimating Fever* (Philadelphia: Joseph M. Wilson, 1859), p. 14.

22. George S. Brown, *Brown's Abridged Journal* (Troy, N.Y.: Prescott and Wilson, 1849), p. 370.

23. Stanley, *The Congo and the Founding of Its Free State*, 2:8.

24. Ibid., 374–75.

25. Ibid., 1:391; and also Stanley, *In Darkest Africa*, 2 vols. (New York: Charles Scribner's Sons, 1890), 1:155.

26. Samuel Phillips Verner, "The Development of Africa," *Forum* 32 (November, 1901), 366–82.

27. Samuel P. Verner, "The White Man's Zone in Africa," *World's Work* 13 (November, 1906), 8233.

28. Verner, "Development of Africa," p. 374.

29. Verner, "The White Man's Zone in Africa," p. 8229.

30. Ibid., p. 8236.

31. Sanford, "American Interests in Africa," p. 429.

32. Ibid., p. 428.

33. Ibid., p. 429.

34. Samuel P. Verner, *Pioneering in Central Africa* (Richmond, Va.: Presbyterian Committee of Publication, 1903), pp. 24–25.

35. Samuel J. Whiton, *Glimpses of West Africa, with Sketches of Missionary Labor* (Boston: American Tract Society, 1866), p. 67.

36. A. H. Godbey, *Stanley in Africa: The Paladin of the Nineteenth Century* (Chicago: Donohue Brothers, 1902), p. 328.

37. Joseph King Goodrich, *Africa of To-day* (Chicago: A. C. McClurg and Co., 1912), pp. 231–32.

38. Reading, *Voyage*, p. 85.

39. Wilson S. Naylor, *Daybreak in the Dark Continent* (New York: Eaton and Mains, 1905), p. 70.

40. Caroline Kirkland, *Some African Highways: A Journey of Two American Women to Uganda and the Transvaal* (Boston: Dana Estes and Co., 1908), p. 93. See also Hubbard, "Africa, Its Past and Future," p. 112; and William Stephen Rainsford, *The Land of the Lion* (London: William Heinemann, 1909), p. 349.

41. Cyrus C. Adams, "Africa in Transformation," *Missionary Review of the World*, n.s. 22 (June, 1909), 457; and also Stewart Edward White, *African Camp Fires* (Garden City, N.Y.: Doubleday, Page and Co., 1913), p. 155.

42. Rainsford, *Land of the Lion*, pp. 349–50; and Cyrus C. Adams, "Foundations of Economic Progress in Tropical Africa," *Journal of Race Development* 2 (July, 1911), 9.

43. Stanley, *The Congo and the Founding of Its Free State*, 2:193. See also Verner, "Development of Africa," pp. 366–82; George Thompson, *Thompson in Africa; or, An Account of the Missionary Labors, Sufferings, Travels, and Observations, of George Thompson, in Western Africa, at the Mendi Mission* (New York: Printed for the Author, 1854), p. 210; and Samuel P. Verner, "Africa Fifty Years Hence," *World's Work* 13 (April, 1907), 8736.

44. Poultney Bigelow, *White Man's Africa* (New York: Harper and Brothers, 1900), p. 219.

45. Answers to these questions can also be found throughout such works as William Astor Chanler, *Through Jungle and Desert; Travels in Eastern Africa* (New York: Macmillan Co., 1896).

46. Henry M. Stanley, *Through South Africa* (London: Sampson Low, 1898), p. xii; and Stanley, *How I Found Livingstone; Travels, Adventures, and Discoveries in Central Africa* (New York: Charles Scribner's Sons, 1890), p. 234.

47. E. Alexander Powell, *The Last Frontier: The White Man's War for Civilisation in Africa* (New York: Charles Scribner's Sons, 1912), p. 195; and also Bigelow, *White Man's Africa*, p. 20.

48. Edgar Beecher Bronson, *In Closed Territory* (Chicago: A. C. McClurg and Co., 1910), p. 225.

49. Verner, "Development of Africa," p. 366.

50. Bigelow, *White Man's Africa*, pp. 106–7.

51. A more complete history can be found in Vincent Harlow, E. M. Chilver, Alison Smith, eds., *History of East Africa*, vol. 2 (Oxford: Clarendon Press, 1963); and Monica Wilson and Leonard Thompson, eds., *The Oxford History of South Africa*, 2 vols. (New York and Oxford: Oxford University Press, 1969–1971).

52. Charles Spencer Smith, *Glimpses of Africa; West and Southwest Coast* (Nashville, Tenn.: Publishing House, African Methodist Episcopal Church Sunday School Union, 1895), p. 213.

6

Africa: Land of Ignobility

As a result of experiencing Africa directly, Americans wrote memorable and sometimes extensive accounts of the natural environment of the continent. They also recorded in detail the appearance of the landscape of Africa, noting significant contributions made by Africans and non-Africans alike to the designed environment of the continent. Although the task was much more difficult than mere description, they defined the continent intellectually as an undeveloped wilderness of great potential wealth that needed to be exploited commercially by the West. However, since the customs, behavior, and societal values of Africans intersected so many of these pursuits, the cultural environment of Africa was the subject of much of their writing as well. Americans were puzzled, for example, by African religious practices; they were interested in knowing more about the idiosyncrasies of the "African" personality and in general asked: Why do Africans appear to be so different from us? Explaining Africans and their cultural world, then, both to themselves and for inquisitive Americans at home, formed an important part of American reports from Africa.

The importance of this task should not be underestimated. How a land is viewed is inseparably linked to explanations of its peoples and their cultures. One influences the other; one determines how the other is ultimately understood. For example, current views of the Japanese influence our understanding of Japan, and thoughts about the Swiss shape our larger impressions of Switzerland.[1] Although explaining Africans was not restricted to any one individual or class of individuals, one particular group of Americans who were especially involved in cultural description in Africa were American missionaries. Even though some missionaries were selectively attentive, while others were not attentive at all, to many of the details of life in Africa, by touching so many facets of African life they became an important means through which the outside non-African world learned about Africa and Africans.

Africa had been the object of American missionary efforts since the time Samuel Hopkins and Ezra Stiles of Newport, Rhode Island, had proposed in 1773 to evangelize the continent by sending ex-slaves to Africa.[2] Their impetus for conversion, like that of so many others, came from the institution of slavery: Christianizing Africa was viewed as a form of reparation, a means of discharging responsibility toward Africa. However, the zeal of Americans for converting Africans arose from a special set of religious conditions associated with the evangelical revival and the Great Awakening of 1734, and a body of racial attitudes that had developed in America concerning the "pagan" peoples of the world.

From its inception, foreign missionary activity had been an outlet for the release of evangelical energies. Oriented toward the active religious life, missionary work combined adventure with duty. As part of the humanitarian crusade of antislavery, temperance, and peace, it proposed a vision of a better world to be achieved by saving heathen souls, transforming pagan societies, and converting all nations to Christianity. Within such a perspective Africa was seen as an unusual opportunity for saving Africans from themselves. Africa was unredeemed, but capable of being saved, and as a land obviously beset by idolatrous practices, it qualified for massive foreign aid. Africa offered spiritually motivated American missionaries a focal point for their socially useful actions. Missionaries believed that they could transform this "land of ignobility," as they called Africa, into a Christian enterprise. If individuals could be improved spiritually, then why not attempt to perfect an entire continent? Surprisingly, for such a noble crusade there was no grand strategy. As the chief handbook of mission work, the Bible furnished assurance of, though not a plan for, ultimate victory. The Christian conquest of Africa was interpreted solely in light of the biblical promise contained in Psalms 68:31: "Ethiopia shall soon stretch out her hands unto God."

By the early part of the nineteenth century, however, establishing Christianity in Africa involved setting up missionary stations and placing missionaries throughout the continent. In West Africa a number of American missionary societies were especially active. The American Baptist Missionary Union had established a church in Monrovia, Liberia, in 1822. Lott Carey, a former slave born in Virginia in 1780, and Colin Teague, his companion, were instrumental in its success. Additional churches were based at Edina, Bexley, and Bassa Cove. In 1833 the Missionary Society of the Methodist Episcopal Church sent Melville Cox to Liberia, while Agnes McAllister began a church in Liberia at Garraway in 1888. The General Conference of the Methodist Episcopal Church of Philadelphia in 1884 made Wiliam Taylor responsible for starting new missions in Angola at Luanda, Pungo Andongo, and Malange. Taylor was eventually succeeded in 1896 by Joseph Hartzell, who presided over a number of missionary activities in Liberia, Angola, Mozambique, and Rhodesia.

The work of the Domestic and Foreign Missionary Society of the Protestant Episcopal Church had begun in Africa at Cape Palmas, Liberia, in 1836. At that same site, only two years earlier, the American Board of Commissioners for Foreign Missions had located a missionary station in Liberia under the direction of J. Leighton Wilson. The mission was transferred in 1842 to Baraka, eight miles from the mouth of the Gabon River in Gabon, where it functioned successfully until 1870.[3] Nearby, on Corisco Island, off the coast of Gabon, the Board of Foreign Missions of the Presbyterian Church, North, began a missionary station in 1842, where two missionaries, Robert W. Mulligan and Robert Hamill Nassau lived for a number of years.[4] Finally, the Foreign Missions Board of the Southern Baptist Convention was active both in Liberia and in Nigeria, where Thomas Jefferson Bowen established a church among the Yoruba and Egba peoples in 1853 at Ogbomosho.[5]

In Central Africa, missionaries labored primarily in the "Congo Free State" where the Presbyterian Church, South, had begun its missionary work. William Henry Sheppard, author of *Presbyterian Pioneers in the Congo* and a graduate of the Stillman Institute in

Tuscaloosa, Alabama, a school founded specifically to train black Americans as missionaries, lived in the Congo from approximately 1889 to 1910.[6] Sheppard was joined by Samuel Norval Lapsley, a graduate of the University of Alabama and the McCormick Theological Seminary in Chicago who worked in the Congo from the time of his appointment in 1889 until his death in 1892.[7] Between 1892 and 1900, thirteen additional missionaries were appointed, with two individuals being especially noteworthy: DeWitt Snyder of Brooklyn, New York, a missionary and physician who lived in Central Africa from 1892 to 1901, and William Morrison, who arrived in Africa in 1896 and remained until 1918.

In southern Africa, missionaries from the American Board of Commissioners for Foreign Missions settled in Cape Town in 1835. Daniel Lindley, an Ohio-born pastor of a church in North Carolina, Alexander Erwin Wilson, a physician and minister from North Carolina, and Henry I. Venable of Kentucky worked among the Matabele peoples at Moseka. A second group of missionaries, which included Newton Adams, a physician from New York, Aldin Grout, a graduate of Amherst College, and George Champion of Yale University, was stationed in Natal among the Zulu. In addition, the African Methodist Episcopal Church had established a missionary site in South Africa, with Henry M. Turner the first member of the church to visit the area and Levi J. Coppin its initial resident clergyman. Proclaimed the "First Resident Bishop of South Africa," Coppin founded a church in Arensdale, near Cape Town, in 1901.[8]

Although American missionaries such as these had been stationed in various parts of Africa at different times, they looked upon themselves as martyrs who had to endure great trials and even greater temptations. Living in Africa presented real obstacles to saintliness, and the early death of many missionaries served to reinforce the difficulty of their work. In the numerous popular biographies that were published in America, they were portrayed as genuine heroes.[9] Although most American missionaries came from the smaller towns and farm villages of America, and were not affluent but mostly college trained, they achieved special status in America because of the difficult work they were willing to do. Their job in essence was nothing less than a spiritual errand into a pagan wilderness, where they had to contend with unfamiliar terrains and uncooperative Africans, while the enormity of their task was expressed in the kinds of rhetoric they used to describe it: "spreading new light on the Dark Continent" by bringing the "light of Christianity to the benighted souls of Africa." Such a perspective on the "unredeemed" was not wholly a religious one, but was shaped by a number of racial attitudes about black people in general that missionaries brought with them to Africa.

When American missionaries, most of whom were white, came to Africa during their most active period in the late nineteenth and early twentieth centuries, race was a central cultural predictor of their responses to Africans.[10] Religious institutions and missionary societies had to face the implications of Darwin's *On the Origin of Species* concerning the supposed superiority and inferiority of various races. Generated by the idea of evolution, human races, it was argued, represented different stages in the evolutionary cycle, and therefore some were innately unequal. Many missionaries believed that the nonwhite races were varieties of a species that was in a relatively primitive stage of evolution. Although the idea of hereditary inequality had adherents of its own, Josiah Strong, among other religious leaders in America, believed that the inequality of races was divinely ordained. Better races emerge, as the inferior is replaced with the superior, all under the providential direction of God. Strong's popular book *Our Country*, published in 1885, sold 175,000 copies, and his writings were generally distributed widely and well received because they fit the race prejudices of many white Americans. In addition, Horace Bushnell, another religious reformer of the time, lent credence to many of Strong's ideas, but also stated that God's word must be extended by the conversion of the heathen and the expansion of Christianity throughout the world. The Caucasian race possessed a brilliant future, with the advance of Western civilization being only a matter of good winning out over bad, of the advance of progress over stagnation, of the higher over the lower, of white over black.

Missionaries in Africa were nearly always expansionists who were supported by powerful religious leaders in America. In many cases, however, they were unwilling to echo the message that it was the destiny of the nonwhite races to melt away entirely. Despite their opposition to the sentiment for the disappearance of nonwhite races through outright oppression and dispossession, they supported the ideas of racial inferiority and a hierarchy of humankind determined by race, a viewpoint that shaped their responses to Africans. As a consequence, missionaries in Africa conveyed a strong impression of heathen depravity in their writings. By defining Africans as savage, and by emphasizing only the most exotic elements of African life, missionaries legitimized the importance of their work. In dwelling on the low standards of African sexual morality, they shocked Protestant sensibilities in America, and by condemning the religion and customs of Africans, they pointed to the need for Christian salvation. Their writings, in effect, were a means of classifying Africans as religiously and culturally inferior. By demonstrating how Africans lacked a worthwhile religious system of their own, and by describing just how savage the African truly was, they created a highly pejorative portrait of African peoples.

The life and work of Willis R. Hotchkiss is representative of the American missionary view of Africa. Hotchkiss was born in 1873 and ordained a missionary of the Society of Friends. In the 1890s he established a missionary station in West Central Africa, and after spending several years there he returned to the United States. In 1901 Hotchkiss wrote *Sketches From the Dark Continent* in which he composed an allegorical story about what he had come to know best: Africa, Africans, and the attitude of missionaries toward both. In it he likened Africa to a "great giant" who had fallen "asleep" for a long time, but who was now "waking up," "rubbing his eyes," and wondering how the rest of the world had "acquired so much power while he slept." Although Africa, in the past, had been more advanced than most other countries "in several branches of learning," it was currently "an object of pity." Hotchkiss noted that the progeny of this "great giant," the present generation of Africans, was "growing up uncared for, untaught—a wild, lazy, reckless horde at the mercy of every adventurer." He concluded by stating that missionaries had an obligation to uplift the children of this "unredeemed" giant, to extricate them from their obvious state of moral decay, and to offer them freely the saving graces of Christianity.[11]

Missionaries like Hotchkiss devoted considerable space in their writings to describing and condemning the idolatrous nature of African religious practices, and worked from the premise that there were no "false structures" in Africa to inhibit the spread of Christianity.[12] Whatever evidence there was of "a native" religion clearly suggested a world of unmitigated heathenism which an African system of morality encouraged:

Lying, stealing, polygamy, slavery, and promiscuous living have the countenance and approbation of Pagan religion. Drunkenness, gluttony, every form of licentious debauchery, and even murder are features of the festivals of Pagan religion. The unspeakable, unthinkable horrors of witchcraft, human sacrifice, burial alive, and cannibalism are inextricably intertwined with Pagan religion. The reflex influence is inevitably a callousness to suffering and a fiendish gloating in brutalities. Heredity and continued practice through thousands of years have steeped the people in inbred superstitions and animal passions. Intrenched ever more deeply, the accumulating depravity increases from generation to generation with manifold power.[13]

Since Africans lacked a "moral nature" of their own, the "heathen priests" who were responsible for Africa's spiritual depravity were singled out for special condemnation. As the chief rivals of American missionaries, the African "clergy" were seen as crafty individuals, skillful in the use of magic and cunning, who manipulated and controlled the lives of their people. Robert Nassau, for example, documented that they were referred to by many names, but especially as "witch doctors, magicians, diviners, medicine men, and devil-doctors."[14] Through the use of elaborate rituals, or "disgusting ceremonies" as they were often called, "witch doctors" shrewdly handled the lives of an already superstitious African people:

> A cunning set of rascals are these priests; well skilled in ventriloquism and legerdemain, they have great power over the people, and can bring even princes to their feet. They enter the priesthood early in life, and so complete are their deceptions, that they deceive even themselves, and are, therefore, often conscientious in blinding and deceiving their followers.[15]

Although several religious customs were encouraged by African "priests," according to Robert Mulligan, who wrote a popular article entitled "Heathenism As It Is in West Africa" for *Missionary Review of the World* in 1904, two of the most pervasive practices were the custom of "fetishism" and the worship of animals.[16] The first, the worship of or belief in fetiches or a material object thought to have magical powers, was actually an all-inclusive category used by missionaries to designate anything within the realm of the supernatural. In its most restricted sense, the term referred to the practice of collecting teeth, hair, fingernails, strips of flesh, and even skulls, which were then strategically placed about by Africans to properly honor the dead. But fetiches, it seemed, were everywhere:

> One of the first things which salutes the eyes of a stranger after planting his feet upon the shores of Africa, is the symbols of this religion. He steps forth from the boat under a canopy of fetiches, not only as a security for his own safety, but as a guaranty that he does not carry the elements of mischief among the people; he finds them suspended along every path he walks; at every junction of two or more roads; at the crossing-place of every stream; at the base of every large rock or overgrown forest tree; at the gate of every village; over the door of every house, and around the neck of every human being whom he meets. They are set up on their farms, tied around their fruit trees, and are fastened to the necks of sheep and goats, to prevent them from being stolen. If a man trespasses upon the property of his neighbor in defiance of fetiches he has set up to protect it, he is confidently expected to suffer the penalty of his temerity at some time or other. If he is overtaken by a formidable malady or lingering sickness afterward, even should it be after the lapse of twenty, thirty, or forty years, he is known to be suffering the consequences of his own rashness.[17]

Notwithstanding the fact that missionaries considered the worship of fetiches to be vile, sensual, and repulsive, the second custom—the veneration of animals—was even more seriously condemned.[18] Because the doctrine of transmigration, or the passing of a soul into another body after death, was generally accepted in Africa, such animals as the monkey and crocodile were widely respected, and as the objects of worship, snakes were revered for their magical powers.[19] Since Africans believed that animals were animated by the spirit of the dead that lived within them, certain places they happened to frequent were considered sacred areas. Stripped of all romantic notions about the simplicity of primitive life, missionaries agreed that African religion as displayed in these two practices revealed the true nature of spiritual life on the continent.[20]

In essence, then, missionaries considered the religious practices of Africans a debasing system of worship: They degraded the minds of people by making them extremely superstitious; they fostered dependence on wizards, charms, and amulets for explanations; they accorded witchcraft a position of undeserved eminence, and they made Africans slaves to a "canopy of fetiches," turning Africa into a land where fetiches might be randomly found on paths, on fences, or around the necks of people.[21] It was a world "gone mad," as Robert Milligan, a missionary who had spent a number of years in the southern Cameroon, reported, a wild and strange place that might be encountered "on the brink of sleep."[22]

In order to establish further a justification for their interests in the religious life of Africans, however, missionaries had to argue that Islam had done little to improve conditions among Africans, although Islam had been a part of the religious life of Africa for centuries. Even though it had been successful in adapting itself "to the peoples it sought to convert," as Christianity's chief competitor for the spiritual allegiance of Africans, Islam's spread throughout the continent needed to be checked. Not through force nor by coercion would Christianity succeed, but only by offering an alternative to Islam, where necessary, would the essential work of American missionaries be able to move forward.[23] As the readers of *Harper's Weekly* were asked in 1895 by one missionary: "Shall the factors and forces" determining Africa's future be "Christian or Moslem?"[24]

By emphasizing the idolatrous nature of African religion, missionaries conceptually lumped all Africans together as being outside the doctrines of Christianity. The rhetoric of missionary accounts, in presenting the accepted image of non-Christian religion, reflected the presumption of evolutionary stasis. Even such a universal human institution as religion was considered to be only rudimentary in form or merely a mix of weird rituals, and African "witchcraft" simply became an expression of the irrational fears of superstitious Africans. American foreign missionary activity, however, was at best a precarious undertaking in terms of converts and contributions. While the image of the impulsive African savage served to bolster the missionary desire for dominance and control of Africans, the need for continuing financial support also made it imperative to evoke constantly the moral degradation of the heathen African through extensive descriptions of subjects prized by missionaries for their power to excite: cannibalism, nudity, and the status of women in Africa.

American missionaries considered cannibalism to be the direct result of moral decay and a graphic demonstration of the savage, impulsive, irrational behavior of Africans. Although several arguments were advanced to explain its prevalence in Africa, one theory stated that Africans consumed human flesh because they liked to:

> Cannibalism was popular with the true negro simply as a matter of taste. He ate human flesh whenever he could get it because he liked it, not for any religious or sentimental reason. Good luck had nothing to do with the performance and rarely was it a case of necessity, because usually it would have been much easier to kill wild game or butcher a domestic animal than to catch an enemy, with the possibility always of having the tables turned and himself put into the pot to satisfy the appetite of his enemy! Indeed, it has been established as a fact that the negroes who were, and it may be proper to say *are*, most addicted to this horrible practice of cannibalism are the very ones who inhabit districts where game is most plentiful.[25]

A second explanation stated that Africans actually considered the human body a delicacy, to be consumed to satisfy a craving for flesh in an African diet where meat was scarce.[26] Missionaries reported that stealing a person from a neighboring village to eat was a common occurrence, and even among the more "polished cannibals" of Africa, the practice was so widespread that complex business transactions evolved around it. To illustrate, very often some hapless person was auctioned off to the highest bidder. The human trophy was then divided into "a culinary map" by making marks on the ground with a stick. After indicating the parts most preferred, such as an arm, a leg, or a thigh, and after all the flesh was sold, the unlucky person was butchered up like so much meat. Missionaries were quick to point out, nevertheless, that in many cases women were exempt from the practice because of their economic value, while the sick, the injured, and children were sometimes spared. The head was rejected outright since it contained little flesh; however, hands soaked in water were prized for their taste.

Examples of other shocking behavior seemed to be in plentiful supply for missionaries to deliver to the reading public in America. After coming upon a partially eaten carcass hanging from the branch of a tree, J. Leighton Wilson learned that, only a short time before, the victim had been convicted by his peers for mere petty theft.[27] Decapitation and dismemberment of an enemy's body was widespread, while collecting and displaying an adversary's skull and bones was reported to be a well-established custom. Skulls sat atop the walls of many African villages as badges of victory. Although missionaries often misread signs of brutality as evidence of cannibalism, its very existence in African life was symptomatic of the absence of discipline and the acceptance of unfettered impulse.

Lack of moral restraint was also demonstrated by the prevalence of nudity. To the missionary entering Africa for the very first time, bare breasts and uncovered buttocks rivalled the lack of religion and the presence of cannibalism as sure signs that Africans were in need of redemption. Not only did these facts of life in a tropical climate present a number of moral questions, but they also made clothing Africans an immediate concern for the missionary, since clothing had something to do with modesty and everything to do with sin. There was, in fact, a twofold reason why dressing Africans in pants and skirts was so important: Africans in Western-style clothing actually looked more "civilized," while the adoption of this particular kind of dress was interpreted as proof that Christianity was becoming an accepted part of African life. Helen Chapman Springer, who had accompanied her husband to Africa as a missionary of the Methodist Episcopal Church, related how she had never known "a mission girl" to revert to heathenism "as long as she wore her foreign clothing." But as soon as any young African woman decided to stray from Christianity and reject its teachings, the "first sign" of defection was "a return to the native garment or loin cloth."[28] Despite the fact that the relationship between clothing and conversion was a difficult one to establish and progress may have been more illusory than real, since outward dress was not synonymous with inward salvation, belief in the significance of the connection was not easily abandoned.[29]

Besides nudity, one of the chief emotional appeals made by missionaries was through descriptions of the degraded position of women in Africa. Polygyny in particular was singled out for special attention since missionaries essentially viewed the custom as indicative of the lack of tenderness for women in African life.[30] Polygyny was antithetical to "domestic happiness" and had a disruptive effect on the "deep foundations of society."[31] True affection between a husband and wife was difficult to achieve when there was more than one partner, and how could children know their parents if there were multiple choices? For the missionary who sought to create in Africa replicas of an idealized American family in which women and men played specific roles, polygyny was an obvious source of frustration.

But polygyny aside, missionaries were vivid in their commentary on the place of women in African society, convinced that they were unwilling victims of African men.[32]

On many occasions, missionaries recalled seeing women treated as either "beasts" or the objects of unrestrained sexual passion:

> The African husband, as a rule, is a lazy, exacting, indolent man. Woman is his drudge. While her lord and master lounges, snuffs, smokes, hunts, guzzles beer, or gads from kraal to kraal discussing a recent case of witchcraft, or gorges himself with meat like a boa-constrictor, she, with a child on her back, and a heavy hoe on her shoulders, goes to the fields, digs the hard soil all day long or pulls the rank weeds from the garden, for she is both miller and baker, cook and farmer, and beast of burden.[33]

Moreover, as a missionary of the Presbyterian Church, James S. Dennis noted that African women were often excluded from the affairs of men and relegated to the company of animals where they were forced to eat "with the dogs." Even after such a humiliating experience, upon the death of her husband a woman might be fortunate indeed if she were spared the fate of being tossed "into the same grave" with her dead spouse.[34]

In other instances, individuals like George Thompson reported how some women had been burned alive for disobeying their husbands, while others were handled perhaps even less compassionately:

> One woman had parts of her body *roasted*! Another had her *breasts burned off*! One was delivered of a premature child under the sufferings! One had a split stick put on her head, over the tops of the ears, and tied together tight in front, till the stick had *cut off* the ears, and sunk into the head![35]

The sexual exploitation of women, moreover, was attributed to heathen practices that dulled the consciences of African men. Corrupt marriage laws and "legalized" forms of slavery forced women into submissive positions, while child marriages and cases in which fathers sold their daughters to the highest bidder were nothing more than culturally sanctioned forms of prostitution.[36] African wives were little better than slaves who had no other functions than to satisfy the wanton desires and passions of men who were their "owners rather than husbands."[37] As a result, "Ere middle life is reached you have a hag with pendent breasts, bleared eyes, and hideous yellow teeth, with features of an ape; a wretched, toiling slave, beaten by the man whose savage passions have drained her of her youth and beauty before her time."[38]

Constant reassertions of the moral degradation of Africa, as reflected by discussions of cannibalism, nudity, and the status of women, served to exploit the idea of African inferiority and to justify American missionary intervention in Africa. The future financial stability of foreign missionary activity created a vested interest in perpetuating the idea of African heathenism by carefully charting the sources of such moral decay. Although it would be misleading to assert that missionaries admired nothing about Africans—the Masai, for example, were praised for their "military" bearing, the Kru for their strength, and the Zulu for bravery—emphasis in missionary accounts was placed elsewhere. In attempting to arouse interest in bringing the "dark souls" of Africa the "light of the true knowledge of God," American foreign missionaries created a particular vision of Africans and their cultures that functioned as an explanation for what life in Africa was actually like.

We know today that the missionary view was not the cultural experience of Africans. The term "religion" as used by missionaries during the late nineteenth and early twentieth centuries was an impoverished word for social analysis since it did not adequately convey the African perception of reality. However exotic the "disgusting ceremonies" of Africans appeared, and however bizarre their "spiritual beliefs" seemed, they functioned to safeguard a community's welfare and survival by providing social control through spiritual explanation. The placing of fetiches—those objects often discussed by missionaries as the most prominent material artifacts of heathenism—not only reveal an intense attention to place by Africans but also demonstrate a concern for prediction and order. Gruesomeness was not the issue concerning the infamous practice of cannibalism. By eating flesh, a new leader might ritualistically acquire the knowledge and strength of a former one, thereby giving form to the human desires for continuity and perpetuity. Polygyny was not tied to male concupiscence but had a great deal to do with providing a sense of social stability by creating complex familial relationships.

Nonetheless, missionaries in Africa worked from the premise that

Africans could be converted through the efforts of dedicated individuals. They sought to establish nothing less than "grand Christian civilizations" throughout the continent.[39] As agents of change, they believed they could effect social progress and religious regeneration for both individual Africans and African society generally. Armed with the "subtle power of their faith," the "backward races" of Africa could be permanently reshaped by altering social conditions through the creation of a religious environment.

Such an attitude, however, also assumed that the African, as the object of conversion, possessed an "unformed" mind. To missionaries, Africans were interesting but they were essentially primitive, and if civilized then only partially so. They were fascinating and curious but not curious enough for most missionaries to study them well nor fascinating enough to ever be completely understood. Since they had few wants and even fewer cares, Africans were seen as a simple people unencumbered by the burdens of civilized Western society. They were jovial and carefree, reacting to events and people in a lighthearted way. They were "always ready to dance and sing, or laugh and play."[40] One American observed:

When I first looked out upon Durban from the piazza of its comfortable club, I saw a gathering of young Zulus in charge of jinrikishas similar to those of Japan. I felt as I did when first taken to the monkey cage at the Zoological Gardens—my wonder was not at their animal, but their human appearance. The Zulus before me were compelled by the English authorities to wear a white linen tunic and loose white trousers cut off above the knee. The trimming was red braid around the edges of the short sleeves, around the neck, and at the extremities of the trunks. The effect in contrast with their natural skin was striking, though possibly uncomfortable to men who considered themselves clothed when they had slipped through the lobe of their ear a long horn spoon with which to ladle their snuff. These Zulus were dancing up and down like children playing at horse in the nursery; and they uttered continuous native gurglings, partly like turtledoves and partly like the hallelujah ejaculations at one of our African Methodist camp-meetings. They all appeared very happy during this performance, which continued so long that I calculated the amount of energy expended to represent about ten miles of unpaid travel.[41]

The disposition of missionaries to see Africans as "children" developed out of the ideology of Social Darwinism. As stated previously, according to Darwin's theory, biological organisms change their physical characteristics throughout a slowly developing process of evolution. Although as a scientist Darwin was concerned primarily with the natural world of plants and animals, his idea of natural selection and his concept of struggle were seen as explanations for understanding the differences that exist in human societies. Struggle and competition between individual members of a society, between members of classes of society, between different nations, and especially between races was nature's indispensable method of producing superior people, nations, and races, while variation through natural selection ensured "the survival of the fittest."

As the chief proponent of the application of Darwinian theory to society, or Social Darwinism, Herbert Spencer reasoned that little or nothing could be done for primitive peoples. Their civilizations merely reflected the stages of biological evolution, just as in the natural world some species of life were more developed than others. By analogy, Spencer further argued that the mind of a child recapitulates the history of the human races in their development from savagery to civilization. To understand primitive races, study children; and to know children, look to the primitive races of the world. In addition, in equating primitive peoples with children, Spencer was supported in his reasoning by G. Stanley Hall, a specialist in child psychology, who theorized that the primitive races of the world were actually in an early evolutionary stage, something comparable to an arrested childhood.

The doctrine of natural selection, as originally proposed by Darwin, simplified by Spencer, and supplemented by Hall, was used to underline the differences that existed between human groups. Although most missionaries subscribed to the idea that Africans had all the limitations of the minds of children and that their intellectual development might even be permanent, they believed that an African's spiritual life could be greatly enhanced through the teachings of Christianity, and that Africans could be radically improved socially through Christianization. In many ways, missionaries' accounts are indistinguishable in their generalizations and sense of moral superiority from the verdicts of other American visitors to Africa, and their allegations of the "childishness" of Africans were a common means of comprehending if not condoning behavior. However, their emphasis on African heathenism and its eradication through spiritual enlightenment was their distinguishing feature and the central premise upon which their work in Africa rested.[42]

As a place to which their religiously motivated efforts could be channelled, Africa and its transformation generated predictable amounts of enthusiasm and difficulties within the American missionary movement, not only in Africa but in American society as well. At home, missionaries influenced the popular attitudes of Americans and shaped their conception of Africans in a number of ways. They made frequent visits to host churches, as living embodiments of Christianity's concern for Africa. For reasons of health, personal affairs, or furloughs, they returned to America where they spoke at annual meetings of their missionary associations about their labors in Africa. Sometimes returning missionaries brought with them living examples of redeemed heathenism: a once idolatrous African now saved by Christianity.

Missionaries, in addition, captured a large share of the popular imagination of Americans by having their reports from the field regularly promulgated through ecclesiastical channels. From the pulpit, at prayer meetings, and by the publication of their books, pamphlets, broadsheets, and Sunday school tracts in the religious press, they became major interpreters of African cultures. Missionary promoters recorded news and accounts of religious activities in Africa, and in turn, religious journals, such as the *Missionary Review of the World*, which drew freely upon other publications for information, multiplied the total impact of missionary intelligence, thereby providing Americans with many opportunities both to read and to hear about Africa and Africans. The organizational conferences of missionary societies, moreover, were major outlets for views on Africa, and in particular, the subject of Africa was the focus of three important conferences in America: the Chicago Congress on Africa of 1893, held in conjunction with the Columbian Exposition; the Congress on Africa, convened in Atlanta, Georgia, in 1895; and the Ecumenical Conference on Foreign Missions, which took place in New York City in 1900.

Not surprisingly, the principal theme of all three meetings was also the major assumption upon which American missionary activity in Africa was based: a belief in the heathen depravity of African peoples who were desperately in need of salvation. Originally termed the "African Ethnological Congress," the Chicago Congress on Africa was sponsored by the American Missionary Association. Under the leadership of Joseph Roy, an officer in the American Missionary Association, and Frederic Perry Noble, who served as the congress's secretary, the convention lasted eight days, from August 14 through August 21, 1893.[43] Morning, afternoon, and evening sessions were held. From a panel on African and Afro-American arts and literature to the nature of natural science, sociology, and political science as they related to Africa, the talks included discussions of "Disease and Medicine in Africa," "Native Customs and Popular Life," "The Arabs in Africa," "African Religions," "Methods and Policies of African Missions," "Principles of Colonization," and "Africa as a New Factor in Civilization."[44] The program, in short, was structured to include a complete range of topics, covering nothing less than "themes vitally linking Africa in all its aspects and relations to humanity in every sphere of thought and action."[45]

The conference attracted an assortment of individuals who shared an interest in Africa, including Frederick Douglass, Alexander Crummell, William Taylor, and Bishop Henry M. Turner. Representing a variety of perspectives, over one hundred experts and specialists attended the congress, while fifty participants either spoke or sent papers to be read at the sessions—or as Frederic Perry Noble put it:

> Man and woman; negro and white; Christianity and Islam; Africa, America, Europe and Oceania; North and South; high and low; rich and poor; Austria, Angola, Belgium and Congo, Denmark, England, Egypt, France, Gabun, Germany, Garenganze, Haiti, Ibea, Italy, Lagos, Liberia, Scotland; Uganda, the United States, Victoria and Zululand; artists, authors, editors, divines, diplomatists, educators, explorers, jurists, legislators, physicians, missionaries, rulers and statesmen, scholars, scientists and soldiers, former slaves and former slave-holders, ex-Confederate and Union veterans—in short, THE WORLD—made the Chicago Congress on Africa a senate of representative men and races, and the world's supreme court of deliberation on its once-lost continent.[46]

The keynote address was delivered by Joseph Cook, an American missionary, who set the tone for the conference by cataloguing the chief causes for Africa's present religious distress. Cook believed that the "chief miseries of the Dark Continent" were attributable to no less than twelve factors: isolation from civilization, climatic conditions, the impact of slavery, the traffic in rum, cannibalism, polygamy, paganism, Mohammedanism, tribal wars, foreign aggression, the lack of Christianity, and finally, the absence of an able native leadership.[47] To remove the causes of Africa's troubles, Cook argued for a vigorous program of missionary activity involving greater numbers of missionaries and the establishment of industrial schools.[48] Collectively, missionaries and their schools would function like "lighthouses of civilization amid inland seas of savagery."[49] Brightening the dark horizons of Africa's spiritual world, inculcating a continent without God with a sense of morality, imparting the Christian faith to one of the most debased people on earth, and ministering to Africa's spiritual needs were the lofty aims that characterized this the first important congress on Africa.[50]

The common themes of the Chicago Congress were cast into new perspectives and given added prominence at a subsequent conference. Atlanta's Congress on Africa, sponsored in conjunction with the Cotton States and International Exposition of 1895, was convened for three days in December under the auspices of the Stewart Missionary Foundation for Africa of the Gammon Theological Seminary.[51] Wilbur Thirkield, president of the Gammon Theological Seminary, William Stewart, founder of the Stewart Missionary Foundation for Africa, and J.W.E. Bowen of the Gammon Theological Seminary served as the conference's leaders. Many of the participants at the Chicago Congress also attended the conference in Atlanta, including William Taylor of the Methodist Episcopal Church, Joseph Roy of the Chicago Congress on Africa, and Cyrus Adams, editor of the *New York Sun*. In addition, parallels between the Atlanta and Chicago meetings were obvious. Many participants argued that missionaries had a "duty" to save Africans from their "filthy performances," which passed for religious ceremonies, and from their peculiar customs, which were merely barbaric rituals.[52] While such points of commonality indicated agreement about the Africans' spiritual state, there was an important distinguishing feature about the Atlanta meeting: In the redemption of Africa it allocated a greater role to the black American missionary.

Black American missionaries were thought to be amply suited for the work for several reasons: Where climatic conditions were considered too extreme and diseases too deadly for white missionaries to bear, they could survive; and since Africans might welcome Afro-Americans because of a shared racial affinity, establishing mission stations would be an easier task. The continent, moreover, would be "recompensed" for its loss through slavery by having black American missionaries make over Africa not in the image of its idolatrous past but by creating a spiritually liberated continent. Although sometimes branded as subversive by white European settlers and colonial officials in Africa, black American missionaries were successful in establishing schools and churches and providing for African students to come to America to study. Nevertheless, they considered themselves to be, above all, Christians first and of African descent only secondarily, and essentially reflected in their writings the pejorative attitudes toward Africans that they shared with their white missionary colleagues.

A number of participants at the Atlanta meeting felt that "educated" Africans, individuals who were trained as Christians, were actually the most effective agents for Africa's salvation, and not the black American. "Native converts" knew the "mind," "modes of thinking," and "rude primal faith" of their people, a point that was well made by Orishetukeh Faduma, a converted Christian minister of Yoruba descent.[53] While acknowledging that Africans needed religious help, Faduma stressed the importance of instructing Africans in their native tongues and of allowing potential converts to retain their own African "name, dress, and food." American missionaries, he thought, had retarded their efforts in Africa by requiring Africans to subordinate their identities to their own, and Christianity would eventually fail if it brought about a loss of either personal, racial, or national self-consciousness. Moreover, Faduma believed that "denominational rivalry" had been a divisive element, serving to weaken the Christian crusade and the success of missionary activity in general.[54]

As central themes of the conferences in Chicago and Atlanta, the heathen conditions of African life and the need for Christian redemption were emphasized in the third organizational missionary meeting, the Ecumenical Conference on Foreign Missions. Over an eleven-day period in 1900, the convocation attracted more than two hundred thousand people to various sessions held at Carnegie Hall and surrounding churches, with the total number of delegates and missionaries attending the conference estimated at nearly thirty-two hundred.[55] An indication of the importance of the meeting can be gauged from the prominence of those individuals who came: Theodore Roosevelt, then governor of New York, Benjamin Harrison, former United States President and honorary head of the conference, and President William McKinley.

The Ecumenical Conference was auspiciously convened, just as the political and commercial aspirations of America were directing "the thought of Christendom to distant parts of the earth," and as a reflection of that interest, a major part of the agenda was devoted to showing how "human progress" was "inseparably bound up with Christian missions."[56] President McKinley, for example, in his opening remarks, stated that missionaries

> have been among the pioneers of civilization. They have illumined the darkness of idolatry and superstition with the light of intelligence and truth. They have been messengers of righteousness and love. They have braved disease, and danger, and death, and in their exile have suffered unspeakable hardships, but their noble spirits have never wavered.[57]

As with the two former conferences, the delegates agreed that Africa fully qualified as a promising missionary field because of its heathen idolatry. However, they also thought that Africa's "old culture" was changing to meet the "standards" of the new order advanced by missionaries, and from this core of traditional African ideas, values, and institutions, a new "set of customs," in basic harmony with the precepts of Western culture, would emerge.

As the conference statements of Chicago, Atlanta, and New York and reports from the field indicated, American missionaries disparaged African life for its lack of spiritual growth. In proclaiming the superiority of Christianity by comparing the debased state of heathenism to the enlightened status of their own faith, missionaries established a precise measurement against which Africa's religious progress was measured. They saw very little in Africa that resembled their vision of what a Christian civilization should be. To the contrary, Africa was the embodiment of savagery and idolatry, a mirror image of what America was not or should never become. However, apart from their analyses of the peculiar characteristics of African life, missionaries also revealed something significant about themselves: When they attempted to describe the spiritual world of Africans, they said as much about their own country as they did about Africa.

Toward the latter part of the nineteenth century, as it began to develop into an industrialized and urbanized society, America embarked upon an imperialistic course of action that prompted religious leaders in America to call for their country's presence abroad in the battle for heathen souls. Consequently, foreign missionaries confronted the outside world with a self-image borne of confidence in their country's identity, and one to which they resorted when faced with the task of explaining America to others. It was a conception not so much of what America actually was but of what they thought it to be: a living model of spiritual enlightenment for the rest of the world to emulate. Nowhere, except in America, had a people been given the chance to work out Christianity's ideals. In addition, unlike earlier periods in their country's past when missionaries had set out to convert the pagan by spreading the gospel, several characteristics distinguished the late-nineteenth- and early-twentieth-century period. Missionary crusades to save "the heathen" from their "idolatrous" practices in "savage" parts of the world, undertaken on a grand scale, were seen as continuations of an American sense of national purpose and as expressive outlets for a nation's energy.[58]

Cleansing primitive lands of sinister forces had always been one of the aims of missionary societies. For spiritually motivated individuals, the idea of converting the heathen was a powerful incentive to go out and teach all nations the gospel, wherever they might be. American missionaries made repeated efforts in Africa, although Africans never did embrace Christianity with the same amount of zeal with which missionaries had approached the continent. Converts were few for the years of work involved, and the toll that Africa exacted was great. With the possibility of a quick death, the inevitability of a number of hardships, and the certainty of difficult work, Africa was seen by missionaries as a place to test their faith. However, in their reports from Africa, missionaries who emphasized the intense "heathenism" of this "land of ignobility" created an exaggerated vision of Africa and the cultural life of its peoples—both for other missionaries who were about to go to Africa and for inquiring Americans at home.

Notes

1. See, for example, Harold R. Isaacs, *Scratches on Our Minds: American Images of China and India* (New York: John Day Co., 1958); Robert McClellan, *The Heathen Chinee: A Study of American Attitudes Toward China, 1890–1905* (Columbus: Ohio State University Press, 1971); and Stuart Creighton Miller, *The Unwelcome Immigrant: The American Image of the Chinese, 1785–1882* (Berkeley: University of California Press, 1969).

2. Archibald Alexander, *A History of Colonization on the Western Coast of Africa* (Philadelphia: William S. Martien, 1846), pp. 48–55.

3. See J. Leighton Wilson, *Western Africa: Its History, Condition, and Prospects* (New York: Harper and Brothers, 1856); and also J. Leighton Wilson, "Comparative Vocabularies of Some of the Principal Negro Dialects of Africa," *Journal of the American Oriental Society* 1 (1849), 337–81.

4. See Robert Hamill Nassau, *Fānwe Primer and Vocabulary* (New York: E. O. Jenkins, 1881); R. H. Nassau, *Fetichism in West Africa: Forty Years' Observation of Native Customs and Superstitions* (New York: Charles Scribner's Sons, 1904); R. H. Nassau, *Corisco Days: The First Thirty Years of the West African Mission* (Philadelphia: Allen, Lane and Scott, 1910); and R. H. Nassau, *Africa: An Essay* (Philadelphia: Allen, Lane and Scott, 1911).

5. See T. J. Bowen, *Central Africa: Adventures and Missionary Labors in Several Countries in the Interior of Africa, From 1849 to 1856* (Charleston, S.C.: Southern Baptist Publication Society, 1857); Bowen, *Meroke; or, Missionary Life in Africa* (Philadelphia: American Sunday-School Union, 1858); and Bowen, *Grammar and Dictionary of the Yoruba Language* (Washington, D.C.: Smithsonian Institution, 1858).

6. William Henry Sheppard, *Presbyterian Pioneers in the Congo* (Richmond, Va.: Presbyterian Commission of Publication, 1917).

7. Samuel Norval Lapsley, *Life and Letters of Samuel Norval Lapsley, Missionary to the Congo Valley, West Africa, 1866–1892* (Richmond, Va.: Whittet and Shepperson, 1893).

8. See Levi Coppin, *Observations of Persons and Things in South Africa, 1900–1904* (Philadelphia: A.M.E. Book Concern, n.d.).

9. See, for example, E. T. Wharton, *Led in Triumph: Sixty Years of Southern Presbyterian Missions in the Belgian Congo* (Nashville, Tenn.: Board of World Missions, Presbyterian Church, U.S., 1952).

10. Thomas F. Gossett, *Race: The History of an Idea in America* (Dallas: Southern Methodist University Press, 1963), pp. 176–97.

11. Willis R. Hotchkiss, *Sketches from the Dark Continent* (Cleveland: Friends Bible Institute and Training School, 1901), pp. 9–10.

12. DeWitt C. Snyder, "Beginning Work in Central Africa," *Missionary Review of the World* 16 (June, 1903), 437.

13. Wilson S. Naylor, *Daybreak in the Dark Continent* (New York: Eaton and Mains, 1905), p. 108.

14. Robert Nassau, "Spiritual Beings in West Africa: Their Class and Functions," *Bulletin of the American Geographical Society* 35 (1903), 120; and James S. Dennis, *Christian Missions and Social Progress: A Sociological Study of Foreign Missions,* 3 vols. (New York: Fleming H. Revell Co., 1897–1906), 1:193.

15. Charles W. Thomas, *Adventures and Observations on the West Coast of Africa, and Its Islands* (New York: Derby and Jackson, 1860), p. 302.

16. Robert W. Mulligan, "Heathenism As It Is In West Africa," *Missionary Review of the World* 17 (June, 1904), 405.

17. Wilson, *Western Africa*, p. 214.

18. Josiah Tyler, "Fetishism in Africa," *Missionary Review of the World* 8 (June, 1895), 408–9; and also Mulligan, "Heathenism As It Is In West Africa," pp. 401–7.

19. Wilson, *Western Africa*, p. 207.

20. Helen Springer, *Snap Shots from Sunny Africa* (New York: Fleming H. Revell Co., 1909), p. 85.

21. See, for example, Lewis Grout, *Zulu-Land; or, Life Among the Zulu-Kafirs of Natal and Zulu-Land, South Africa* (Philadelphia: Presbyterian Publication Committee, 1864), p. 174.

22. Robert H. Milligan, *The Fetish Folk of West Africa* (New York: Fleming H. Revell Co., 1912), pp. 5–6.

23. James Hupfield, "Islam in West Africa," *Missionary Review of the World* 13 (January, 1900), pp. 47–48.

24. George Schodde, "The Struggle of the Christian and the Moslem in Africa," *Harper's Weekly* 39 (July 13, 1895), 664.

25. Joseph King Goodrich, *Africa of To-Day* (Chicago: A. C. McClurg and Co., 1912), p. 225.

26. Naylor, *Daybreak*, p. 80.

27. Wilson, *Western Africa*, p. 288.

28. Springer, *Snap Shots*, p. 122.

29. DeWitt C. Snyder, "Missionary Experiences in the Heart of Africa," *Missionary Review of the World* 16 (July, 1903), 515; and also George S. Brown, *Brown's Abridged Journal* (Troy, N.Y.: Prescott and Wilson, 1849), p. 114; and Samuel J. Whiton, *Glimpses of West Africa, with Sketches of Missionary Labor* (Boston: American Tract Society, 1866), p. 84.

30. Thomas, *Adventures and Observations*, p. 289.

31. Wilson, *Western Africa*, p. 265.

32. See, for example, Naylor, *Daybreak*, p. 16; Edward Warren Capen, *Sociological Progress in Mission Lands* (New York: Fleming H. Revell, Co., 1914), p. 97; and Hotchkiss, *Sketches*, p. 165.

33. "Woman's Life in Africa," *Missionary Review of the World* 24 (June, 1911), 429.

34. Dennis, *Christian Missions*, 1:107.

35. George Thompson, *Thompson in Africa; or, An Account of the Missionary Labors, Sufferings, Travels, and Observations of George Thompson, in Western Africa, at the Mendi Mission* (New York: Printed for the author, 1854), p. 224.

36. Robert Dabney Bedinger, *Triumphs of the Gospel in the Belgian Congo* (Richmond, Va.: Presbyterian Committee of Publication, 1920), pp. 56–57; and Hotchkiss, *Sketches*, p. 47.

37. Wilson, *Western Africa*, p. 112.

38. A. H. Godbey, *Stanley in Africa: The Paladin of the Nineteenth Century* (Chicago: Donohue Brothers, 1902), p. 332.

39. Milligan, *Fetish Folk*, p. v.

40. Grout, *Zulu-Land*, p. 181.

41. Poultney Bigelow, *White Man's Africa* (New York: Harper and Brothers, 1900), p. 224.

42. Gossett, *Race*, pp. 144–75.

43. Unfortunately there exists no official publication of the congress; information has been gathered from the following sources: Frederic Perry Noble, "Africa at the Columbian Exposition," *Our Day* 9 (November, 1892), 773–89; "The Chicago Congress on Africa," *Our Day* 12 (October, 1893), 279–300; Joseph Cook, "The Divine Program in the Dark Continent," *Our Day* 12 (September, 1893), 193–202; and Cook, "American Opportunities in Africa," *Our Day* 5 (June, 1890), 490–99.

44. Noble, "Africa at the Columbian Exposition," pp. 785–86.

45. Ibid., p. 785.

46. Noble, "Chicago Congress," p. 299.

47. Cook, "Divine Program," pp. 194–95; and Cook, "American Opportunities," pp. 490–99.

48. Booker T. Washington was an advocate of this approach. Writing in 1906, Washington confessed that his personal knowledge of Africa was not extensive; it had come mainly from "the reports of missionaries and travellers" and from the advice of his Tuskegee students who had travelled to Togo, West Africa. Despite a lack of direct contact, Washington was convinced that the "surest way" of saving Africans was by making them useful. Placing industrial schools throughout the continent ensured the "permanent establishment of Christian religion and Christian civilization," a perspective endorsed by many missionaries who also felt that the success of their work was dependent on educating the "head, heart, and hand" of the African. According to the plan, each African settlement had an industrial school, serving as a focal point for spiritual instruction; and through industrial

training Africans were introduced to the virtues of productivity and efficiency. Only after learning to work were the subtleties of "ethics and theology" then taught. Rote adherence to Christian ceremonies accomplished little, while industrial education generated feelings of "self-respect, stability, and earnestness." See Booker T. Washington, "Industrial Education in Africa," *Independent* 60 (March 15, 1906), 617–18.

49. Noble, "Africa at the Columbian Exposition," p. 774.

50. See, for example, ibid., pp. 778–79; and Noble, "Chicago Congress," p. 300.

51. The program of the congress and selected papers are contained in J.W.E. Bowen, ed., *Africa and the American Negro; Addresses and Proceedings of the Congress on Africa* (Atlanta: Gammon Theological Seminary, 1896).

52. Ibid., pp. 13, 143.

53. Ibid., p. 138.

54. Ibid., pp. 126–28, 132–34.

55. In volume 2 of the *Ecumenical Missionary Conference, New York, 1900* (New York: American Tract Society, 1900), the names of delegates and missionaries who attended the conference are listed on pp. 395–418.

56. Ibid., 1:9–10.

57. Ibid., p. 39.

58. See, for example, the best-selling work by the Congregational minister Josiah Strong, *Our Country: Its Possible Future and Its Present Crisis* (New York: Baker and Taylor, 1885).

7

Africa in America

By the end of the First World War, inquiring Americans had access to a substantial body of information about Africa, written by individuals who had actually travelled to the continent. This material was published as exploration narratives, travel accounts, articles written for popular magazines, instructional manuals compiled for missionary societies, and personal reminiscences of time spent in Africa. Adventurers, scientists, missionaries, and travellers recorded their impressions and shared their experiences with a larger reading audience. Their observations, nevertheless, did not constitute the sole source of information about Africa and Africans, but were complemented by a collection of popular secondary materials: writings about Africa based directly on primary works or publications that were wholly the invention of a creative editor or a resourceful scholar. Particularly noteworthy during the late nineteenth and early twentieth centuries were two groups of documents, arbitrarily chosen to demonstrate the diversity of audience for whom publications about Africa were intended. The first group, which includes geography textbooks, literature designed for children, and American travel books, represents the beginnings of an American tradition of using popular secondary sources to explain Africa. Since such materials were new—and were not as dominant then as they were later on—they only supplemented and did not exceed the primary importance of direct reports from Africa in determining America's understanding of the continent. Nonetheless, it has been well documented that educational texts are basic tools for learning about the world, that children's literature is influential in shaping the attitudes of the young toward other people, and that travel books are significant indices to a writer's impressions of a new environment. But regarding Americans and Africa, when and how did this tradition begin?

The Afro-American press and the writings of black American scholars on Africa make up the second group. There is a good deal of complexity to the subject of black responses to Africa, ranging from outright repudiation to complete association with the continent. However, the Afro-American press generally portrayed Africa in unfavorable terms, while a number of black American writers sought to document the positive elements in Africa's past. These two elements, in representing opposite poles of opinion, can be considered extremes, but by juxtaposing the polarities of rejection and identification, a sense of the dialogue taking place among black Americans concerning Africa can be gauged.

The geography textbook was one of the earliest sources of information about Africa, and one of the most influential geographers in late-nineteenth-century America was Arnold Guyot. As professor of geology and physical geography at Princeton University and a friend of naturalist Louis Agassiz, Guyot wrote a number of texts. Through his work, schoolchildren learned that the African continent was "in a very low state of civilization." Compared to America and the modern nations of Europe, Africa was still very much a "savage" land. Guyot pointed out, for example, that West Africa was a region where large congregations of "heathen idol worshipers" still lived. Other primitive practices, such as cannibalism and witchcraft, gave the area a distinctly barbaric character. Guyot stressed that Africans were incapable of establishing effective controls to regulate the affairs of their cities and governments, and though he acknowledged in many of his textbooks that there were some African cities of note, many with large populations and definable urban features, most of Africa had taken only "the first steps" toward civilizing itself. The great bulk of Africa, according to Guyot, remained "still in the savage state."[1]

The American Book Company published another widely used and

well-received text. Unlike the works of Guyot, however, *Harper's School Geography* attempted to survey and classify all the nations of the world by assigning each country to one of five categories: savage, barbarous, half-civilized, civilized, and enlightened. Although distinctions between "savage" and "barbarous" were never clearly made in the text, Africa was nonetheless designated "barbarous" because it surpassed "all the rest of the world together" in the number of its inhabitants who deserved the title "barbarian." Africans, the text pointed out, had done little throughout their history to improve social conditions or to create civilizations worthy of praise. According to *Harper's*, what saved Africa from being designated "savage"—the lowest classification—was the presence of Europeans and Americans who controlled parts of the African economy and whose numbers, as they grew during the late nineteenth century, increased the chances of Africa's being reassigned to a higher category.[2]

Alexis E. Frye offered a third approach to Africa for the schoolchildren of America. In contrast to the broad sweep of *Harper's*, in *Elements of Geography* Frye described in detail a typical day as lived in the "Kongo." Most people in Central Africa, the young American reader learned, no longer lived in caves or mud dwellings as in former times. Nevertheless, the "Kongo" was still a very strange place. To convey that sense in terms schoolchildren might understand, Frye described parts of the African countryside at night as being dark, foreboding, and inhabited by any number of dangerous animals. Because it was overrun by so many wild creatures, the environment caused Africans to behave unusually. Why else, Frye asked, would so many Africans be in bed so early in the evening?[3]

Implicit in the work of Frye and other authors was the approval of imperialism and colonialism as logical and inevitable developments in the history of Africa. Cyrus C. Adams, considered one of America's leading authorities on Africa, authored *An Elementary Commercial Geography* in 1902. Colonies in foreign lands, he argued, had proved historically to be of great value to the conquering nations of the world. They were storehouses of raw materials, ready markets for finished goods, and ideal spots for industrial and agricultural expansion, and since the African continent still needed to be developed commercially, it was imperative that all of its geographical features be explored immediately.[4] The conclusion, of course, to be reached by American schoolchildren was that European and American interests in Africa were legitimate. Moreover, by 1914 American writers of geography textbooks for children had become more consistent in their condemnation of Africa, with a number of assumptions about the continent being issued almost unreflectively: Africa was an underutilized land that lacked manufacturing, industry, and modern technology. In *Africa, A Supplementary Geography*, for example, James and Arthur Chamberlain pointed out that Africa was indeed far from civilization, since most Africans "have never seen a locomotive, a street car, an automobile, a telephone, an electric light, a typewriter," or any number of "other things" traditionally associated with everyday life in twentieth-century America.[5]

Geography texts were not restricted to an elementary clientele. Textbooks designed for the American university student were built upon the informational foundation laid by the more basic texts. To cite one example, college students were exposed to the licentious and lazy character of Africans throughout Ralph S. Tarr and Frank M. McMurry's *World Geography*. The only difference between the college texts and the elementary works was that Africa was presented more exhaustively for the university audience. Social scientific methods were introduced for the first time and impressionistic thoughts were supported by graphs and statistics. In order to illustrate the superstitious nature of African life, Tarr and McMurry reported that four million, of approximately eighty million, pagans had been slaughtered over a short period of time in an effort to rid Africa of evil spirits.[6] Thus, at the very least, geography textbooks for schoolchildren and young adults projected a view of the continent that coincided with the more direct observations of Americans in Africa.

A second major source of information about Africa was literature written for children. Because of its obvious potential for excitement and adventure, the "exotic world of Africa" became a natural part of this genre. As a distant land, separated from the security of familiar places, far removed from the influences of parents, long associated with slave ships and capturing slaves, and inhabited by other small people called "pygmies," Africa had a strong appeal for the young imagination. Thomas Knox structured a series of travel books around the exploits of two "boy travellers" who travelled around the world in search of adventure. In 1883 they entered Africa for the first time, exploring many of the continent's mysteries, but by 1888 the young travellers had joined Henry M. Stanley on a journey through the

Congo in *The Boy Travellers on the Congo: Adventures of Two Youths in a Journey with Henry M. Stanley (Through the Dark Continent)*, a book that contained a parenthetical reminder of and reference to one of Stanley's most famous works. By 1895 the two youths had made it safely through the Sahara desert, despite numerous sandstorms and trackless terrain.

The writings of William James Morrison and his youthful hero Willie Wyld soon appeared. Between 1911 and 1912, Morrison wrote no less than three African adventures for his young readers, beginning with Willie Wyld sailing out of New York on a "wonderful" voyage to Zanzibar. A year later, Willie is found on safari in East Africa, an attempt by Morrison to capitalize on the interest in "big game" and safaris generated by Theodore Roosevelt's expedition of two years earlier. In 1912, unfortunately, Willie vanishes in *Willie Wyld: Lost in the Jungles of Africa*, never to be heard from again.[7] Although American children were never at a loss for adventurous stories about Africa because of writers like Knox and Morrison, the most prolific and readable author was an individual who had spent considerable time in Africa: Paul Belloni Du Chaillu.

Beginning with the publication of *Stories of the Gorilla Country: Narrated for Young People*, Du Chaillu warned his young readers that it was impossible to live or travel in Africa without experiencing several unforgettable adventures.[8] Africans were introduced by Du Chaillu as a peculiar group of people who not only dressed differently but also lived in "queer little huts" made from the bark of trees.[9] Du Chaillu, in addition, compiled elaborate descriptions of Africa's animal population and mentioned throughout his writings how startled he had been by the "strange, discordant, half human, devilish cry" of the gorilla.[10] Having barely escaped with his life intact from the menacing onslaught of the animal, he recalled the anxiety and terror he had experienced in confronting one of the world's most ferocious beasts—which was not the only exotic creature to populate Africa.

American children were simultaneously delighted and frightened by Du Chaillu's presentation of the practices of cannibals. Armed with spears and shields, their bodies were heavily tattooed and nearly naked. How dreadful they looked, Du Chaillu remarked, and to increase the intensity of the narrative even further, the young reader was brought into the midst of a cannibal ceremony. At a "war-dance

of Cannibals," portrayed as "the wildest scene" ever witnessed in
Africa, the "fantastic forms" of "wild men" emerged from the darkness of the jungle night.[11] They made unusual contortions with their
bodies. They screamed and yelled and made themselves appear "like
demons." Midway through the ceremony, the cannibals approach a
corpse bartered for in a neighboring town, their shining skins giving
the jungle an eerie feeling. Finally, with drawn knives, they take
possession of the body. At this point Du Chaillu stated that he could
no longer tolerate looking at the scene, although he still could hear
the cannibals "growing noisy over the division of their horrid spoil."[12]

Life in Africa involved other aspects of the macabre as well. Du
Chaillu described his own battle with African fever and the "violent
returns" of the disease that played with his mind and body, making
his head seem as if it were actually on fire. In one instance in particular, he became "mad with pain" and, thinking he was about to
die, prayed for relief from the debilitating disease that afflicted him.[13]
In addition, in *Lost in the Jungle*, Du Chaillu presented a number
of gruesome themes for his young readers to consider: idol worship,
involving the veneration of the skulls of dead elephants, leopards,
and monkeys, mixed with the skins of snakes, leaves, and charred
bones; and a victory celebration, upon the death of a gorilla, in which
drums beat so "furiously" that the participants appeared to be "almost out of their senses."[14] As in all his tales of Africa "narrated
for young people," Du Chaillu emphasized the "wonders" encountered, the perils endured, the "warlike tribes" met, and the dangers
"seen and unseen," and he reminded his readers: "I have told you
many things about Africa, about its strange animals, its terrible
gorillas, its savage Cannibals; and all that I have told you is true,
for it is what I have seen with my own eyes."[15]

Du Chaillu ended his child's excursion through Africa on a somber
note. In *The Country of the Dwarfs* he related how at one time he lay
on his back on the ground in the cold and misty night air, recalling
how an "intense feeling of sadness" had come over him.[16] He was
far from home, and the heat of the jungle made him think of the
"northern climes," of the changing seasons, of snowflakes, "of a
happy home, of girls and boys, of friends, of schoolmates." For the
young reader, it was perhaps comforting to know that any of Du
Chaillu's "thrilling" adventures about Africa could be ended by
simply closing a book. However, for the adult reader, numerous

travel books that complemented the books designed for children as popular sources on Africa, began to be published in unprecedented numbers throughout the late nineteenth and early twentieth centuries. Based on the primary works of individuals who had been to Africa, writers and publishers compiled an impressive string of secondary texts. Writing in the *North American Review*, for example, Gilbert Haven pointed out that even by 1877 Africa had entered "the realm of romance" and was rapidly becoming the "central fascination" of a diverse group of people, including explorers, adventurers, and scholars. It was, as Haven claimed, a land that "draws all eyes and hearts to its majestic mysteries," with the result that "books of travel, voluminous and costly, are pouring constantly from the presses of Europe and America."[17]

Many of the most widely circulated accounts of Africa, which poured from European and American publishers, were the work of retailers. Either as individual writers or as editors for large publishing houses, retailers were responsible for assembling under a single title excerpts from the works of many others. A good example of this type of publication is the work of Charles H. Jones. Entitled *Africa: The History of Exploration and Adventure as Given in the Leading Authorities from Herodotus to Livingstone*, the book was organized by chapters around the lives and adventures of the most illustrious explorers of Africa: Heinrich Barth, David Livingstone, Paul Belloni Du Chaillu, Richard Burton, and Henry Morton Stanley, among others.[18] The subject matter of the book, however, contained selected passages that were chosen to attract the most attention from the reader because of their sensational content.

Two excerpts from the writings of Du Chaillu illustrate this point. Jones, for example, extracted Du Chaillu's portrait of a particular group of African people, the Fon, for the American reading public to consider:

> The men were almost naked. They had no cloth about the middle, but used instead the soft inside bark of a tree, over which, in front, was suspended the skin of some wild-cat or tiger. They had their teeth filed, which gives the face a ghastly and ferocious look, and some had the teeth blackened besides. Their hair, or "wool," was drawn out into long thin plaits; on the end of each stiff plait were strung some white beads, or copper or iron rings. Some wore feather

caps, but others wore long queues made of their own wool and a kind of tow, dyed black and mixed with it, and giving the wearer a most grotesque appearance. Over their shoulders was suspended the huge country knife, and in their hands were spears and the great shield of elephant hide, and about the necks and bodies of all were hung a variety of fetiches and greegrees, which rattled as they walked.[19]

In another selection, chosen for its ability to excite and entertain, Jones confronted the reader with the following description of Du Chaillu's encounter with a gorilla:

His eyes began to flash fiercer fire as we stood motionless on the defensive, and the crest of short hair which stands on his forehead began to twitch rapidly up and down, while his powerful fangs were shown as he again sent forth a thunderous roar. And now truly he reminded me of nothing but some hellish dream creature—a being of that hideous order, half man half beast, which we find pictured by old artists in some representations of the infernal regions. He advanced a few steps—then stopped to utter that hideous roar again—advanced again, and finally stopped when at a distance of about six yards from us. And here, as he began another of his roars and beating his breast in rage, we fired, and killed him.[20]

Although selections from the African narratives of Du Chaillu were so memorable as to be often reproduced, the writings of Henry M. Stanley inspired the most replication in America, for as Stanley's fame in Africa grew, so also did the retailers' interest in him increase.

J. T. Headley invited readers of *The Achievements of Stanley and Other African Explorers* to follow "the daring and intrepid Stanley in facing a thousand perils by savages, cataracts, disease, wild beasts and starvation" throughout a great many pages. They did. The generous number of illustrations, together with its large size, made it a best-seller. In addition to Headley's successful format, A. G. Feather exploited Stanley's writings and captured an even greater audience of readers.[21] Entitled *Stanley's Story or Through the Wilds of Africa; A Thrilling Narrative of His Remarkable Adventures, Terrible Experiences, Wonderful Discoveries and Amazing Achievements in the Dark Continent*, only the most exciting aspects of Stanley's experiences in Africa were presented, as promised by the author:

In *Stanley's Story* the reader is presented a most trilling narrative of the terrible experiences encountered, as well as a graphic account of the wonderful discoveries and the amazing achievements accomplished by Mr. Stanley during his career in Africa. The subject—one of unparalleled interest—is presented in the characteristic style of the writer, from thoroughly reliable information, data, and the official reports of Mr. Stanley himself. It favorably commends itself to every lover of geographical science, as well as to the admirer of the marvellous in life and nature.[22]

Feather, by way of Stanley, treated his readers to the following sketch of a "native" celebration, held immediately after the defeat of an enemy:

They had barely died before the medicine men came up, and with their scalpels had skinned their faces and their abdominal portions, and had extracted what they call "mafuta," or fat, and their genital organs. With this matter which they had extracted from the dead bodies the native doctors or waganga made a powerful medicine, by boiling it in large earthen pots for many hours, with many incantations and shakings of the wonderful gourd that was only filled with pebbles. This medicine was drunk that evening with great ceremony, with dances, drum beating and general fervor of heart.[23]

In many aspects, the work of Bayard Taylor, the famous American writer and traveller, typified the retailer approach to the subject of Africa. Taylor initially had written about the continent in *A Journey to Central Africa; or, Life and Landscapes From Egypt to the Negro Kingdoms of the White Nile* in which he revealed his approach to the topic of Africa by stating, "Although I cannot hope to add much to the general stock of information concerning Central Africa, I may serve, at least, as an additional witness, to confirm or illustrate the evidence of others."[24] As editor of *The Illustrated Library of Travel, Exploration, and Adventure,* however, a travel series sponsored by the publishing firm of Scribner, Armstrong and Company, Taylor set forth both a method for selection and a well-conceived aim for the series:

Each volume will be complete in itself, and will contain, first, a brief preliminary sketch of the country to which it is devoted: next, such an outline of previous explorations as may be necessary to explain what has been achieved by later ones; and finally, a condensation of one or more of the most important narratives of recent travel, accompanied with illustrations of the scenery, architecture, and life of the races, drawn only from the most authentic sources. An occasional volume will also be introduced in the LIBRARY, detailing the exploits of individual adventurers. The entire series will thus furnish a clear, picturesque, and practical survey of our present knowledge of lands and races as supplied by the accounts of travellers and explorers. The LIBRARY will therefore be both entertaining and instructive to young as well as old, and the publishers intend to make it a necessity in every family of culture and in every private and public library in America.[25]

As a result of the widespread acceptance of Taylor and his *Illustrated Library* by the general reading public, together with the writings of Jones, Headley, and Feather, among others, Africa emerged from the retailers' hands as a continent just too thrilling to be believed, despite the fact that they claimed that their intention was to inform the public about the "mysteries" of the continent. They extrapolated only the most exciting parts of selected narratives, and by condensing and compiling the most sensational episodes from much larger works into a single volume, they helped to create a distorted view of the continent for the reading public in America. However, a second group of documents, consisting of the Afro-American press and the work of black American scholars, offered other perspectives on Africa and added to the complexity of the discussion in America about the nature of the continent and the characteristics of its people.

Along a spectrum of responses ranging from total rejection to complete identification, the majority of black newspapers in America portrayed Africa in unfavorable terms.[26] On occasion, sympathetic views of Africa were stimulated by the realization that life in America had become oppressive. Newspaper editors, in response, projected onto Africa the ideas of freedom and opportunity, concepts that had been promised but were withheld from many black Americans. Editorial opinion suggested that as the bearers of Western civilization black Americans might even become the future economic, educational, and religious leaders of Africa. Such discussion, however, was the exception. The consensus about Africa in the Afro-American press was found throughout the pages of the *Freeman, An Illustrated*

Colored Newspaper. Published in Indianapolis, Indiana, it was the single most important newspaper in terms of circulation and sustained commentary on Africa. During the late nineteenth and early twentieth centuries, the *Freeman*'s approach to Africa was threefold: It presented excerpts from the writings of famous explorers just as retailers did; it printed eyewitness accounts from the less celebrated who had been to Africa and returned; and it offered its readers biting attempts at humor.

An illustration of the first approach came from the work of Henry M. Stanley, whose narratives about Africa were often reprinted in a number of black American newspapers. Through Stanley, the readers of the *Freeman*, however, were given many glimpses of Africa and, in particular, a sketch of the Congo, which was described as having

> briars and thorns abundant; lazy creeks, meandering through the depths of the jungle. . .ants and insects of all kinds, sizes and colors, murmuring around; monkeys and chimpanzees above, queer noises of birds and animals, crashes in the jungle as troops of elephants rush away; dwarfs with poisoned arrows securely hidden. . .standing poised, still as dead stumps, rain puttering down on you every other day in the year; an impure atmosphere, with its dread consequences, fever and dysentery; gloom throughout the day, and darkness, almost palpable, throughout the night. . . . The aborigines are wild, utterly savage, and incorrigibly vindictive. The dwarfs—called Wambutti—are worse still, far worse. . . . The gloom of the forest is perpetual.[27]

A less-than-negative response to this African landscape of fear would be difficult for any reader of the *Freeman* to achieve.

Short articles and letters to the editor comprised the *Freeman*'s second approach to Africa: its publication of eyewitness accounts of the continent. For example, the British consul at Cameroon, H. H. Johnstone, was the source of a report from Africa entitled "Cannibals of the Niger." On a trip into the Congo basin, Johnstone claimed that he had seen "some of the worst cannibals in the world," perhaps numbering into "the millions." At one stop in his travels, he reported entering a hut where "a smoked human ham was hanging from the smoke blackened rafters, and above a hundred skulls were ranged around the upper part of the clay walls." Johnstone noted for the readers of the *Freeman* that Congo cannibals "habitually eat human flesh" and recalled that as he was about to leave "the natives were debating the question whether to treat" him and his party "as honored guests or to eat them."[28] In addition, in 1889 the *Freeman* published a letter from a "Major Goldsmith" headlined, "Cannibalism: How Tayonga, an African Chief, Luxuriates on Human Flesh." In many sections of Africa, Goldsmith observed that human flesh was "sometimes boiled, but generally it was baked in a covered oven," with the "preferred" pieces being the "upper parts of the arms and thighs." However, Goldsmith added that a particular African chief, Tayonga, "used to take great delight in pointing out to me certain persons whom he had made up his mind to eat," especially babies "recently born" who were considered "delicacies."[29]

African life, finally, was also the subject of ridicule in many of the editorial cartoons published in the *Freeman*. A favorite caricature of the paper featured two Africans, Nijiji and Hojojo. With bones through their noses, rings in the ears, and bedecked with necklaces made of teeth, they were always captured discussing matters of importance to them. The caption of one cartoon read:

The Age of Ornament

NIJIJI:. Say, I've lost one of my tooties off my neck ornamentish.
HOJOJO: Well dats all right, one won't be missed.
NIJIJI: Yes'a it will'a. I wan'ny you to pully one a mine to put on it.[30]

A second example of the pictorial joke was a bit more sophisticated, since it played upon the different meanings of the word "fair" and made reference to the "World Committee," an important missionary organization. Two Africans, once again clothed in skulls, bones, and rings but suffering this time with bellyaches, are interrogated by a third African, with the situation being structured around the following conversation:

The Columbian Fair

MR. HAJOJO: Oh! Oh! I'se dun eat one 'er dem wurl' 'mittee!
MR. UJIJI: How you know you'se eat 'im?
MR. HAJOJO: Him don't agree.[31]

In reacting to editorial endorsements of this kind, W. D. Boyce, the editor of the influential black newspaper, the *Blade*, pointed out that little could be done

to wean the popular imagination from picturing Africa in pigments
of shadow-drenched jungles, viciously charging animals, superstitious
savages and black slavery. From the days of misty tradition, thru [*sic*]
the comparatively short period of recorded history to the present day,
Africa, the second largest continent on the globe, has been a land of
fascinating mystery. Imagination and speculation have been so thoroly
[*sic*] mixed with facts, that those who do not know the country as I do
have absorbed more fancy and grotesque notions than truth.[32]

While the Afro-American press as represented by the *Freeman* continued to be an important conduit for negative commentary on Africa, there was also a growing counterforce operating in America
that searched for a more complete understanding of Africa's past.

In all historical periods there are exceptions to popular trends. In
contrast to the negative view of Africa published in the black American press, a number of Afro-American scholars searched for positive
elements in Africa's history throughout the nineteenth century. This
fact has been commented upon recently by St. Clair Drake:

> An image was in the making throughout the nineteenth century which
> stressed the deadly character of Africa's climate, the menace of its
> fauna, and the "savagery" of its peoples. This image *did* eventually,
> have a negative effect upon American Negro attitudes toward Africa,
> but it also spurred some Negroes to try to change the image to what
> they conceived of as the African reality.[33]

Although there are numerous examples of this quest for understanding, the efforts of Hosea Easton, Robert Benjamin Lewis, William
Wells Brown, George W. Williams, and W.E.B. Du Bois reveal that
there was a genuine divergency of approach to the subjects of Africa
and Africans among black American writers.[34]

An early point of departure, advanced by Hosea Easton, the author
of *A Treatise on the Intellectual Character and Civil and Political Condition of the Colored People of the United States*, consisted of acknowledging the eminence of ancient Africa and then of ascribing blame
for its subordinate condition to the actions of hostile, non-African
forces during the nineteenth century:

> Africa could once boast of several states of eminence, among which
> are Egypt, Ethiopia, and Carthage; the latter supported an extensive
> commerce, which was extended to every part of the then known world.

Her fleets even visited the British shores, and was every where pros-
perous, until she was visited with the scourge of war, which opened
the way for nations whose life depended on plunder. The Romans
have the honor, by the assistance of the Mauritonians, of subduing
Carthage; after which the North of Africa was overrun by the Vandals,
who, in their march destroyed all arts and sciences; and, to add to
the calamity of this quarter of the world, the Saracens made a sudden
conquest of all the coasts of Egypt and Barbary, in the seventh century.
And these were succeeded by the Turks, both being of the Maho-
medan [*sic*] religion, whose professors carried desolation wherever
they went; and thus the ruin of that once flourishing part of the world
was completed.

From that time on, Easton concluded, "Africa has been robbed of
her riches and honor and sons and daughters, to glut 'the rapacity
of the great minds of European bigots.'"[35]

A second approach was to catalogue the positive contributions that
Africa had made to world history from earliest times to the present.
Starting from the very beginning, Robert Benjamin Lewis located
the "fall of man" in Africa and then argued that Adam and Eve
were, in fact, black people:

The transgression of Adam and Eve, commonly called the fall of man,
took place, probably, soon after the creation, and has been most awful
in its consequences. For their transgression, Adam and his companion
were driven out of the garden, to till the ground of Ethiopia, it needing
cultivation in consequence of the curse.—(Gen. iii.17.) Adam and his
posterity settled on the river Gihon, that went out of the Garden of
Eden, and compassed the whole land (or country) of Ethiopia; and
they tilled the ground, from which Adam was taken.—(Gen. ii.13:
iii.23.)

The word *Adam* is derived as follows: Adam, Adamah, Adami,
Admah—which means *earthy*. The earth is a rich, dark substance and
from it our first parents were taken. Now if we admit that Dr. Brown's
and other Bible Dictionaries are correct in their explanations of the
meanings of terms, then the deduction must be that Ethiopia (Gen.
ii.13) was *black*, and the first people were Ethiopians, or blacks.[36]

In relying upon the Bible for evidence, Lewis in effect reverted to
a tactic pioneered by members of the white clergy in America who

had used the Bible and its teachings to justify the institution of slavery and to legitimize the subordination of black people.

Evaluations of contemporary Africa supplemented judgments about the continent of a more distant past. In *The Rising Son; or, the Antecedents and Advancements of the Colored Race*, William Wells Brown compared the creative abilities of Africans "with the best workmanship of English and American manufacturers":

> Civilization is receiving an impetus from the manufacturing of various kinds of goods as carried on by the people through Africa, and especially in the Egba, Yoruba, and Senegambia countries. Iron-smelting villages, towns devoted entirely to the manufacturing of a particular kind of ware, and workers in leather, tailors, weavers, hat, basket, and matmakers, also workers in silk and worsted may be seen in many of the large places....[37]

Since many Americans believed that most Africans were either unable or disinclined toward productivity, especially in the mid-nineteenth century as America began the process of industrializing itself in earnest, Brown's research pointed to specific examples to disprove the validity of such a premise. Although Brown sought to demonstrate the black American's capacity for citizenship throughout his life, his writings accomplished a great deal in rehabilitating Africa's past as well.

As exemplified in the work of Brown, George Washington Williams continued the reconstruction of Africa's history and the search for positive aspects in the continent's past. Williams, who has the distinction of being the first black American to be elected to the Ohio legislature, is also credited with writing the first history of black Americans to be given serious attention by white American scholars. Although the focus of the *History of the Negro Race in America from 1619 to 1880* was not Africa but America, Williams began his study by discussing the "Ashantee" peoples of West Africa:

> The king of Ashantee has a fair government. His power is well-nigh absolute. He has a House of Lords, who have a check-power. Coomassi is the famous city of gold, situated in the centre of the empire. The communication through to the seacoast is unobstructed; and it is rather remarkable that the Ashantees are the only nation in Africa, who, living in the interior, have direct communication with the Cau-

casian. They have felt the somewhat elevating influence of Mohammedanism, and are not unconscious of the benefits derived by the
literature and contact of the outside world. They are a remarkable
people: brave, generous, industrious, and mentally capable.[38]

The writings of Williams were well received in America, including
a later work, *A Report Upon the Congo-State and Country to the President of the Republic of the United States of America*, the result of a
trip to the Congo undertaken for the United States government.
Because of the efforts of Williams, the writing of black history in
general achieved a scholarly and professional status. However, with
the publication in 1915 of *The Negro*, W.E.B. Du Bois began to
define more fully both the context and the nature of the debate about
the true dimensions of Africa's heritage.

Born in Great Barrington, Massachusetts, in 1868 and educated
at Fisk, Harvard, and the University of Berlin, Du Bois was exposed
at an early age to the larger world of diverse peoples and competing
ideas. His thoughts about Africa, nevertheless, were ambivalent and
idealized at first. Early in his career he conceived of Africa as a
"happy" land, contrasted the concept of Western "efficiency" with
the idea of African "leisure," and reflected the difficulties experienced by many other black Americans who wished to identify with
Africa. His concern for Africa, however, involved more than a long-
ing for a new spiritual home and nothing less than a search for a
realistic African history. In *The Negro*, for example, Du Bois chal-
lenged the idea that any artistic achievement or creative development
in Africa was the primary result of non-African influences, and asked
why so much "misinformation and contempt is widespread concerning Africa and its people, not simply among the unthinking mass,
but among men of education and knowledge?"[39] He attempted to
rehabilitate Africa's past by establishing a positive relationship between Americans and Africa by countering the claims of the de-
bunkers of African creativity. To do so, Du Bois cited the works of
others who had travelled to Africa:

West of the Great Lakes, Stanley (1878) found wonderful examples
of smith work: figures worked out of brass and much work in copper.
Cameron (1878) saw vases made near Lake Tanganyika which reminded him of the amphorae in the Villa of Diomedes, Pompeii. Horn
(1882) praises tribes here for iron and copper work. Livingstone (1871)

passed thirty smelting houses in one journey, and Cameron came across bellows with valves, and tribes who used knives in eating. He found tribes which no Europeans had ever visited, who made ingots of copper in the form of the St. Andrew's cross, which circulated even to the coast. In the southern Congo basin iron and copper are worked; also wood and ivory carving and pottery making are pursued.[40]

It is important to remember, nevertheless, that Du Bois represented only one point of view on Africa. Individuals who shared his vision, starting with Hosea Easton and continuing down to George Washington Williams, were countered by an opposing perspective. The Afro-American press, particularly the *Freeman*, which conceived of Africa in unfavorable terms, was supported by other popular secondhand accounts of Africa. Geography textbooks, children's literature, and American travel books were significant in shaping a pejorative and distorted perspective on Africa. They were disseminated throughout different segments of American society and were, in many cases, the prime sources of information through which Americans learned about Africa. However, because only elements that played upon the public's love for the exotic were chosen, they reveal a bias in description and interpretation that favored the bizarre and the unusual over the commonplace and the ordinary. The result has been an unsatisfactory intellectual compression of vast geographical expanses and diverse cultural customs into a series of images that have served to simplify and distort the reality of a complex land for the reading public of America.

Notes

1. Arnold Guyot, *Guyot's Grammar-School Geography* (New York: Scribner, Armstrong and Co., 1874), p. 174; Arnold Guyot, *The Earth and Its Inhabitants: Common-School Geography* (New York: Scribner, Armstrong and Co., 1875), pp. 49–50; and Arnold Guyot, *Physical Geography* (New York: American Book Co., 1885), p. 118.

2. *Harper's School Geography* (New York: American Book Co., 1894), pp. 18, 116–17.

3. Alexis E. Frye, *Elements of Geography* (Boston: Ginn and Co., 1898), pp. 35–36.

4. See Cyrus C. Adams, *An Elementary Commercial Geography* (New York: D. Appleton, 1902).

5. James Franklin Chamberlain and Arthur Henry Chamberlain, *Africa: A Supplementary Geography* (New York: Macmillan Co., 1914), p. 204.

6. Ralph S. Tarr and Frank M. McMurry, *World Geography: One-Volume Edition* (New York: Macmillan Co., 1912), p. 450.

7. The following children's books deal with Africa explicitly: G. T. Day, *African Adventure and Adventurers* (Boston: D. Lothrop, 1906?); Thomas W. Knox, *The Boy Travellers on the Congo: Adventures of Two Youths in a Journey with Henry M. Stanley (Through the Dark Continent)* (New York: Harper and Brothers, 1888); *In Wild Africa: Adventures of Two Youths in a Journey Through the Sahara Desert* (Boston: W. A. Wilde, 1895); Mary Muller (Lenore E. Mulets), *The Story of Akimakoo an African Boy* (New York: A. Flanagan, 1904); William James Morrison, *Willie Wyld: His Wonderful Voyage to the Island of Zanzibar* (Nashville, Tenn.: Publishing House, Methodist Episcopal Church, South, 1911); *Willie Wyld: Hunting Big Game in Africa* (Nashville, Tenn.: Publishing House, Methodist Church, South, 1912); and *Willie Wyld: Lost in the Jungles of Africa* (Nashville, Tenn.: Publishing House, Methodist Church, South, 1912); Herbert Strang, *Fighting on the Congo: The Story of an American Boy Among the Rubber Slaves* (Indianapolis: Bobbs-Merrill, 1906).

8. See, for example, Paul Belloni Du Chaillu, *Stories of the Gorilla Country; Narrated for Young People* (New York: Harper and Brothers, 1895).

9. Ibid., p. 17.

10. Ibid., p. 68.

11. Ibid., p. 81.

12. Ibid., p. 92.

13. Ibid., p. 278.

14. Paul Du Chaillu, *Lost in the Jungle; Narrated for Young People* (New York: Harper and Brothers, 1869), p. 40.

15. Paul Du Chaillu, *My Apingi Kingdom; With Life in the Great Sahara* (New York: Harper and Brothers, 1871), p. 147, and also Paul Du Chaillu, *Stories of the Gorilla Country*, p. 292.

16. Paul Du Chaillu, *The Country of the Dwarfs* (New York: Harper and Brothers, 1872), p. 303.

17. Gilbert Haven, "America in Africa," *North American Review* 125 (July–August, 1877), 147–58.

18. Charles H. Jones, *Africa: The History of Exploration and Adventure as Given in the Leading Authorities from Herodotus to Livingstone* (New York: Henry Holt and Co., 1875), p. iv.

19. Ibid., p. 194.

20. Ibid., p. 196.

21. See, front matter, Joel Tyler Headley, *The Achievements of Stanley and Other African Explorers* (Philadelphia: Hubbard Brothers, 1878).

22. A. G. Feather, *Stanley's Story or Through the Wilds of Africa; A Thrilling Narrative of His Remarkable Adventures, Terrible Experiences, Wonderful Discoveries and Amazing Achievements in the Dark Continent* (Chicago: Thompson and Thomas, 1890), p. vi.

23. Ibid., p. 132.

24. Bayard Taylor, *A Journey to Central Africa; or, Life and Landscapes From Egypt to the Negro Kingdoms of the White Nile* (New York: G. P. Putnam, 1859), p. 1.

25. Bayard Taylor, *Travels in South Africa* (New York: Scribner, Armstrong and Co., 1872), n.p. [end matter].

26. On the subject of Afro-American responses to Africa, see William Bittle and Gilbert Geis, *The Longest Way Home: Chief Alfred C. Sam's Back-to-Africa Movement* (Detroit: Wayne State University Press, 1964); Margerite Cartwright, "Teaching About Africa," *Negro History Bulletin* 19 (January, 1956), 77–78; C. A. Chick, Sr., "The American Negroes' Changing Attitude Toward Africa," *Journal of Negro Education* 31 (Fall, 1962), 531–35; John Henrik Clarke, ed., *Marcus Garvey and the Vision of Africa* (New York: Vintage Books, 1974); Henry E. Cobb, "The African Background of the American Negro: Myth and Reality," *Bulletin of Southern University and A.M. College* 55 (June, 1969), 9–20; John A. Davis, ed., *Africa Seen by American Negroes* (Paris: Présence africaine, 1958); St. Clair Drake, "Negro Americans and the Africa Interest," in *The American Negro Reference Book*, ed. John P. Davis, 2 vols. (Englewood Cliffs, N.J.: Prentice-Hall, 1966); George Edmund Haynes, "Americans Look at Africa," *Journal of Negro Education* 27 (Winter, 1958), 94–100; Harold R. Isaacs, *The New World of Negro Americans* (New York: John Day, 1963); Louis R. Mehlinger, "The Attitude of the Free Negro Toward African Colonization," *Journal of Negro History* 1 (July, 1916), 276–301; Edwin S. Redkey, *Black Exodus: Black Nationalist and Back-to-Africa Movements, 1890–1910* (New Haven: Yale University Press, 1969); Edwin S. Redkey, "The Meaning of Africa to Afro-Americans, 1890–1914," *Black Academy Review* 3 (Spring–Summer, 1972), 5–37; Sterling Stuckey, "DuBois, Woodson, and the Spell of Africa," *Negro Digest* 16 (February, 1967), 60–74; Earl E. Thorpe, "Africa in the Thought of Negro Americans," *Negro History Bulletin* (October, 1959), 5–10, 22; Robert G. Weisbord, "The Back-to-Africa Idea," *History Today* 18 (January, 1968), 30–37; and Weisbord, *Ebony Kinship: Africa, Africans, and the Afro-American* (Westport, Conn.: Greenwood Press, 1973).

27. *Freeman*, May 4, 1889, p. 7.

28. Ibid., August 11, 1888, p. 2.

29. Ibid., February 16, 1889, p. 3.

30. Ibid., July 26, 1890, p. 5.

31. Ibid., October 4, 1890, p. 8.

32. *Blade,* July 31, 1890, p. xv.

33. St. Clair Drake, "Negro Americans and the African Interest," in John P. Davis, ed., *The American Negro Reference Book,* 1:630.

34. George Shepperson, "The Afro-American Contribution to African Studies," *Journal of American Studies* 8 (1975), 281–301.

35. Hosea Easton, *A Treatise on the Intellectual Character and Civil and Political Condition of the Colored People of the United States. . .* (Boston: Isaac Knapp, 1837), p. 14.

36. Robert Benjamin Lewis, *Light and Truth: Collected from the Bible and Ancient and Modern History, Containing the Universal History of the Colored and the Indian Race, from the Creation of the World to the Present Time* (Boston: Benjamin F. Roberts, 1844), p. 10.

37. William Wells Brown, *The Rising Son; or, the Antecedents and Advancement of the Colored Race* (Boston: A. G. Brown and Co., 1874), p. 137. See also William Wells Brown, *The Black Man, His Antecedents, His Genius and His Achievements* (New York: T. Hamilton, 1863).

38. George W. Williams, *History of the Negro Race in America from 1619 to 1880* (New York: G. Putnam's Sons, 1883; reprint, New York: Arno Press, 1968), p. 44.

39. W. E. Burghardt Du Bois, *The Negro* (New York: Henry Holt and Co., 1915), p. 138.

40. Ibid., p. 112.

8

Conclusion and Epilogue: Africa and Americans

Despite the number of reports that attempted to describe the continent in all its complexity, the American image of Africa was highly unfavorable. Detailed information about the continent was delivered within the context of arrogance, contempt, and condescension. When comparisons were made between Africa and America—and they were frequently—little recognition of African achievements emerged in the balance. Americans more easily assessed the topography of Africa than the human dimensions of the continent, with the result that the natural scene was pluralistically described. The unexpected beauty of West Africa as well as the region's association with heat and disease was noted, while in Central Africa the jungle terrain was portrayed in graphic detail. In eastern and southeastern Africa, Americans encountered a part of the continent that appeared to be familiar to them in many ways, but with an animal population that gave the region a distinctive character. However, when either implicit or explicit references were made to Africans, the tone of analysis changed.

Americans divided the built environment of Africa into two distinct landscape elements: a non-African, expansive, and progressive landscape and a primitively designed African one. On the level of intellectual definition, they transformed Africa into a symbol of the economically uncivilized parts of the world, an undeveloped wilderness that needed to be exploited by outside forces. Americans, like their European counterparts, considered Africans incapable of doing so themselves because of certain racial assumptions Americans held about the dark-skinned people of the world. American missionaries, in addition, transmitted a strong impression of heathen depravity by classifying Africans as religiously and culturally inferior. By demonstrating that Africans lacked a worthwhile religious system of their own and by describing just how savage the African truly was, missionaries created a degraded portrait of the peoples they wished to convert. But to what effect?

American reports from Africa, in many instances, were simply reinventions of a well-established cultural stereotype: The desire to entertain as well as to inform was as much a part of the intention of Herodotus as it was of Theodore Roosevelt. Nonetheless, American descriptions of Africa were significant in their own right for the sense they conveyed about Africa. Although their impact on American society in general was substantial during the late nineteenth and early twentieth centuries, the problem was more complex at that time for black Americans, since negative views of Africa were directly tied to the concept of a negative self-image.

Victims of prejudice and discrimination often internalize the grossly perverted stereotypes handed them by others. The popular British caricature of the Irish, for example, as pug-nosed, pickled leprechauns has had special meaning for Irish people as well as for Americans of Irish descent. Similarly, black Americans have been indoctrinated with the idea that their African ancestors—as essential links with both a history and a heritage—belonged to a backward, primitive race of people. During the late nineteenth and early twentieth centuries especially, a majority of black Americans subscribed either consciously or unconsciously to the dangerous and fallacious idea of African inferiority.[1] They were forced to react to a derogatory image of Africa not only because of the abundance of material that was being published at that time but also because the predominantly white society in which they lived would not allow them to forget it. A negative image of Africa, supported by ideas derived from the theory of evolution, provided a convenient underpinning for racist ideas about black people.

In essence, the psychological sustenance to be gained from bonds forged by a positive heritage was lacking. Africa became a source of shame for many and even self-hatred for some. Although psychological scarring is difficult to measure, examples of how the process works can be found in the past, with the writings of Booker T. Washington being particularly instructive. In one instance, Washington recalled how he was shocked by the way in which pictures of Africa and African life were placed "in an unnecessarily cruel contrast with the picture of the civilized and highly cultured Europeans and Americans." He noted how a likeness of George Washington was "placed side by side with a naked African, having a ring in his nose and a dagger in his hand." In reaction to what he saw, Washington then revealed how he himself unconsciously sensed that there must be something wrong and degraded about any person who was different from the customary white, European-American standard.[2] Without a past worthy of emulation, feelings of mortification and degradation, as Washington sensed, can easily arise in a pluralistic society where ancestry serves an important function.

Besides being linked to issues involving identity, however, Africa has provided the basis for the status of black Americans as an exploited group, with all the political, social, and economic abuses that accrue to such a discriminated minority. Like other immigrant people, black Americans have been directly affected by the nature of their lineage. Racial difficulties between blacks and whites in America have had an historical foundation, not only in terms of events but also by the manner in which races have conceived of each other. In America, white views of black Americans in part have been built upon the implied assumptions of innate African inferiority. In colonial America, for example, slave traders who sought to justify their traffic in human lives depicted Africans as a thoroughly debased and barbaric people. They argued that their trade in slaves was actually saving Africans by transporting them out of the "heathen jungles" of their African homeland. When Europeans and Americans confronted Africans in the eighteenth century, theories about the origins of races were developed in order to classify Africans as subordinate. The image of Africa as a "savage land," moreover, was marshalled by the defenders of slavery in the mid-nineteenth century in support of continuing the "peculiar institution." Since Africans were a "beastly" lot to begin with, it was only just and proper for Africans to be enslaved.

While the predominance of this material has produced an un-
healthy supply of misconceptions about Africa, it has had a more
immediate effect as well, for once a perception of a land and its
peoples exists in the minds of another group, it becomes a part of
the real world for them. Perceptions, in short, influence behavior;
they not only can precipitate action for positive ends, but they can
also strike out, maim, and sometimes even cripple. Although dis-
paraging views of Africa and Africans were not the principal reason
so many hangmen's nooses were so easily slipped around black necks
in America, denigrating, distorted, and misinformed ideas about
Africa made the task an easier one. By portraying Africa as a savage
land and Africans as a barbaric people, it was less complicated to
deny people of African descent a meaningful place in American
society.

As a point of illustration, in 1894, Prince Momolu Massaquoi of
Sierra Leone spoke before a distinguished audience of American
clergy in Boston, telling them that Africa was a continent that "has
been misrepresented in America." The son of Sierra Leonean roy-
alty, Massaquoi was educated at a mission school and baptized and
confirmed into the Protestant Episcopal Church. In 1888, when only
sixteen, he came to the United States and entered Central Tennessee
College at Nashville. In 1893 he addressed the Chicago Congress on
Africa at the Columbian Exposition.[3] In Boston, however, he pointed
out that although Americans spoke about the "savage in Africa" he
believed that in America there was "more savagery than I have seen
all my days in Africa." Massaquoi then went on to describe the
following incident he had witnessed:

In the spring of 1872 I stood in a public square in the city of Nashville,
and there I saw a black man torn out of prison. A rope was tied around
his neck, he was dragged to the bridge, and they pushed him over.
And I stood there and saw hundreds and hundreds of men and women
of your race waving handkerchiefs and laughing at that man as he
hung under the bridge. And his body was cut loose a few minutes
afterwards and thrown away. I saw that with my own eyes.[4]

The significance of Massaquoi's juxtaposition of two seemingly
unconnected matters—racial violence in America and the American
view of Africa as a "savage" land—cannot be easily dismissed. Al-

though it would do violence to logic itself to argue a direct causal link between negative ideas of Africa and the treatment of black people in America, there is no guarantee that such a connection did not exist. To the contrary, it seems reasonable to assume that one phenomenon did affect the development of the other. In America, ideas about Africa and Africans were not only powerful in their own right, inasmuch as they molded people's opinions about Africa and Africans, but they were also products of a particular set of social and racial conditions that engendered their expression.[5] People subscribe to and articulate ideas, not necessarily because they think they are true, but because they wish to believe in those ideas in order to justify certain societal policies. The generation and expression of ideas about Africa and Africans, together with the political and social ramifications that accrued to black Americans because of them, reinforced and reaffirmed one another in a pernicious interlocking manner. Such a hypothesis suggests that discrimination has had a transatlantic dimension, thus broadening our understanding of race prejudice in America by enlarging the milieu within which it thrived.

More recently, the potency of the original perspective in shaping a fixed cultural tradition for viewing Africa, though begun and developed in America during the late nineteenth and early twentieth centuries especially, has manifested itself in several ways. As a founder of the first university program in African Studies in the United States, Melville Herskovits noted in 1962:

> [For] many years the predominant image of Africa was of a continent hot and humid, overgrown with jungles and roamed by herds of wild animals. Its peoples were held to have fallen behind in the march of progress, with ways of life representing early stages in the evolution of human civilizations. This is the "darkest Africa" picture.[6]

A short time later, Basil Davidson, a British journalist and scholar, reaffirmed Herskovits's sentiments. Davidson believed that "old views about Africa are worth recalling for another reason. Though vanished from serious discussion, they still retain a kind of underground existence." Davidson added that the "stercoraceous sediment" of misinformed opinion about Africa "has settled like a layer of dust and ashes on the minds of large numbers of otherwise thoughtful people, and is constantly being swirled about."[7]

Besides Herskovits and Davidson, two scholars of Africa, Paul Bohannan and Philip Curtin, have summarized some of the "oldest and most pervasive myths" about the continent in *Africa and Africans*:

> That Africa is a series of jungles filled with lions. In reality, lions do not live in jungles, and only five percent of the African continent can be called jungle. This myth, according to the authors, is a "symbol for the unrecognized fear that Americans have of Africa."

> That Africa is a "Dark Continent" is a "subject-object confusion." Since Europe did not know about Africa, the assumption was that Africa was not known. In fact, during the Middle Ages, Africans, Arabs, and Indians had been trading with each other, across the Sahara Desert and the Indian Ocean, for many years.

> That Africa is "savage" is actually the result of a need to justify a number of commercial, philosophical, and religious movements which were begun both in Europe and in America.[8]

A tradition of viewing Africa from an established perspective has also had a more immediate effect. In 1963, perhaps the most complete study of the impact of Africa on the lives of black Americans was undertaken by Harold R. Isaacs of the Center for International Studies at the Massachusetts Institute of Technology. As part of a larger inquiry into the "New World of Negro Americans," Isaacs questioned over a hundred black Americans—writers, scholars, educators, and business and church people. Interview sessions conducted by Isaacs lasted from four to eight hours each, and sometimes there were two or three sessions per person.[9] Sample interviews were supplemented by more extensive meetings with such prominent black Americans as James Baldwin, Kenneth B. Clark, W.E.B. Du Bois, Ralph Ellison, John Hope Franklin, Martin Luther King, Thurgood Marshall, A. Phillip Randolph, and Jackie Robinson, among others. Isaacs's intent, in general, was to study within a changing world "all the important ways" in which black Americans "have viewed themselves until now," and more particularly, in a section of the study called "Negroes and Africa," Isaacs attempted to determine through what means black Americans first learned about Africa and the relationship of that knowledge to their own self-conception.[10]

It became clear, by the nature of the responses, that one of the most influential sources of information about Africa available to the people interviewed were the writings of American missionaries. Some of the more detailed statements given by the respondents and collected by Isaacs were these:

In the church I went to in Americus, Georgia, when I was a little boy...I was given the missionary's concept, and the picture we got of African people was of ugly, unkempt, naked savages who had to be civilized. We had to take them Christianity and the Bible....

Returning missionaries painted a very disturbing picture...cannibalism, polygamy, illiteracy, primitive way of life, and worst of all, not Christians.

I used to go to missionary meetings and always heard such horrible things about Africa....I imagined it as a horrible place to live....

As a young boy (what I got was) all negative, cannibalism, Sunday-school literature, naked women, heathen, tribal masks, shame, savages.

Missionaries spoke of the Dark Continent, the noble missionaries, the poor Africans eager to get the word of God. I am afraid they supported in the main the initial images from the geographies of wild, savage peoples....[11]

Isaacs further noted the importance of "literary" sources in shaping initial impressions of Africa, since "wherever there was exposure to books or reading in Negro homes, an important part of it had to do with Africa."[12] Again the recorded responses of the individuals interviewed are revealing:

As a child I read the Stanley story. I had a red book about the strange and exotic things in Africa, pygmies. My father had lots of missionary books about Africa. The *In Darkest Africa* sort of thing....

When I was a little boy and could first read, I had books on Stanley, Livingstone and things like that....

I knew about Livingstone; we had Stanley's book illustrated, a fat brown book....

> I read Stanley's *In Darkest Africa* when I was about twelve or thirteen,
> I read everything he wrote....[13]

A familiarity with Stanley and Livingstone, however, was only part of the story. Early in life, many black Americans confronted Africa in school, where they met for the first time a "naked, savage, uncivilized African" in a textbook:

> I opened a geography and saw Africa represented by a naked African with a headdress, some feathers around his middle and a spear....
>
> We were shown people, wild, pagan, hopelessly inferior, heathen-looking animalist types. Even the Indian was painted with greater dignity than the Africans in these books. It must have been in the primary grade at six or seven that I saw these pictures.[14]

Statements such as these are not just random responses from selected black Americans; they form the basis for something much greater. Isaacs concluded in his study: "In nearly every instance the early discovery of the African background was in a fact a prime element in the shaping of each individual's knowledge of himself and his world and his attitudes toward both."[15]

Africa is a developing part of the world, an economically poor continent that suffers from poverty, ignorance, and disease. It is also, however, a land where events have been rapidly changing. The emergence of Africa as a geopolitical force of sovereign states with national aspirations and foreign policies was a development for which many Western nations were unprepared. In the constantly shifting scales of international power and ideological allegiances, the newly independent nations of modern Africa have become integral parts, and the movement of Africa toward self-determination has altered the traditional perspective from which the continent has been viewed. With the demise of colonialism, earlier views and previous attitudes require reexamination, as Africa faces the problems of implementing growth while preserving its cultural traditions.

However, Africa's development has been slowed by a harsh physical environment. Communications are problematic because of the landscape, and there are vast areas of the continent that are arid or semiarid. Rainfall is poorly distributed throughout the year. Soils are poor; important mineral resources, such as coal and oil, are in short supply; and the majority of Africans in tropical regions suffer from the effects of one or more diseases. "Africa has little manufacturing industry, few people with industrial skills, and limited capital with which to finance the building of hospitals, roads, dams and factories."[16] Thus, in a real sense, Africa and America represent the polarities of economic development—between the poorest and the richest continents, "between those who have a high standard of living with access to health, education, and comfort and those who do not." Compared to Americans, "most Africans are extremely poor; their lives are generally hard, frequently short, and with few material rewards."[17] Africa, moreover, is a continent of such magnitude and intricacy that no single picture or analysis can more than hint at its true nature. It is a land that even Malcolm X, toward the end of his short life, realized as being much more than a continent of "naked savages, cannibals, monkeys and tigers and steaming jungles"—and much more complex than the way in which he had imagined it to be in his youth.

Notes

1. I am grateful here to Robert Weisbord and his important work, *Ebony Kinship: Africa, Africans, and the Afro-American* (Westport, Conn.: Greenwood Press, 1973).

2. Booker T. Washington, *The Story of the Negro*, 2 vols. (New York: Doubleday, Page and Co., 1909), 1: 8.

3. See Prince Momolu Massaquoi of Ghendimah (Gallinas), "Africa's Appeal to Christendom," *Century Magazine* 69 (April, 1905), 927–36.

4. "Address of Prince Momolu Massaquoi, of Vei, Africa, in the Boston Monday Lectureship, February, 1894," *Our Day* 13 (May–June, 1894), 272–73.

5. I. A. Newby, *Jim Crow's Defense: Anti-Negro Thought in America, 1900–1930* (Baton Rouge: Louisiana State University Press, 1965), esp. pp. 19–51.

6. Melville J. Herskovits, "The Image of Africa in the United States," *Journal of Human Relations* 10 (Winter and Spring, 1962), 236–45.

7. Basil Davidson, *The African Genius* (Boston: Little, Brown and Co., 1969), p. 25.

8. Paul Bohannan and Philip Curtin, *Africa and Africans* (Garden City, N.Y.: Natural History Press, 1971), pp. 6–7.

9. Harold R. Isaacs, *The New World of Negro Americans* (New York: John Day Co., 1963).

10. Despite Horace Mann Bond's criticism of Isaacs's methodology, what is important is the content of the statements made by the individuals interviewed concerning their impressions of Africa. See Horace Mann Bond, "Howe and Isaacs in the Bush: The Ram in the Thicket," reprinted in *Apropos of Africa: Sentiments of Negro American Leaders on Africa from the 1800s to the 1950s*, ed. Adelaide Cromwell Hill and Martin Kilson (London: Frank Cass and Co., 1969), 278–88.

11. Isaacs, *New World*, p. 128.

12. Ibid., p. 146.

13. Ibid., pp. 146–47.

14. Ibid., p. 162.

15. Ibid., p. 159.

16. David Kilingray, *A Plague of Europeans: Westerners in Africa Since the Fifteenth Century* (Baltimore: Penguin Books, 1973), p. 116.

17. Ibid., p. 118.

Selected Bibliography

Earlier Published Works

Books

Adams, Cyrus C. *An Elementary Commercial Geography*. New York: D. Appleton and Co., 1902.

Africa Illustrated: Scenes from Daily Life on the Dark Continent from Photographs Secured in Africa by Bishop William Taylor, Dr. Emil Holub and the Missionary Superintendents. New York: Illustrated Africa, 1895.

Alexander, Archibald. *A History of Colonization on the Western Coast of Africa*. Philadelphia: William S. Martien, 1846.

Alexander, Sam. *Photographic Scenery of South Africa*. Syracuse, N.Y.: Sam Alexander and Co., 1882.

Anderson, Benjamin. *Narrative of a Journey to Musardu, the Capital of the Western Mandingoes*. New York: S. W. Green, 1870.

Arnett, Benjamin William. *Bishop Abraham Grant's Trip to the West Coast of Africa*. New York: Published by order of the Bishop's Council by Rev. H. B. Parks, 1899.

Ashmun, Jehudi. *History of the American Colony in Liberia, From December, 1821, to 1823*. Washington City, [D.C.]: Way and Gideon, 1826.

Babe, Jerome L. *The South African Diamond Fields*. New York: D. Wesley, 1872.

Bacon, David Francis. *Wanderings on the Seas and Shores of Africa*. New York: Joseph W. Harrison, 1843.

Bacon, Ephraim. *Abstract of a Journal Kept by E. Bacon, Assistant Agent of the United States, to Africa*. 3d ed. Philadelphia: Clark and Raser, 1824.

Barnes, James. *Through Central Africa from Coast to Coast*. New York: D. Appleton and Co., 1915.

Beach, Harlan P. *A Geography and Atlas of Protestant Missions*. 2 vols. New York: Student Volunteer Movement for Foreign Missions, 1901.

Beck, Henry Houghton. *History of South Africa and the Boer-British War*. Philadelphia: Globe Bible Publishing Co., 1900.

Bedinger, Robert Dabney. *Triumphs of the Gospel in the Belgian Congo*. Richmond, Va.: Presbyterian Committee of Publication, 1920.

Beehler, W. H. *The Cruise of the Brooklyn*. Philadelphia: J. B. Lippincott Co., 1885.

Bell, Solomon [Samuel G. Goodrich]. *Tales of Travels in Central Africa*. Boston: Gray and Bowen, 1831.

Benezet, Anthony. *A Short Account of That Part of Africa Inhabited by the Negroes*. Philadelphia: W. Dunlap, 1762.

————. *Some Historical Account of Guinea*. Philadelphia: Joseph Crukshank, 1771.

Bennett, Norman R., ed. *Stanley's Despatches to the New York Herald 1871-1872, 1874-1877*. Boston: Boston University Press, 1970.

Besolow, Thomas Edward. *From the Darkness of Africa to the Light of America*. Boston: F. Wood, 1891.

Bigelow, Poultney. *Seventy Summers*. 2 vols. London: Edward Arnold and Co., 1925.

————. *White Man's Africa*. New York: Harper and Brothers, 1900.

Blake, J.Y.F. *A West Pointer with the Boers*. Boston: Angel Guardian Press, 1903.

Boas, Franz. *The Mind of Primitive Man*. New York: Macmillan Co., 1911.

Booth, Alan R., ed. *Journal of the Rev. George Champion, American Missionary in Zululand 1835-39*. Cape Town: C. Struik, 1967.

Bosman, Willem. *A New and Accurate Description of the Coast of Guinea: Divided Into the Gold, the Slave, and the Ivory Coasts*. Translated from the Dutch. 2d ed. London: J. Knapton, D. Midwinter, 1721.

Bowen, J.W.E., ed. *Africa and the American Negro; Addresses and Proceedings of the Congress on Africa*. Atlanta: Gammon Theological Seminary, 1896.

Bowen, T. J. *Central Africa: Adventures and Missionary Labors in Several*

Countries in the Interior of Africa, From 1849 to 1856. Charleston, S.C.: Southern Baptist Publication Society, 1857.

———. *Grammar and Dictionary of the Yoruba Language*. Washington, D.C.: Smithsonian Institution, 1858.

———. *Meroke; or, Missionary Life in Africa*. Philadelphia: American Sunday-School Union, 1858.

Bridge, Horatio [Nathaniel Hawthorne, ed.]. *Journal of an African Cruiser. Comprising Sketches of the Canaries, the Cape de Verds, Liberia, Madeira, Sierra Leone, and Other Places of Interest on the West Coast of Africa*. New York: George P. Putnam and Co., 1853.

Brittan, Harriette G. *Scenes and Incidents of Every-day Life in Africa*. New York: Pudney and Russell, 1860.

Bronson, Edgar Beecher. *In Closed Territory*. Chicago: A. C. McClurg and Co., 1910.

Brown, George S. *Brown's Abridged Journal*. Troy, N.Y.: Prescott and Wilson, 1849.

Brown, William H. *On the South African Frontier: The Adventures and Observations of an American in Mashonaland and Matabeleland*. New York: Charles Scribner's Sons, 1899.

Brown, William Wells. *The Black Man, His Antecedents, His Genius, and His Achievements*. New York: T. Hamilton, 1863.

———. *The Rising Son; or, the Antecedents and Advancement of the Colored Race*. Boston: A. G. Brown and Co., 1874.

Buel, J. W. *Heroes of the Dark Continent*. Richmond, Va.: B. F. Johnson and Co., 1890.

Burnham, Frederick Russell. *Scouting on Two Continents*. New York: Garden City Publishing Co., 1926.

Campbell, Robert. *A Few Facts, Relating to Lagos, Abbeokuta, and Other Sections of Central Africa*. Philadelphia: King and Baird, 1860.

———. *A Pilgrimage to My Motherland: An Account of a Journey Among the Egbas and Yorubas of Central Africa in 1859-60*. New York: T. Hamilton, 1861.

Capen, Edward Warren. *Sociological Progress in Mission Lands*. New York: Fleming H. Revell Co., 1914.

Carnes, J. A. *Journal of a Voyage from Boston to the West Coast of Africa*. Boston: John P. Jewett and Co., 1852.

Carpenter, Frank G. *Africa*. New York: American Book Co., 1905.

Chaillé-Long, Charles. *Central Africa: Naked Truths of Naked People*. London: Sampson Low, Marston, Searle and Rivington, 1876.

———. *My Life in Four Continents*. 2 vols. London: Hutchinson and Co., 1912.

Chamberlain, James Franklin, and Chamberlain, Arthur Henry. *Africa: A Supplementary Geography*. New York: Macmillan Co., 1914.

Chambers, Henry E. *A Higher History of the United States for Schools and Academies*. New York: University Publishing Co., 1898.

Champion, Sarah Elizabeth [Booth]. *Rev. George Champion, Pioneer Missionary to the Zulus*. New Haven: Tuttle, Morehouse and Taylor, 1896.

Chanler, William Astor. *Through Jungle and Desert; Travels in Eastern Africa*. New York: Macmillan Co., 1896.

Chatelain, Heli. *Folk-Tales of Angola*. Boston and New York: Houghton Mifflin Co., 1894.

Christy, David. *Ethiopia: Her Gloom and Glory*. Cincinnati: Rickey, Mallory and Webb, 1857.

———. *Lectures on African Colonization*. Columbus, Ohio: J. H. Riley and Co. 1853.

Clough, Ethlyn T. *Africa: An Account of Past and Contemporary Conditions and Progress*. Detroit: Bay View Reading Club, 1911.

Coker, Daniel. *Journal of Daniel Coker, a Descendant of Africa*. Baltimore: Edward J. Coale, 1820.

Cole, J. Augustus. *A Revelation of the Secret Orders of Western Africa*. Dayton, Ohio: United Brethren Publishing House, 1886.

Coppin, Levi Jenkins. *Observations of Persons and Things in South Africa, 1900-1904*. Philadelphia: A.M.E. Book Concern, n.d.

Cox, Melville B. *Remains of Melville B. Cox, Late Missionary to Liberia. With a Memoir*. Boston: Light and Horton, 1835.

Crummell, Alexander. *Africa and America: Addresses and Discourses*. Springfield, Mass.: Willey and Co., 1891.

———. *The Future of Africa*. New York: Charles Scribner, 1862.

———. *The Relations and Duties of Free Colored Men in America to Africa*. Hartford, Conn.: Case, Lockwood and Co., 1861.

Cuffe, Paul. *A Brief Account of the Settlement and Present Situation of the Colony of Sierra Leone in Africa*. New York: Samuel Wood, 1812.

Daly, Charles P. *The Commercial Importance of Central Africa and the Free Navigation of the Congo*. New York: H. Bessey, 1884.

Davies, Edward. *The Bishop of Africa; or, the Life of William Taylor, D.D.* Reading, Mass.: Holiness Book Concern, 1885.

———. *An Illustrated Handbook on Africa*. Reading, Mass.: Holiness Book Concern, 1886.

Davis, Richard Harding. *The Congo and Coasts of Africa*. New York: Charles Scribner's Sons, 1907.

Day, G. T. *African Adventure and Adventurers*. Boston: D. Lothrop and Co., 1906?

Delany, M. R. *Official Report of the Niger Valley Exploring Party*. New York: T. Hamilton, 1861.

Dennis, James S. *Christian Missions and Social Progress: A Sociological Study of Foreign Missions.* 3 vols. New York: Fleming H. Revell Co., 1897-1906.

Dodge, Richard E., and Grady, William E. *Home Geography and World Relations.* Chicago: Rand, McNally and Co., 1914.

Dowd, Jerome. *The Negro Races: A Sociological Study.* New York: Macmillan Co., 1907.

Du Chaillu, Paul Belloni. *Adventures in the Great Forest of Equatorial Africa and the Country of the Dwarfs.* New York: Harper and Brothers, 1871.

————. *L'Afrique Savvage.* Paris: Michel Lévy, 1868.

————. *Explorations and Adventures in Equatorial Africa; with Accounts of the Manners and Customs of the People, and of the Chase of the Gorilla, the Crocodile, Leopard, Elephant, Hippopotamus, and other Animals.* New York: Harper and Brothers, 1861.

————. *In African Forest and Jungle.* New York: Charles Scribner's Sons, 1903.

————. *A Journey to Ashango-Land: and Further Penetration into Equatorial Africa.* New York: D. Appleton and Co., 1867.

————. *King Mombo.* New York: Charles Scribner's Sons, 1902.

————. *Lost in the Jungle. Narrated for Young People.* New York: Harper and Brothers, 1877.

————. *My Apingi Kingdom; With Life in the Great Sahara.* New York: Harper and Brothers, 1871.

————. *Stories of the Gorilla Country; Narrrated for Young People.* New York: Harper and Brothers, 1895.

————. *Wild Life Under the Equator; Narrated for Young People.* New York: Harper and Brothers, 1896.

Ecumenical Missionary Conference, New York, 1900. 2 vols. New York: American Tract Society, 1900.

Ellis, George W. *Negro Culture in West Africa.* New York: Neale Publishing Co., 1914.

Elmslie, W. A. *Among the Wild Ngoni.* New York: Fleming H. Revell Co., 1899.

Everett, Marshall [Henry Neil]. *Roosevelt's Thrilling Experiences in the Wilds of Africa Hunting Big Game.* Chicago, 1910.

Farini, G. A. *Through the Kalahari Desert: A Narrative of a Journey with Gun, Camera, and Note-book to Lake N'Gami and Back.* London: Sampson Low, Marston, Searle and Rivington, 1886.

Feather, A. G. *Stanley's Story or Through the Wilds of Africa.* Chicago: Thompson and Thomas, 1890.

Ferris, William Henry. *The African Abroad.* New Haven: Tuttle, Morehouse, and Taylor Press, 1913.

Flickinger, D. K. *Ethiopia: or, Twenty Years of Missionary Life in Western Africa*. Dayton, Ohio: United Brethren Publishing House, 1877.

――――. *Fifty-five Years of Active Ministerial Life*. Dayton, Ohio: United Brethren Publishing House, 1907.

――――. *History of the Origin, Development and Condition of Missions Among the Sherbo and Mendi Tribes in Western Africa*. Dayton, Ohio: United Brethren Publishing House, 1885.

――――. *Off Hand Sketches of Men and Things in Western Africa*. Dayton, Ohio: United Brethren Printing Establishment, 1857.

Foard, John F. *North America and Africa: Their Past, Present, and Future and Key to the Negro Problem*. Statesville, N.C.: Brady, 1904.

Foote, Andrew H. *Africa and the American Flag*. New York: D. Appleton and Co., 1854.

Forbes, Edgar Allen. *The Land of the White Helmet*. New York: Fleming H. Revell Co., 1910.

Ford, Henry A. *Observations on the Fevers of the West Coast of Africa*. New York: E. O. Jenkins, 1856.

Foster, John Watson. *The Relation of Diplomacy to Foreign Missions*. Sewanee, Tenn.: University Press, 1906.

French-Sheldon, M. *Sultan to Sultan: Adventures Among the Masai and Other Tribes of East Africa*. Boston: Arena Publishing Co., 1892.

Frye, Alexis E. *Elements of Geography*. Boston: Ginn and Co., 1898.

Geil, William Edgar. *Adventures in the African Jungle Hunting Pigmies*. New York: Doubleday, Page and Co., 1917.

――――. *A Yankee in Pigmy Land*. London: Hodder and Stoughton, 1905.

A Geographical Present: Being Descriptions of the Several Countries of Africa. New York: William Burgess Juvenile Emporium, 1831.

Godbey, A. H. *Stanley in Africa: The Paladin of the Nineteenth Century*. Chicago: Donohue Brothers, 1902.

Godbey, J. M., and Godbey, A. H. *Light in Darkness*. Indianapolis: World Publishing Co., 1892.

Goodrich, Joseph King. *Africa of To-Day*. Chicago: A. C. McClurg and Co., 1912.

Goodrich, Samuel G. *Lights and Shadows of African History*. Boston: Bradbury, Soden, and Co., 1844.

――――. *The Tales of Peter Parley*. Boston: Carter, Hendee and Co., 1833.

Gore, James H. *The Congo: A Report of the Commission of Enquiry Appointed by the Congo Free State Government*. New York, 1906.

Grout, Lewis. *Autobiography of the Rev. Lewis Grout*. Brattleboro, Vt.: Clapp and Jones, 1905.

――――. *The Isizulu: A Grammar of the Zulu Language*. London: Trübner and Co., 1859.

———. *Zulu-land; or, Life Among the Zulu-Kafirs of Natal and Zulu-land, South Africa.* Philadelphia: Presbyterian Publication Committee, 1864.

Gurley, Ralph Randolph. *Life of Jehudi Ashmun, Late Colonial Agent in Liberia.* Washington, D.C.: J. C. Dunn, 1835.

Guyot, Arnold. *The Earth and Its Inhabitants: Common-School Geography.* New York: Scribner, Armstrong and Co., 1875.

———. *Guyot's Grammar-School Geography.* New York: Scribner, Armstrong and Co., 1874.

———. *Physical Geography.* New York: American Book Co., 1885.

Hamilton, J. T. *Twenty Years of Pioneer Missions in Nyassaland.* Bethlehem, Pa.: Society for Propagating the Gospel, 1912.

Hance, Gertrude Rachel. *The Zulu Yesterday and Today.* New York: Fleming H. Revell Co., 1916.

Harding, William. *War In South Africa and the Dark Continent from Savagery to Civilization.* New Haven: Butler and Alger, 1899.

Harper's School Geography. New York: American Book Co., 1894.

Harris, Norman D. *Intervention and Colonization in Africa.* Boston: Houghton Mifflin Co., 1914.

Hawkins, Joseph. *A History of a Voyage to the Coast of Africa and Travels into the Interior of That Country.* Troy, N.Y.: Luther Pratt, 1797.

Headley, Joel Tyler. *The Achievements of Stanley and Other African Explorers.* Philadelphia: Hubbard Brothers, 1878.

———. *Stanley's Adventures in the Wilds of Africa.* Philadelphia: Hubbard Brothers, 1882.

Helper, Hinton Rowan, *The Negroes in Negroland.* New York: G. W. Carleton, 1868.

Hepburn, A. Barton. *The Story of an Outing.* New York: Harper and Brothers, 1913.

Hodgson, William Brown. *The Foulahs of Central Africa, and the African Slave Trade.* New York, 1843.

Holmes, Prescott. *The Story of Exploration and Adventure in Africa.* Philadelphia: Henry Altemus Co., 1898.

Hornaday, William T. *Free Rum on the Congo and What It Is Doing There.* Chicago: Women's Christian Temperance Union, 1887.

Hotchkiss, Willis R. *Sketches from the Dark Continent.* Cleveland, Ohio: Friends Bible Institute and Training School, 1901.

Humphrey, Edward P. *Africa and Colonization.* Washington, D.C.: McGill and Witherow, 1873.

Ireland, William. *Historical Sketch of the Zulu Mission, In South Africa, As Also of the Gaboon Mission, In Western Africa.* Boston: American Board of Commissioners for Foreign Missions, n.d.

Jack, James. W. *Daybreak in Livingstonia.* New York: Fleming H. Revell Co., 1900.

Johnson, R. M. *Liberia As It Is*. Philadelphia: Brown's Steam-Power Book and Job Printing Office, 1853.

Johnston, James. *Missionary Landscapes in the Dark Continent*. New York: A.D.F. Randolph and Co., 1892.

Jones, Charles H. *Africa: The History of Exploration and Adventure as Given in the Leading Authorities from Herodotus to Livingstone*. New York: Henry Holt and Co., 1875.

————. *Negroland; or, Light Thrown Upon the Dark Continent*. New York: Hurst and Co., 1881.

Jordan, David Starr. *Imperial Democracy*. New York: D. Appleton and Co., 1901.

Kidd, Benjamin, *The Control of the Tropics*. New York: Macmillan Co., 1898.

Kirkland, Caroline. *Some African Highways: A Journey of Two American Women to Uganda and the Transvaal*. Boston: Dana Estes and Co., 1908.

Knox, Thomas W. *The Boy Travellers on the Congo: Adventures of Two Youths in a Journey with Henry M. Stanley (Through the Dark Continent)*. New York: Harper and Brothers, 1888.

————. *In Wild Africa: Adventures of Two Youths in a Journey Through the Sahara Desert*. Boston: W. A. Wilde Co., 1895.

Kotzé, D. J., ed. *Letters of the American Missionaries, 1835-1838*. Cape Town: Van Riebeeck Society, 1950.

Lapsley, Samuel Norval. *Life and Letters of Samuel Norval Lapsley, Missionary to the Congo Valley, West Africa, 1866-1892*. Richmond, Va.: Whittet and Shepperson, 1893.

Latimer, Elizabeth Wormeley. *Europe in Africa in the Nineteenth Century*. Chicago: A. C. McClurg and Co., 1895.

Leo Africanus, Joannes. *History and Description of Africa*. Translated by John Pory. London: 1600 and reprinted Amsterdam: Da Capo Press, 1969.

Lewis, Robert Benjamin. *Light and Truth: Collected from the Bible and Ancient and Modern History, Containing the Universal History of the Colored and the Indian Race, from the Creation of the World to the Present Time*. Boston: Benjamin F. Roberts, 1844.

Loomis, Eben J. *An Eclipse Party in Africa*. Boston: Roberts Brothers, 1896.

Loring, J. Alden. *African Adventure Stories*. New York: Charles Scribner's Sons, 1914.

Lugenbeel, J. W. *Sketches of Liberia: Comprising a Brief Account of the Geography, Climate, Productions, and Diseases, of the Republic of Liberia*. Washington, D.C.: C. Alexander, 1850.

Lundeberg, Axel, and Seymour, Frederick. *The Great Roosevelt African Hunt and the Wild Animals of Africa. Their Appearance, Habits, Traits of Character, and Every Detail of Their Wild Life, with Thrilling, Exciting, Daring, and Dangerous Exploits of Hunters of Big Game in Wildest Africa.* New York: D. B. McCurdy, 1910.

McAllister, Agnes. *A Lone Woman in Africa: Six Years on the Kroo Coast.* New York: Eaton and Mains, 1896.

McCutcheon, John T. *In Africa: Hunting Adventures in the Big Game Country.* Indianapolis: Bobbs-Merrill Co., 1910.

MacQueen, Peter. *In Wildest Africa.* Boston: L. C. Page and Co., 1909.

Madeira, Percy C. *Hunting in British East Africa.* Philadelphia: J. B. Lippincott Co., 1909.

Martin, Lawrence. *A Laboratory Manual of College Geography.* Madison, Wis.: The University, 1913.

Medbery, R. B. *Memoir of William G. Crocker.* Boston: Gould, Kendall, and Lincoln, 1848.

Merriam, Edmund F. *A History of American Baptist Missions.* Philadelphia: American Baptist Publication Society, 1900.

Miller, Armistead. *Liberia Described; A Discourse Embracing a Description of the Climate, Soil, Productions, Animals, Missionary Work, Improvement, Etc., with a Full Description of the Acclimating Fever.* Philadelphia: Joseph M. Wilson, 1859.

Milligan, Robert H. *The Fetish Folk of West Africa.* New York: Fleming H. Revell Co., 1912.

———. *The Jungle Folk of Africa.* New York: Fleming H. Revell Co., 1908.

Mills, J. S. *Africa and Mission Work in Sierra Leone, West Africa.* Dayton, Ohio: United Brethren Publishing House, 1898.

Mitchell, S. Augustus. *First Lessons in Geography for Young Children.* Philadelphia: E. H. Butler and Co., 1864.

Morris, Charles. *Home Life in All Lands.* Philadelphia: J. B. Lippincott Co., 1907-11.

Morrison, William James. *Willie Wyld: His Wonderful Voyage to the Island of Zanzibar.* Nashville, Tenn.: Publishing House, Methodist Episcopal Church, South, 1911.

———. *Willie Wyld: Hunting Big Game in Africa.* Nashville, Tenn.: Publishing House, Methodist Episcopal Church, South, 1912.

———. *Willie Wyld: Lost in the Jungles of Africa.* Nashville, Tenn.: Publishing House, Methodist Episcopal Church, South, 1912.

Morton, Eliza H. *Morton's Elementary Geography.* New York: Butler, Sheldon, and Co., 1900.

Mowbray, Jay Henry. *Roosevelt's Marvelous Exploits in the Wilds of Africa.* Washington, D.C.: George W. Berton, 1909.

Muller, Mary [Lenore E. Mulets]. *The Story of Akimakoo an African Boy.* New York: A. Flanagan Co., 1904.

Nassau, Robert Hamill. *Africa, an Essay*. Philadelphia: Allen, Lane and Scott, 1911.

———. *Corisco Days: The First Thirty Years of the West African Mission*. Philadelphia: Allen, Lane and Scott, 1910.

———. *Fänwe Primer and Vocabulary*. New York: E. O. Jenkins, 1881.

———. *Fetichism in West Africa: Forty Years' Observation of Native Customs and Superstitions*. New York: Charles Scribner's Sons, 1904.

———. *In an Elephant Corral and Other Tales of West African Experiences*. New York: Neale Publishing Co., 1912.

———. *Where Animals Talk: West African Folk Lore Tales*. Boston: Richard G. Badger, Gorham Press, 1912.

Naylor, Wilson S. *Daybreak in the Dark Continent*. New York: Eaton and Mains, 1905.

Nesbit, William. *Four Months in Liberia; or, African Colonization Exposed*. Pittsburgh: J. T. Shryock, 1855.

Noble, Frederic Perry. *The Redemption of Africa. A Story of Civilization*. 2 vols. Chicago: Fleming H. Revell Co., 1899.

Officer, Morris. *African Bible Pictures; or, Scripture Scenes and Customs in Africa*. Philadelphia: Lutheran Board of Publication, 1859.

———. *Western Africa, a Mission Field*. Pittsburgh: U. S. Haven, 1856.

Osborne, E. W. *Anglican Church Missions in Africa*. Hartford, Conn.: Church Missions Publication Co., 1908.

Parks, H. B. *Africa: The Problem of the New Century*. New York: Bible House, 1899.

Peterson, Daniel H. *Through a Looking-Glass: Being a True Report and Narrative of the Life, Travels, and Labors of the Rev. Daniel H. Peterson, A Colored Clergyman....* New York: Wright, 1854.

Pierson, H. W., ed. *American Missionary Memorial*. New York: Harper and Brothers, 1853.

Powell, E. Alexander. *Beyond the Utmost Purple Rim: Abyssinia, Somaliland, Kenya Colony, Zanzibar, the Comoros, Madagascar*. New York: Century Co., 1925.

———. *The Last Frontier: The White Man's War for Civilisation in Africa*. New York: Charles Scribner's Sons, 1912.

———. *The Map That Is Half Unrolled: Equatorial Africa from the Indian Ocean to the Atlantic*. New York: Century, 1925.

Pratt, Mary H. S. *The Guyot Geographical Reader and Primer: A Series of Journeys Around the World*. New York: American Book Co., 1898.

Rainsford, William Stephen. *The Land of the Lion*. London: William Heinemann, 1909.

Ralph, Julian. *An American with Lord Roberts*. New York: Frederick A. Stokes Co., 1901.

————. *Towards Pretoria: A Record of the War Between Briton and Boer to the Relief of Kimberley*. New York: Frederick A. Stokes Co., 1900.

Reading, Joseph H. *The Ogowe Band; a Narrative of African Travel*. Philadelphia: Reading and Co., 1890.

————. *A Voyage Along the Western Coast or Newest Africa*. Philadelphia: Reading and Co., 1901.

Reid, J. M. *Missions and Missionary Society of the Methodist Episcopal Church*. 3 vols. New York: Hunt and Eaton, 1895.

Reynolds, Jeremiah N. *Voyage of the United States Frigate Potomac, Under the Command of Commodore John Downes. . . .* New York: Harper and Brothers, 1835.

Richards, Erwin H. *The African, European, and Latin American Fields: Addresses Delivered Before the Eastern Missionary Convention of the Methodist Episcopal Church, Philadelphia, Pa., October 13-15, 1903*. New York: Eaton and Mains, 1904.

Robbins, Archibald. *A Journal, Comprising an Account of the Brig Commerce, of Hartford, (Con.) James Riley, Master, Upon the Western Coast of Africa, August 28th, 1815*. Hartford, Conn.: Silas Andrus, 1824.

Roosevelt, Theodore. *African and European Addresses*. New York: G. P. Putnam's Sons, 1910.

————. *African Game Trails: An Account of the African Wanderings of an American Hunter-Naturalist*. New York: Charles Scribner's Sons, 1910.

————, and Heller, Edmund. *Life Histories of African Game Animals*. 2 vols. New York: Charles Scribner's Sons, 1914.

Ruffner, William Henry. *Africa's Redemption: A Discourse on African Colonization*. Philadelphia: William S. Martin, 1852.

Scull, Guy H. *Lassoing Wild Animals in Africa*. New York: Frederick A. Stokes Co., 1911.

Shaw, Edward R. *Big People and Little People of Other Lands*. New York: American Book Co., 1900.

Sheppard, Rosco Burton. *Islamic Africa*. New York: Methodist Book Concern, 1914.

Sheppard, W. H. *Presbyterian Pioneers in the Congo*. Richmond, Va.: Presbyterian Commission of Publication, 1917.

Shufeldt, Robert W. *America's Greatest Problem: The Negro*. Philadelphia: F. A. Davis, 1915.

————. *The Negro: A Menace to American Civilization*. Boston: Badger, 1907.

Simonton, Ida Vera. *Hell's Playground*. New York: Brentano's, 1912.

Smith, A. Donaldson. *Through Unknown African Countries: The First Expedition from Somaliland to Lake Lamu*. London: Edward Arnold, 1897.

Smith, Charles Spencer. *Glimpses of Africa; West and Southwest Coast*. Nashville, Tenn.: Publishing House, African Methodist Episcopal Church Sunday School Union, 1895.

Sparks, Jared. *A Historical Outline of the American Colonization Society.* Boston: O. Everett, 1824.

Springer, Helen Chapman. *Snap Shots from Sunny Africa.* New York: Fleming H. Revell Co., 1909.

Springer, John McKendree. *The Heart of Central Africa: Mineral Wealth and Missionary Opportunity.* New York: Methodist Book Concern, 1909.

―――. *Pioneering in the Congo.* New York: Methodist Book Concern, 1916.

Stanley, Henry M. *The Congo and the Founding of Its Free State; A Story of Work and Exploration.* 2 vols. New York: Harper and Brothers, 1885.

―――. *Coomassie and Magdala; The Story of Two British Campaigns in Africa.* London: Sampson Low, Marston and Co., 1874.

―――. *How I Found Livingstone; Travels, Adventures, and Discoveries in Central Africa.* New York: Charles Scribner's Sons, 1899.

―――. *In Darkest Africa.* 2 vols. New York: Charles Scribner's Sons, 1890.

―――. *Through South Africa.* London: Sampson Low, Marston and Co., 1898.

―――. *Through the Dark Continent.* 2 vols. New York: Harper and Brothers, 1879.

Starr, Frederick. *A Bibliography of Congo Languages.* Chicago: University Press, 1908.

―――. *Congo Natives: An Ethnographic Album.* Chicago: Lakeside, 1912.

―――. *The Truth About the Congo.* Chicago: Forbes and Co., 1907.

Stevens, Thomas. *Africa As Seen by Thomas Stevens and the Hawke-Eye.* Boston: Blair Camera Co., 1890.

―――. *Scouting for Stanley in East Africa.* New York: Cassell Publishing Co., 1890.

Stone, R. H. *In Africa's Forest and Jungle or Six Years Among the Yorubans.* New York: Fleming H. Revell Co., 1899.

Strang, Herbert. *Fighting on the Congo: The Story of an American Boy Among the Rubber Slaves.* Indianapolis: Bobbs-Merrill Co., 1906.

Strickland, W. P. *History of the Missions of the Methodist Episcopal Church.* Cincinnati: L. Swormstedt and J. H. Power, 1850.

Strong, Josiah. *Our Country: Its Possible Future and Its Present Crisis.* New York: Baker and Taylor, 1885.

Strong, William E. *The Story of the American Board.* Boston: Pilgrim Press, 1910.

Swann, Alfred James. *Fighting the Slave-Hunters in Central Africa.* Philadelphia: J. B. Lippincott Co., 1910.

Tarbell, Horace S. *The Werner Grammar School Geography.* New York, Werner School Book Co., 1896.

Tarr, Ralph S., and McMurry, Frank M., *World Geography*. New York: Macmillan Co., 1912.

Taylor, Bayard. *A Journey to Central Africa; or, Life and Landscapes from Egypt to the Negro Kingdom of the White Nile*. New York: G. P. Putnam and Co., 1854.

————, ed. *The Lake Region of Central Africa*. New York: Scribner, Armstrong and Co., 1873.

————. *Travels in South Africa*. New York: Scribner, Armstrong and Co., 1872.

Taylor, Earl. *The Price of Africa*. New York: Young People's Missionary Movement, 1902.

Taylor, William. *Christian Adventures in South Africa*. New York: Phillips and Hunt, 1881.

————. *The Flaming Torch in Darkest Africa*. New York: Eaton and Mains, 1898.

————. *William Taylor of California, Bishop of Africa*. London: Hodder and Stoughton, 1897.

Thomas, Charles W. *Adventures and Observations on the West Coast of Africa, and Its Islands*. New York: Derby and Jackson, 1860.

Thompson, George. *Africa in a Nutshell, for the Million; or, Light on the "Dark Continent."* Oberlin, Ohio: New Press, W. H. Pearce, 1883.

————. *The Palm Land or West Africa, Illustrated*. London: Dawsons of Pall Mall, 1858.

————. *Thompson in Africa; or, an Account of the Missionary Labors, Sufferings, Travels, and Observations, of George Thompson, in Western Africa, at the Mendi Mission*. New York, printed for the author, 1854.

Thorpe, Durant. *The Universal Guide of Standard Routes and Itineraries of Tourist Travel All over the World*. Boston: D. Thorpe, 1907.

Tiffany, Otis H. *Africa for Africans*. Washington City [D.C.]: Colonization Building, 1884.

Tjader, Richard. *The Big Game of Africa*. New York: D. Appleton and Co., 1910.

Tupper, Henry Allen. *American Baptist Missions in Africa*. Philadelphia: American Baptist Publication Society, 1895.

Tuttle, Sarah. *The African Traveller; or, Prospective Missions in Central Africa*. Boston: Massachusetts Sabbath School Society, 1832.

Twain, Mark. *Following the Equator: A Journey Around the World*. Hartford, Conn.: American Publishing Co., 1897.

————. *King Leopold's Soliloquy, a Defense of His Congo Rule*. Boston: P. R. Warren Co., 1905.

Tyler, Josiah. *Forty Years Among the Zulus*. Boston: Congregational Sunday-School and Publishing Society, 1891.

———. *Livingstone Lost and Found; or, Africa and Its Explorers.* Hartford, Conn.: Mutual Publishing Co., 1873.

Unger, Frederick W. *Roosevelt's African Trip.* New York: W. E. Scull, 1909.

Verner, Samuel P. *Pioneering in Central Africa.* Richmond, Va.: Presbyterian Committee of Publication, 1903.

Vescelius-Sheldon, Louise. *Yankee Girls in Zulu Land.* New York: Worthington Co., 1888.

Vincent, Frank. *Actual Africa, or the Coming Continent. A Tour of Exploration.* New York: D. Appleton and Co., 1895.

Wack, Henry Wellington. *The Story of the Congo Free State.* New York: G. P. Putnam's Sons, 1905.

Ward, Herbert. *A Voice from the Congo.* New York: Charles Scribner's Sons, 1910.

White, Stewart Edward. *African Camp Fires.* Garden City, N.Y.: Doubleday, Page and Co., 1913.

———. *The Land of Footprints.* Garden City, N.Y.: Doubleday, Page and Co., 1913.

———. *The Rediscovered Country.* New York: Doubleday, Page and Co., 1915.

White, William S. *The African Preacher; an Authentic Narrative.* Philadelphia: Presbyterian Board of Education, 1849.

Whiton, Samuel J. *Glimpses of West Africa, with Sketches of Missionary Labor.* Boston: American Tract Society, 1866.

Williams, Gardner. *The Diamond Mines of South Africa.* New York: Macmillan Co., 1902.

Williams, George W. *History of the Negro Race in America from 1619 to 1880.* New York: G. P. Putnam's Sons, 1883.

———. *A Report Upon the Congo-State and Country to the President of the Republic of the United States of America.* N.p., 1890.

Williams, Samuel. *Four Years in Liberia.* Philadelphia: King and Baird, 1857.

Wilson, John Leighton. *Western Africa: Its History, Condition, and Prospects.* New York: Harper and Brothers, 1856.

World Missionary Conference, Edinburgh, 1910. Report of Commission I. *Carrying the Gospel to All the Non-Christian World.* New York: Fleming H. Revell Co., 1910.

Articles

Adams, Charles Francis. "Reflex Light from Africa." *Century Magazine* 72 (n.s. 50) (May, 1906), 101–11.

Adams, Cyrus C. "Africa in Transformation." *Missionary Review of the World*, n.s. 22 (June, 1909), 456-57.

———. "The Doom of the Lion in Africa." *American Review of Reviews* 46 (August, 1912), 219-21.

———. "Foundations of Economic Progress in Tropical Africa." *Journal of Race Development* 2 (July, 1911), 1-17.

———. "Railroad Development in Africa." *Engineering Magazine* 4 (February, 1893), 693-707.

———. "Studying the Dark Continent: Recent Remarkable Change in the Methods and Purposes of African Research." *Chautauquan* 19 (n.s. 10) (September, 1894), 701-3.

———. "Tropical Africa as a Factor in Civilization." *Our Day* 13 (January-February, 1894), 5-16.

Austin, O. P. "Africa: Present and Future." *Forum* 28 (December, 1899), 427-41.

Balch, Edwin S. "American Explorers of Africa." *Geographical Review* 5 (1918), 274–81.

Bates, Francis W. "Educational Problems in South Africa." *Missionary Review of the World*, n.s. 19 (June, 1906), 438-45.

Bigham, W. R. "Trade Suggestions from United States Consuls." *Scientific American Supplement* 54 (August 9, 1902), 22251.

Blyden, Edward W. "The African Problem." *North American Review* 446 (September, 1895), 327-39.

Boas, Franz. "Industries of the African Negroes." *Southern Workman* 38 (April, 1909), 217-29.

Bowen, T. J. "Yoruba Proverbs." *Christian Review* 23 (1858), 508-28.

"The Commercial Prospects of Africa." *Scientific American* 86 (June 14, 1902), 410-11.

Cook, Joseph. "American Opportunities in Africa." *Our Day* 5 (June, 1890), 490–99.

———. "The Divine Program in the Dark Continent." *Our Day* 12 (September, 1893), 193-202.

Davis, Richard Harding. "Along the East Coast of Africa." *Scribner's Magazine* 29 (March, 1901), 259-77.

Du Bois, W.E.B. "Back to Africa." *Century Magazine* 105 (February, 1923), 539-48.

Du Chaillu, Paul Belloni. "On the Physical Geography and Tribes of Western Equatorial Africa." *Athenaeum* 9 (1866), 341.

———. "Second Journey into Equatorial Western Africa." *Journal of the Royal Geographical Society* 36 (1866), 64-76.

"The Engineering Development of Africa." *Engineering Magazine* 24 (February, 1903), 781-82.

Ford, Henry A. "Annual Report of Missions, 1853." *Missionary Herald* 50 (1854), 129-30.

———. "Health of the Gaboon, African Women." *Missionary Herald* 47 (1851), 221-22.

French, George K. "The Gold Coast, Ashanti, and Kumasi." *National Geographic Magazine* 8 (January, 1897), 1-15.

French-Sheldon, Mary. "Customs Among the Natives of East Africa, from Teita to Kilimegalia, with Special Reference to their Women and Children." *Journal of the Anthropological Institute* 21 (1892), 358-90.

———. "England's Commercial and Industrial Future in Central Africa." *Journal of the Tyneside Geographical Society* 3 (1897), 415-18.

Hammond, John Hays. "South Africa and Its Future." *North American Review* 483 (February, 1897), 233-48.

Haven, Gilbert. "America in Africa (Part I)." *North American Review* 125 (July-August, 1877), 147-58.

———. "America in Africa (Part II)." *North American Review* 125 (November-December, 1877), 517-28.

Hotchkiss, Willis R. "Africa–Old and New." *Missionary Review of the World*, n.s. 15 (June, 1902), 403-7.

Hubbard, Gardiner G. "Africa, Its Past and Future." *National Geographic Magazine* 1 (April, 1889), 99-124.

———. "Africa Since 1888, with Special Reference to South Africa and Abyssinia." *National Geographic Magaizne* 7 (May, 1896), 157-75.

Hubbard, James M. "Stanley's Africa Then and Now." *Atlantic Monthly* 105 (1910), 333-40.

Kerr, David. "Africa's Awakening." *Harper's Monthly Magazine* 72 (March, 1886), 546-58.

Kroeber, A. L. "The Morals of Uncivilized People." *American Anthropologist* 12 (July, 1910), 437-47.

Lueder, A. B. "Building American Bridges in Mid-Africa." *World's Work* 6 (July, 1903), 3657-72.

Mulligan, Robert W. "Heathenism As It Is In West Africa." *Missionary Review of the World*, n.s. 17 (June, 1904), 401-7.

Nassau, Robert Hamill. "Unique Aspects of Missions to West Africa." *Missionary Review of the World*, n.s. 13 (June, 1900), 417-26.

Noble, Frederic Perry. "Africa at the Columbian Exposition." *Our Day* 9 (November, 1892), 773-89.

———. "The Chicago Congress on Africa." *Our Day* 12 (October, 1893), 279-300.

"Our Trade with Africa." *Scientific American* 74 (June 20, 1896), 391.

Parker, Montgomery D. "Sketches in South Africa." *The Knickerbocker, New-York Monthly Magazine* 36 (1850), 65-69, 338-42; 38 (1851), 147-51, 571-77; 39 (1852), 130-36.

Pierson, Arthur T. "The Dark Continent and Its People." *Missionary Review of the World* 19 (June, 1906), 407-12.

Powell, E. Alexander. "All Aboard for Cape Town!" *Outlook* 99 (November 25, 1911), 724-33.

———. "The Reshuffle in Africa." *Collier's Magazine* 48 (November 25, 1911), 20-22.

Ramage, B. J. "The Partition of Africa." *Sewanee Review* 7 (April, 1899), 221-38.

Roosevelt, Theodore. "Elephant Hunting on Mount Kenya." *Scribner's Magazine* 47 (June, 1910), 641-70.

———. "The Guaso Nyero: A River of the Equatorial Desert." *Scribner's Magazine* 48 (July, 1910), 1-33.

———. "On an East African Ranch–Lion-Hunting on the Kapiti Plains." *Scribner's Magazine* 46 (November, 1909), 513-39.

———. "On Safari: Rhinos and Giraffes." *Scribner's Magazine* 46 (December 1909), 652-69.

———. "A Railroad Through the Pleistocene." *Scribner's Magazine* 46 (October, 1909), 385-406.

———. "Wild Man and Wild Beast in Africa." *National Geographic Magazine* 22 (January, 1911), 1–33.

Sanford, Henry S. "American Interests in Africa." *Forum* 9 (June, 1890), 409-29.

Snyder, DeWitt C. "Beginning Work in Central Africa." *Missionary Review of the World*, n.s. 16 (June, 1903), 437-42.

———. "Missionary Experiences in the Heart of Africa." *Missionary Review of the World*, n.s. 16 (July, 1903), 507-15.

———. "Some Peculiarities of the Natives of Central Africa." *Missionary Review of the World*, n.s. 16 (March, 1903), 183-88.

Stanley, Henry M. "The Pigmies of the Great African Forest." *Scribner's Magazine* 9 (January, 1891), 3-17.

———. "The Story of the Development of Africa." *Century Magazine* 51 (February, 1896), 500-509.

———. "Twenty-five Years' Progress in Equatorial Africa." *Atlantic Monthly* 80 (1897), 471-84.

Starbuck, Charles C. "A General View of Missions. Second Series. V. West Africa." *Andover Review* 12 (November, 1889), 536-45.

Start, Edwin A. "The Exploitation of Africa." *Chautauquan* 32 (October, 1900–March, 1901), 601-5.

Stevens, Thomas. "African River and Lake Systems." *Scribner's Magazine* 8 (September, 1890), 335-42.

Strickland, Peter. "Need of Direct Steamship Service to Africa." *Scientific American Supplement* 53 (January 25, 1902), 21794-95.

Thompson, William L. "The Need for Industrial Missions in Africa." *Missionary Review of the World*, n.s. 14 (June, 1901), 412-20.

Tillinghast, Joseph A. "The Negro in Africa and America." *Publications of the American Economic Association*, 3d. ser., 3 (May, 1902), 1-231.

Verner, Samuel P. "The Adventures of an Explorer in Africa: How the Batwa Pygmies Were Brought to the St. Louis Fair." *Harper's Weekly* 48 (October 22, 1904), 1618-20.

———. "Africa Fifty Years Hence." *World's Work* 13 (April, 1907), 8727-37.

———. "Belgian Rule on the Congo." *World's Work* 13 (February, 1907), 8568-75.

———. "Bringing the Pygmies to America." *Independent* 57 (September 1, 1904), 485-89.

———. "The Development of Africa." *Forum* 32 (November, 1901), 366-82.

———. "An Educational Experiment with Cannibals." *World's Work* 4 (July, 1902), 2289-95.

———. "The White Man's Zone in Africa." *World's Work* 13 (November, 1906), 8227-36.

———. "The White Race in the Tropics." *World's Work* 16 (September, 1908), 10715-20.

———. "The Yellow Men of Central Africa." *American Anthropologist* 5 (May, 1903), 539-44.

Washington, Booker, T. "Industrial Education in Africa." *Independent* 60 (March, 1906), 616-19.

Willey, Day Allen. "American Interests in Africa." *Arena* 24 (September, 1900), 293-98.

Wilson, John Leighton, "Comparative Vocabularies of Some of the Principal Negro Dialects of Africa." *Journal of the American Oriental Society* 1 (1849), 337-81.

Later Published Works

Books

Allen, John Logan. *Passage Through the Garden: Lewis and Clark and the Image of the American Northwest*. Urbana: University of Illinois Press, 1975.

Arnheim, R. *Visual Thinking*. Berkeley: University of California Press, 1969.

Ayandele, Emmanual Ayankanmi. *African Historical Studies*. London and Totowa, N.J.: F. Cass, 1979.

Barker, Anthony J. *The African Link: British Attitudes to the Negro in the Era of the Atlantic Slave Trade, 1550-1807*. London and Totowa, N.J.: F. Cass, 1978.

Baudet, Henri. *Paradise on Earth: Some Thoughts on European Images of Non-European Man*. Translated by E. Wentholt. New Haven: Yale University Press, 1965.

Bennett, Norman R. *Africa and Europe from Roman Times to the Present*. New York: Africana, 1975.

———, and Brooks, George E., Jr., eds. *New England Merchants in Africa: A History Through Documents 1802 to 1865*. Boston: Boston University Press, 1965.

Berghahn, Marion. *Images of Africa in Black American Literature*. Totowa, N.J.: Rowman and Littlefield, 1977.

Betts, Raymond F., ed. *The Scramble for Africa: Causes and Dimensions of Empire*. Lexington, Mass.: D. C. Heath and Co., 1972.

Bittle, William, and Geis, Gilbert. *The Longest Way Home: Chief Alfred C. Sam's Back-to-Africa Movement*. Detroit: Wayne State University Press, 1964.

Blake, John W. *European Beginnings in West Africa, 1454-1578*. London: Longmans, Green and Co., 1937.

———. *Europeans in West Africa, 1450-1560*. London: Hakluyt Society, 1942.

Blouet, Brian W., and Lawson, Merlin P., eds. *Images of the Plains: The Role of Human Nature in Settlement*. Lincoln: University of Nebraska Press, 1975.

Bolt, Christine. *Victorian Attitudes to Race*. London: Routledge and Kegan Paul, 1971.

Boulding, Kenneth. *The Image*. Ann Arbor: University of Michigan Press, 1956.

Brain, Robert. *Art and Society in Africa*. London and New York: Longman, 1980.

Brooks, George E., Jr. *Yankee Traders, Old Coasters and African Middlemen: A History of American Legitimate Trade with West Africa in the Nineteenth Century*. Boston: Boston University Press, 1970.

Brown, Ralph H. *Mirror for Americans: Likeness of the Eastern Seaboard (1810)*. New York: American Geographical Society, 1943.

Buchanan, William, and Cantril, Hadley. *How Nations See Each Other*. Urbana: University of Illinois Press, 1953.

Bunbury, E. H. *A History of Ancient Geography Among the Greeks and Roman from the Earliest Ages till the Fall of the Roman Empire*. 2 vols. New York: Dover Publications, 1959.

Carpenter, Charles. *History of American Schoolbooks*. Philadelphia: University of Pennsylvania Press, 1963.

Chester, Edward W. *Clash of Titans: Africa and U.S. Foreign Policy.* Maryknoll, N.Y.: Orbis Books, 1974.

Clarke, John Henrik, ed. *Marcus Garvey and the Vision of Africa.* New York: Vintage Books, 1974.

Clendennen, Clarence C., and Duignan, Peter. *Americans in Black Africa up to 1865.* Stanford, Calif.: Hoover Institution on War, Revolution, and Peace, Stanford University, 1964.

————, and Collins, Robert. *Americans in Africa 1865-1900.* Stanford, Calif.: Hoover Institution on War, Revolution, and Peace, Stanford University, 1966.

Cohen, William. *The French Encounter with Africans: White Response to Blacks, 1530-1880.* Bloomington: Indiana University Press, 1980.

Crapol, Edward P. *America for Americans: Economic Nationalism and Anglophobia in the Late Nineteenth Century.* Westport, Conn.: Greenwood Press, 1973.

Crowe, S. E. *The Berlin West African Conference, 1884-1885.* London: Longmans, Green and Co., 1942.

Curtin, Philip D. *The Image of Africa: British Ideas and Action, 1780-1850.* Madison: University of Wisconsin Press, 1964.

Davis, John A., ed. *Africa Seen by American Negroes.* Paris: Présence africaine, 1958.

Donahue, Benedict. *The Cultural Arts of Africa.* Washington, D.C.: University Press of America, 1979.

Drake, St. Clair. *The Redemption of Africa and Black Religion.* Chicago: Third World Press, 1970.

Du Bois, W.E.B. *The World and Africa: Inquiry into the Part Which Africa Has Played in World History.* New York: International Publishers, 1968.

Du Plessis, J. *The Evangelisation of Pagan Africa: A History of Christian Missions to the Pagan Tribes of Central Africa.* Cape Town: J. C. Juta and Co., 1929.

Eckbo, Garrett. *The Landscape We See.* New York: McGraw-Hill, 1969.

El-Khawas, Mohamed A., and Kornegay, Francis A. *American-Southern African Relations: Bibliographic Essays.* Westport, Conn.: Greenwood Press, 1975.

Erickson, Carrolly. *The Medieval Vision: Essays in History and Perception.* New York: Oxford University Press, 1976.

Forbath, Peter. *The River Congo: The Discovery, Exploration, and Exploitation of the World's Most Dramatic River.* New York: Harper and Row, 1977.

Forde, Daryll, ed. *African Worlds: Studies in the Cosmological Ideas and Social Values of African Peoples.* London: Oxford University Press, 1954.

Franklin, John Hope. *George Washington Williams and Africa*. Washington, D.C.: Howard University Press, 1971.

Frazier, E. Franklin. *Race and Culture Contacts in the Modern World*. New York: Alfred A. Knopf, 1957.

Fredrickson, George M. *The Black Image in the White Mind*. New York: Harper and Row, 1971.

Friedman, Lawrence J. *The White Savage: Racial Fantasies in the Postbellum South*. Englewood Cliffs, N. J.: Prentice-Hall, 1970.

Gailey, Harry A., Jr. *The History of Africa in Maps*. Chicago: Denoyer-Geppert Co., 1967.

Gardner, Joseph L. *Departing Glory: Theodore Roosevelt as Ex-President*. New York: Charles Scribner's Sons, 1973.

Gatewood, Willard B., Jr. *Black Americans and the White Man's Burden, 1898-1903*. Urbana: University of Illinois Press, 1975.

Geertz, Clifford. *The Interpretation of Cultures: Selected Essays*. New York: Basic Books, 1973.

Gibson, James J. *The Perception of the Visual World*. Boston: Houghton, Mifflin Co., 1950.

Glacken, Clarence J. *Traces on the Rhodian Shore: Nature and Culture in Western Thought from Ancient Times to the End of the Eighteenth Century*. Berkeley: University of California Press, 1967.

Gossett, Thomas F. *Race: the History of an Idea in America*. Dallas: Southern Methodist University Press, 1963.

Graber, Linda H. *Wilderness as Sacred Space*. Washington, D.C.: Association of American Geographers, 1976.

Groves, Charles Pelham. *The Planting of Christianity in Africa*. 4 vols. London: Lutterworth Press, 1948-1958.

Haller, John S. *Outcasts from Evolution: Scientific Attitudes of Racial Inferiority, 1859-1900*. Urbana: University of Illinois Press, 1971.

Hammond, Dorothy, and Jablow, Alta. *The Africa That Never Was: Four Centuries of British Writing About Africa*. New York: Twayne Publishers, 1970.

Hance, William A. *The Geography of Modern Africa*. New York: Columbia University Press, 1975.

Hansberry, William Leo. *Africa and Africans as Seen by Classical Writers*. Edited by Joseph E. Harris. Washington, D.C.: Howard University Press, 1977.

Hart, James D. *The Popular Book: A History of America's Literary Taste*. New York: Oxford University Press, 1950.

Hofstadter, Richard. *Social Darwinism in American Thought*. Rev. ed. New York: George Braziller, 1959.

Hoskins, W. G. *The Making of the English Landscape*. London: Hodder and Stoughton, 1955.

Howe, Russell Warren. *Along the Afric Shore: An Historic Review of Two Centuries of U.S.-African Relations*. New York: Barnes and Noble, 1975.

Hull, Richard W. *African Cities and Towns Before the European Conquest*. New York: Norton, 1976.

Huttenback, Robert A. *Racism and Empire: White Settlers and Colored Immigrants in the British Self-Governing Colonies, 1830-1910*. Ithaca, N.Y.: Cornell University Press, 1976.

Huxley, Elspeth. *White Man's Country: Lord Delamere and the Making of Kenya*. 2 vols. London: Chatto and Windus, 1935.

Irvine, William. *Apes, Angels and Victorians: The Story of Darwin, Huxley, and Evolution*. New York: McGraw-Hill, 1955.

Isaacs, Harold R. *The New World of Negro Americans*. New York: John Day Co., 1963.

Jackson, Henry F. *From the Congo to Soweto: U.S. Foreign Policy Toward Africa Since 1960*. New York: W. Morrow, 1982.

Jacobs, Sylvia M. *The African Nexus: Black American Perspectives on the European Partitioning of Africa, 1880-1920*. Westport, Conn.: Greenwood Press, 1981.

Jenkins, William S. *Pro-Slavery Thought in the Old South*. Chapel Hill: University of North Carolina Press, 1935.

Jones, Eldred D. *The Elizabethan Image of Africa*. Charlottesville: University of Virginia Press, 1971.

Jones, Howard Mumford. *The Age of Energy: Varieties of American Experience, 1865-1915*. New York: Viking Press, 1971.

July, Robert William. *A History of the African People*. New York: Charles Scribner's Sons, 1980.

Killingray, David. *A Plague of Europeans: Westerners in Africa Since the Fifteenth Century*. Baltimore: Penguin Books, 1974.

Kilson, Martin L., and Rotberg, Robert I., eds. *The African Diaspora: Interpretive Essays*. Cambridge: Harvard University Press, 1977.

King, Kenneth J. *Pan-Africanism and Education: A Study of Race, Philanthropy, and Education in the Southern States of America and East Africa*. New York: Oxford University Press, 1971.

Kovel, Joel. *White Racism: A Psychohistory*. New York: Pantheon Books, 1970.

LaFeber, Walter, *The New Empire: An Interpretation of American Expansion, 1860-1898*. Ithaca, N.Y.: Cornell University Press, 1963.

Lamar, Howard, and Thompson, Leonard, eds. *The Frontier in History: North America and Southern Africa Compared*. New Haven: Yale University Press, 1981.

Lambert, Wallace E., and Klineberg, Otto. *Children's Views of Foreign Peoples*. New York: Appleton, Century, Crofts, 1967.

Latourette, Kenneth Scott. *Missions and the American Mind*. Indianapolis: National Foundation Press, 1949.

Lewis, Roy, and Foy, Yvonne. *Painting Africa White: The Human Side of British Colonialism*. New York: Universe Books, 1971.

Lovejoy, Arthur O., and Boas, George. *Primitivism and Related Ideas in Antiquity*. New York: Octagon Books, 1965.

Lowenthal, David, and Bowden, Martyn J., eds. *Geographies of the Mind: Essays in Historical Geosophy in Honor of John Kirtland Wright*. New York: Oxford University Press, 1976.

Luard, Nicholas. *The Last Wilderness: A Journey Across the Great Kalahari Desert*. New York: Simon and Schuster, 1981.

Lupton, Kenneth. *Mungo Park: The African Traveler*. New York: Oxford University Press, 1979.

Lyons, Charles H. *To Wash an Aethiop White: British Ideas About Black African Educability, 1530-1960*. New York: Teachers College Press, 1975.

McKinley, Edward H. *The Lure of Africa: American Interests in Tropical Africa, 1919-1939*. Indianapolis: Bobbs-Merrill Co., 1974.

Mannoni, O. *Prospero and Caliban: The Psychology of Colonization*. Translated by Pamela Powesland. New York: Frederick A. Praeger, 1964.

Marx, Leo. *The Machine in the Garden: Technology and the Pastoral Ideal in America*. New York: Oxford University Press, 1964.

Mathurin, Owen Charles. *Henry Sylvester Williams and the Origins of the Pan-African Movement, 1869-1911*. Westport, Conn.: Greenwood Press, 1976.

Mayard, Richard A., ed. *Africa on Film: Myth and Reality*. Rochelle Park, N.J.: Hayden Book Co., 1974.

Mazrui, Ali Al'Amin. *The African Condition: A Political Diagnosis*. New York: Cambridge University Press, 1980.

Meek, Ronald L. *Social Science and the Ignoble Savage*. Cambridge: Cambridge University Press, 1976.

Meier, August. *Negro Thought in America, 1880-1915: Racial Ideologies in the Age of Booker T. Washington*. Ann Arbor: University of Michigan Press, 1963.

———, and Rudwick, Elliott M. *From Plantation to Ghetto: An Interpretive History of American Negroes*. New York: Hill and Wang, 1966.

Meining, D.W., ed. *The Interpretation of Ordinary Landscapes*. New York: Oxford University Press, 1979.

Merleau-Ponty, M. *Phenomenology of Perception*. London: Routledge and Kegan Paul, 1962.

Milbury-Steen, Sarah L. *European and African Stereotypes in Twentieth-Century African Fiction*. New York: New York University Press, 1981.

Mott, Frank L. *Golden Multitudes: The Story of Best Sellers in the United States.* New York: Macmillan Co., 1947.

Nash, Gary B., and Weiss, Richard, eds. *The Great Fear: Race in the Mind of America.* New York: Holt, Rinehart and Winston, 1970.

Nash, Roderick. *Wilderness and the American Mind.* New Haven: Yale University Press, 1972.

Neumark, S. Daniel. *Economic Influences on the South African Frontier, 1652-1836.* Stanford, Calif.: Stanford University Press, 1957.

Newby, I. A. *Jim Crow's Defense: Anti-Negro Thought in America, 1900-1930.* Baton Rouge: Louisiana State University Press, 1965.

Noer, Thomas J. *Briton, Boer, and Yankee: The United States and South Africa, 1870-1914.* Kent, Ohio: Kent State University Press, 1979.

Okoye, Felix N. *The American Image of Africa: Myth and Reality.* Buffalo, N.Y.: Black Academy Press, 1971.

Peil, Margaret. *Consensus and Conflict in African Societies: An Introduction to Sociology.* London: Longman, 1977.

Phillips, Clifton Jackson. *Protestant American and the Pagan World: The First Half Century of the American Board of Commissioners for Foreign Missions, 1810-1860.* Cambridge: East Asian Research Center, Harvard University, 1969.

Porter, Bernard. *Critics of Empire: British Radical Attitudes to Colonialism in Africa, 1895-1914.* London: Macmillan, 1968.

Rai, Kauleshwar. *Indians and British Colonialism in East Africa, 1883-1939.* Patna, India: Associated Book Agency, 1979.

Redkey, Edwin S. *Black Exodus: Black Nationalist and Back-to-Africa Movements, 1890-1910.* New Haven: Yale University Press, 1969.

Relph, E. *Place and Placelessness.* London: Pion Limited, 1976.

Robins, Eric, and Littell, Blaine. *Africa: Images and Realities.* New York: Praeger Publishers, 1971.

Robinson, Ronald, and Gallagher, John. *Africa and the Victorians: The Climax of Imperialism.* New York: St. Martin's Press, 1961.

Rosenthal, Eric. *Stars and Stripes in Africa.* London: George Routledge and Sons, 1938.

Rotberg, Robert I., ed. *Africa and Its Explorers: Motives, Methods, and Impact.* Cambridge: Harvard University Press, 1970.

Samuels, Michael A., ed. *Africa and the West.* Boulder, Colo.: Westview Press, 1980.

Sauer, Carl O. *Morphology of Landscape.* Berkeley: University of California Press, 1925.

Schmidt, Nancy J. *Children's Books on Africa and Their Authors: An Annotated Bibliography.* New York: Africana, 1975.

Schmitt, Peter J. *Back to Nature: The Arcadian Myth in Urban America.* New York: Oxford University Press, 1969.

Schneider, William H. *An Empire for the Masses: The French Popular Image of Africa, 1870-1900.* Westport, Conn.: Greenwood Press, 1982.

Severin, Timothy. *The African Adventure: Four Hundred Years of Exploration in the Dangerous Continent.* New York: Dutton, 1973.

Shepard, Paul. *Man in the Landscape: A Historic View of the Esthetics of Nature.* New York: Alfred A. Knopf, 1967.

Shephard, George W., Jr., ed. *Racial Influences on American Foreign Policy.* New York: Basic Books, 1970.

Shepperson, George, and Price, Thomas. *Independent Africa: John Chilembwe and the Origins, Setting, and Significance of the Nyasaland Native Rising of 1915.* Edinburgh: University Press, 1958.

Simpson, Donald. *Dark Companions: The African Contribution to European Explorations of East Africa.* New York: Barnes and Noble, 1975.

Slade, Ruth M. *English-Speaking Missions in the Congo Independent State, 1878–1908.* Brussels: Académie Royale des Sciences Coloniales, 1958.

Smith, H. Shelton. *In His Image, But . . . ; Racism in Southern Religion, 1780-1910.* Durham, N.C.: Duke University Press, 1972.

Smith, Henry Nash. *Virgin Land: The American West as Symbol and Myth.* Cambridge: Harvard University Press, 1970.

Soyinka, Wole. *Myth, Literature, and the African World.* New York: Cambridge University Press, 1976.

Staudenraus, P. J. *The African Colonization Movement, 1816-1865.* New York: Columbia University Press, 1961.

Stocking, George W. *Race, Culture, and Evolution.* New York: Free Press, 1968.

Strage, Mark. *Cape to Cairo: Rape of a Continent.* New York: Harcourt Brace Jovanovich, 1973.

Streak, Michael. *The Afrikaner As Viewed by the English, 1795-1854.* Cape Town: C. Struik, 1974.

Stuckey, Sterling. *The Ideological Origins of Black Nationalism.* Boston: Beacon Press, 1972.

Tuan, Yi-Fu. *Landscapes of Fear.* New York: Pantheon, 1979.

———. *Space and Place: The Perspective of Experience.* Minneapolis: University of Minnesota Press, 1977.

———. *Topophilia: A Study of Environmental Perception, Attitudes, and Values.* Englewood Cliffs, N.J.: Prentice-Hall, 1974.

van den Berghe, Pierre L. *Race and Racism: A Comparative Perspective.* New York: John Wiley and Sons, 1967.

Walker, Eric A. *The Frontier Tradition in South Africa.* London: Oxford University Press, 1930.

Walvin, James. *Black and White: The Negro and English Society, 1555-1945.* London: Penguin Press, 1973.

Weisbord, Robert. *Ebony Kinship: Africa, Africans, and the Afro-American.* Westport, Conn.: Greenwood Press, 1973.

Weston, Rubin F. *Racism in U.S. Imperialism: The Influence of Racial Assumptions on American Foreign Policy, 1893-1946.* Columbia: University of South Carolina Press, 1972.

Wilson, William J. *Power, Racism, and Privilege: Race Relations in Theoretical and Sociohistorical Perspectives.* New York: Macmillan Co., 1973.

Young, Crawford. *Ideology and Development in Africa.* New Haven: Yale University Press, 1982.

Zelinsky, Wilbur. *The Cultural Geography of the United States.* Englewood Cliffs, N.J.: Prentice-Hall, 1973.

Zuesse, Evan M. *Ritual Cosmos: The Sanctification of Life in African Religions.* Athens: Ohio University Press, 1979.

Articles

Abolfathi, Farid. "The Americans' Image of Africa: An Exploratory Discussion." *Pan-Africanist* 3 (December, 1971), 37-38.

Alford, Terry L. "Letter from Liberia, 1848." *Mississippi Quarterly* 22 (1969), 150-51.

Baker, Donald G. "Black Images: The Afro-American in Popular Novels, 1900-1945." *Journal of Popular Culture* 7 (Fall, 1973), 327-46.

Beidelman, T.O. "Social Theory and the Study of Christian Missions in Africa." *Africa* 44 (1974), 235-49.

Berwanger, Eugene H. "Negrophobia in Northern Proslavery and Antislavery Thought." *Phylon* 33 (Fall, 1972), 266-75.

Blackett, Richard, "Martin R. Delany and Robert Campbell: Black Americans in Search of an African Colony." *Journal of Negro History* 62 (January, 1977), 1–25.

Bunkśe, Edmunds V. "Commoner Attitudes Toward Landscape and Nature." *Annals of the Association of American Geographers* 68 (December, 1978), 551-66.

Chick, C. A., Sr. "The American Negroes' Changing Attitude Toward Africa." *Journal of Negro Education* 31 (Fall, 1962), 531-35.

Clarke, John Henrik. "The Afro-American Image of Africa." *Black World* 23 (February, 1974), 4-21.

Constantine, J. Robert. "The Ignoble Savage: An Eighteenth Century Literary Stereotype." *Phylon* 27 (Summer, 1966), 171-79.

Darby, H. C. "The Problem of Geographical Description." *Transactions and Papers of the Institute of British Geographers* 30 (1962), 1-13.

Dixey, F. "African Landscape." *Geographical Review* 34 (1944), 457-65.

Ernst, Joseph E., and Merrens, H. Roy. "Praxis and Theory in the Writing of American Historical Geography." *Journal of Historical Geography* 4 (July, 1978), 277-90.

Genovese, Eugene D. "A Georgia Slaveholder Looks at Africa." *Georgia Historical Quarterly* 51 (June, 1967), 186-93.

———. "The Negro Laborer in Africa and the Slave South." *Phylon* 21 (Winter, 1960), 343-50.

George, Katherine. "The Civilized West Looks at Primitive Africa: 1400-1800." *Isis* 49 (1958), 62-72.

Gilbert, E. W. "The Idea of the Region." *Geography* 45 (July, 1960), 157-75.

Grantham, Dewey. "The Progressive Movement and the Negro." *South Atlantic Quarterly* 54 (October, 1955), 461-77.

Gregory, Derek. "The Discourse of the Past: Phenomenology, Structuralism and Historical Geography." *Journal of Historical Geography* 4 (April, 1978), 161-73.

Guelke, Leonard. "Frontier Settlement in Early Dutch South Africa." *Annals of the Association of American Geographers* 66 (March, 1976), 25-42.

Hammond, Harold E. "American Interest in the Exploration of the Dark Continent." *Historian* 18 (Spring, 1956), 202-29.

Harris, Sheldon H. "An American's Impressions of Sierra Leone in 1811." *Journal of Negro History* 47 (January, 1962), 35-41.

Herskovits, Melville, J. "The Image of Africa in the United States." *Journal of Human Relations* 10 (Winter-Spring, 1962), 236-45.

Johnson, Hildegard Binder. "The Location of Christian Missions in Africa." *Geographical Review* 57 (1967), 168-202.

King, Kenneth J. "Africa and the Southern States of the U.S.A.: Notes on J. H. Oldham and American Negro Education for Africans." *Journal of African History* 10 (1969), 659-77.

Kirk-Greene, A.H.M. "America in the Niger Valley: A Colonization Centenary." *Phylon* 23 (Fall, 1962), 225-39.

Klineberg, Otto. "Pictures in Our Heads." *UNESCO Courier* 8 (September, 1955), 5-9.

Kumm, H.K.W. "Africa as Known to the Greek and Roman Geographers." *Scottish Geographical Magazine* 42 (January, 1926), 11-22.

Lowenthal, David. "The American Scene." *Geographical Review* 58 (January, 1968), 61-88.

———. "Geography, Experience and Imagination: Towards a Geographical Epistemology." *Annals of the Association of American Geographers* 51 (September, 1961), 241-60.

MacMaster, Richard K. "United States Navy and African Exploration, 1851-1860." *Mid-America* 46 (July, 1964), 187-203.

Malefijt, Annemarie de Waal. "Homo Monstrosus." *Scientific American* 219 (October, 1968), 112-18.

Marable, W. Manning. "Booker T. Washington and African Nationalism." *Phylon* 35 (December, 1974), 398-417.

Meinig, D. W. "Environmental Appreciation: Localities As A Humane Art." *Western Humanities Review* 25 (Winter, 1971), 1-11.

Meyer, Lysle E. "The American Image of South Africa in Historical Perspective." *Social Studies* 67 (January-February, 1976), 19-27.

Minshull, Roger. "The Functions of Geography in American Studies." *Journal of American Studies* 7 (December, 1973), 267-78.

Odum, Herbert H. "Generalizations on Race in 19th Century Anthropology." *Isis* 58 (1967), 5-18.

Overton, J. D. "A Theory of Exploration." *Journal of Historical Geography* 7 (January, 1981), 53-70.

Piersen, William D. "White Cannibals, Black Martyrs: Fear, Depression, and Religious Faith As Causes of Suicide Among New Slaves." *Journal of Negro History* 62 (April, 1977), 147-59.

Prince, Hugh C. "Real, Imagined, and Abstract Worlds of the Past." *Progress in Geography* 3 (1971), 4-86.

Roucek, Joseph. "The Changing Relationship of the American Negro to African History and Politics." *Journal of Human Relations* 14 (1966), 17-27.

Rowntree, Lester B, and Conkey, Margaret W. "Symbolism and the Cultural Landscape." *Annals of the Association of American Geographers* 70 (December, 1980), 459-74.

Rudwick, Elliott M., and Meier, August. "Black Man in the 'White City': Negroes and the Columbia Exposition, 1893." *Phylon* 26 (Winter, 1965), 354-61.

Scheiner, Seth. "President Theodore Roosevelt and the Negro, 1901-1908." *Journal of Negro History* 47 (July, 1962), 169-82.

Shepperson, George. "Africa and America." *Bulletin of the British Association for American Studies* 3 (December, 1961), 25-30.

———. "The American Negro and Africa." *Bulletin of the British Association for American Studies* 8 (June, 1964), 3-20.

———. "The United States and East Africa." *Phylon* 13 (1st Quarter, 1952), 25-34.

Smith, Henry Nash. "The West as an Image of the American Past." *The University of Kansas City Review* 18 (Autumn, 1951), 29-40.

Sonnenfeld, Joseph. "Variable Values in Space and Landscape: An Inquiry Into the Nature of Environmental Necessity." *Journal of Social Issues* 22 (1966), 71-82.

Stuckey, Sterling. "DuBois, Woodson, and the Spell of Africa." *Negro Digest* 16 (February, 1967), 60-74.

Watson, J. Wreford. "Image Geography: The Myth of America in the American Scene." *Advancement of Science* 27 (September, 1971), 71-79.

Wax, Darold D. "A Philadelphia Surgeon on a Slaving Voyage to Africa, 1749-1751." *Pennsylvania Magazine of History and Biography* 92 (October, 1968), 465-93.

Williams, Walter L. "Ethnic Relations of African Students in the United States, with Black Americans, 1870-1900." *Journal of Negro History* 65 (Summer, 1980), 228-49.

Winters, Christopher, "Urban Morphogenesis in Francophone Black Africa." *Geographical Review* 72 (April, 1982), 139-54.

Dissertations

Bodie, Charles A. "The Images of Africa in the Black American Press, 1890-1930." Ph.D. dissertation, Indiana University, 1975.

Coan, Josephus. R. "The Expansion of Missions of the African Methodist Episcopal Church in South Africa, 1896-1908." Ph.D. dissertation, Hartford Seminary, 1961.

Dempsey, Francine Ann. "Afro-American Perspectives on Africa: The Image of Africa Among Afro-American Leaders, Artists, and Scholars, 1915-1940." Ph.D. dissertation, University of Minnesota, 1976.

Dinnerstein, Myra. "American Board Missions to the Zulu, 1835-1900." Ph.D. dissertation, Columbia University, 1970.

Fendall, Lonny Ward. "Theodore Roosevelt and Africa: Deliberate Non-Involvement in the Scramble for Territory and Influence." Ph.D. dissertation, University of Oregon, 1972.

Ferrario, Francesco. "The Tourist Landscape: A Method of Evaluating Tourist Potential and Its Application to South Africa." Ph.D. dissertation, University of California, Berkeley, 1977.

Ford, Richard B. "The Frontier in South Africa: A Comparative Study of the Turner Thesis." Ph.D. dissertation, University of Denver, 1966.

Goldstein, Myra S. "The Genesis of Modern American Relations with South Africa, 1895-1914." Ph.D. dissertation, State University of New York at Buffalo, 1972.

Griffith, Cyril Edgar. "Martin R. Delany and the African Dream, 1812-1885." Ph.D. dissertation, Michigan State University, 1973.

Howard, Lawrence Cabot. "American Involvement in Africa South of the Sahara, 1800-1860." Ph.D. dissertation, Harvard University, 1956.

Johnson, Lillie Molliene. "Black American Missionaries in Colonial Africa, 1900-1940: A Study of Missionary-Government Relations." Ph.D. dissertation, University of Chicago, 1981.

Kasambira, Tafadzwa Silas. "An Analysis of the Treatment of Africa and Africans in American Secondary School Geography Textbooks." Ph.D. dissertation, Kent State University, 1980.

Keto, Clement Tsehloane, "American Involvement in South Africa, 1870-1915: The Role of Americans in the Creation of Modern South Africa." Ph.D. dissertation, Georgetown University, 1972.

Luther, Donald Stephen. "The Vision of Africa: Creation of the Imperialist Mentality, 1854-1894." Ph.D. dissertation, University of Delaware, 1979.

McStallworth, Paul. "The United States and the Congo Question, 1884-1914." Ph.D. dissertation, Ohio State University, 1954.

Magubane, Bernard. "The American Negro's Conception of Africa: A Study in the Ideology of Pride and Prejudice." Ph.D. dissertation, University of California at Los Angeles, 1967.

Olton, Roy. "Africa in American Foreign Relations During the Nineteenth Century." Ph.D. dissertation, Fletcher School of Law and Diplomacy, Tufts University, 1954.

Roberts, Norman Phillip. "The Changing Images of Africa in Some Selected American Media from 1930-1969." Ph.D. dissertation, American University, 1970.

Sahli, John A. "An Analysis of Early American Geography Textbooks from 1784-1840." Ph.D. dissertation, University of Pittsburgh, 1941.

Scott, Clifford Haley. "American Images of Sub-Sahara Africa, 1900-1939." Ph.D. dissertation, University of Iowa, 1968.

Shaloff, Stanley. "The American Presbyterian Congo Mission: A Study in Conflict, 1890-1921." Ph.D. dissertation, Northwestern University, 1966.

Smith, Henry Nash. "American Emotional and Imaginative Attitudes Toward the Great Plains and the Rocky Mountains, 1803-1850." Ph.D. dissertation, Harvard University, 1940.

Soremekun, Fola. "A History of the American Board Missions in Angola, 1880-1940." Ph.D. dissertation, Northwestern University, 1965.

Index

About the Author

MICHAEL McCARTHY is Assistant Professor in the Department of American Studies at the University of Maryland. His interest in Africa began when he lived and taught in Ethiopia. His work has appeared in the *Journal of American Studies*. He is currently writing a book on the American tourist experience in Europe.

Contributions in Afro-American and African Studies
Series Advisers: John W. Blassingame and Henry Louis Gates, Jr.

The Afro-Yankees:
Providence's Black Community in the Antebellum Era
Robert J. Cottrol

A Case of Black and White:
Northern Volunteers and the Southern Freedom Summers, 1964-1965
Mary Aickin Rothschild

Gatekeepers of Black Culture: Black-Owned Book Publishing in the United
States, 1817-1981
Donald Franklin Joyce

The Craft of an Absolute Winner: Characterization and Narratology in the
Novels of Machado de Assis
Maria Luisa Nunes

Black Marriage and Family Therapy
Edited by Constance E. Obudho

The Womb of Space: The Cross-Cultural Imagination
Wilson Harris